1–3 John

Reformed Expository Commentary

A Series

Series Editors

Richard D. Phillips
Philip Graham Ryken

Testament Editors

Iain M. Duguid, Old Testament
Daniel M. Doriani, New Testament

1–3 John

Douglas Sean O'Donnell

P&R
PUBLISHING
P.O. BOX 817 • PHILLIPSBURG • NEW JERSEY 08865-0817

Italics within Scripture quotations indicate emphasis added.

Page design by Lakeside Design Plus

Printed in the United States of America

Library of Congress Cataloging-in-Publication Data

O'Donnell, Douglas Sean, 1972-
1-3 John / Douglas Sean O'Donnell. -- 1st ed.
pages cm. -- (Reformed expository commentary)
Includes bibliographical references and index.
ISBN 978-1-59638-987-8 (cloth)
1. Bible. Epistles of John--Commentaries. I. Title.
BS2805.53.O36 2015
227'.9407--dc23

2015002388

To New Covenant Church, Naperville, Illinois

Contents

Series Introduction

In every generation there is a fresh need for the faithful exposition of God's Word in the church. At the same time, the church must constantly do the work of theology: reflecting on the teaching of Scripture, confessing its doctrines of the Christian faith, and applying them to contemporary culture. We believe that these two tasks—the expositional and the theological—are interdependent. Our doctrine must derive from the biblical text, and our understanding of any particular passage of Scripture must arise from the doctrine taught in Scripture as a whole.

We further believe that these interdependent tasks of biblical exposition and theological reflection are best undertaken in the church, and most specifically in the pulpits of the church. This is all the more true since the study of Scripture properly results in doxology and praxis—that is, in praise to God and practical application in the lives of believers. In pursuit of these ends, we are pleased to present the Reformed Expository Commentary as a fresh exposition of Scripture for our generation in the church. We hope and pray that pastors, teachers, Bible study leaders, and many others will find this series to be a faithful, inspiring, and useful resource for the study of God's infallible, inerrant Word.

The Reformed Expository Commentary has four fundamental commitments. First, these commentaries aim to be *biblical*, presenting a comprehensive exposition characterized by careful attention to the details of the text. They are not exegetical commentaries—commenting word by word or even verse by verse—but integrated expositions of whole passages of Scripture. Each commentary will thus present a sequential, systematic treatment of an entire book of the Bible, passage by passage. Second, these commentaries are unashamedly *doctrinal*. We are committed to the Westminster Confession of Faith and Catechisms as containing the system of doctrine taught in the Scriptures of the Old and New Testaments. Each volume will teach, promote, and defend the doctrines of the Reformed faith as they are found in the Bible. Third, these commentaries are *redemptive-historical* in their orientation. We believe in the unity of the Bible and its central message of salvation in Christ. We are thus committed to a Christ-centered view of the Old Testament, in which its characters, events, regulations, and institutions are properly understood as pointing us to Christ and his gospel, as well as giving us examples to follow in living by faith. Fourth, these commentaries are *practical*, applying the text of Scripture to contemporary challenges of life—both public and private—with appropriate illustrations.

The contributors to the Reformed Expository Commentary are all pastor-scholars. As pastor, each author will first present his expositions in the pulpit ministry of his church. This means that these commentaries are rooted in the teaching of Scripture to real people in the church. While aiming to be scholarly, these expositions are not academic. Our intent is to be faithful, clear, and helpful to Christians who possess various levels of biblical and theological training—as should be true in any effective pulpit ministry. Inevitably this means that some issues of academic interest will not be covered. Nevertheless, we aim to achieve a responsible level of scholarship, seeking to promote and model this for pastors and other teachers in the church. Significant exegetical and theological difficulties, along with such historical and cultural background as is relevant to the text, will be treated with care.

We strive for a high standard of enduring excellence. This begins with the selection of the authors, all of whom have proved to be outstanding communicators of God's Word. But this pursuit of excellence is also reflected in a disciplined editorial process. Each volume is edited by both a series editor and a testament editor. The testament editors, Iain Duguid for the Old Testament and Daniel Doriani for the New Testament, are accomplished pastors and respected scholars who have taught at the seminary level. Their job is to ensure that each volume is sufficiently conversant with up-to-date scholarship and is faithful and accurate in its exposition of the text. As series editors, we oversee each volume to ensure its overall quality—including excellence of writing, soundness of teaching, and usefulness in application. Working together as an editorial team, along with the publisher, we are devoted to ensuring that these are the best commentaries that our gifted authors can provide, so that the church will be served with trustworthy and exemplary expositions of God's Word.

It is our goal and prayer that the Reformed Expository Commentary will serve the church by renewing confidence in the clarity and power of Scripture and by upholding the great doctrinal heritage of the Reformed faith. We hope that pastors who read these commentaries will be encouraged in their own expository preaching ministry, which we believe to be the best and most biblical pattern for teaching God's Word in the church. We hope that lay teachers will find these commentaries among the most useful resources they rely on for understanding and presenting the text of the Bible. And we hope that the devotional quality of these studies of Scripture will instruct and inspire each Christian who reads them in joyful, obedient discipleship to Jesus Christ.

May the Lord bless all who read the Reformed Expository Commentary. We commit these volumes to the Lord Jesus Christ, praying that the Holy Spirit will use them for the instruction and edification of the church, with thanksgiving to God the Father for his unceasing faithfulness in building his church through the ministry of his Word.

Richard D. Phillips
Philip Graham Ryken
Series Editors

Preface

In his *Autobiography*, Mark Twain tells a number of interesting stories about the curious events surrounding his life, most of which are drenched in typical Twain wit. A few stories, however, show some of the sober realities of his tumultuous times and travels. One such story is that of an old African medicine man from the island of Mauritius. This man alone had a cure for a rare "child's disease." Whenever parents were desperate for a cure, they would come to him and beg for his life-saving "herb medicine," a potion that had been passed down from his father and grandfather. He always gladly complied. This dependence, however, had a dark side, for he refused to share the secret formula. As this man neared death, the islanders grew frightful. They feared that he would "die without divulging it." Then what would happen to their dying children? Those who survived him would surely not survive the disease.[1]

In John's letters we find a similar but more generous scenario. The last surviving apostle does not stubbornly suppress his secret; instead, he freely and graciously leaves with the next generation the mystery of the life-saving message of the gospel. Writing fifty to sixty years after Christ's resurrection,[2] John reveals to the churches in and around the city of Ephesus (those churches then under his apostolic oversight) the central ingredients of "the word of life" (1 John 1:1).

1. Recounted in Mark Twain, *Autobiography of Mark Twain*, ed. Charles Neider (New York: HarperPerennial, 1990), 11.

2. While no "temporal indicators are given" and "no explicit geographical" location named, "if we care to assign John's Letters to a particular historical milieu at all, it seems warranted to think of them as reflecting conditions in the region of Ephesus in the closing decades of the first century." Robert W. Yarbrough, *1–3 John*, Baker Exegetical Commentary on the New Testament (Grand Rapids: Baker, 2008), 17. Based on patristic sources, we know that John lived and ministered in Ephesus between A.D. 70 and 100, with 1 John likely written between A.D. 80 and 90.

After Christ's ascension, the apostles planted the seed of the gospel in Asia Minor, and as it grew by God's grace, this seed sprouted into many churches. Yet shortly after those churches began to flourish, impostors infiltrated them, seeking to sever them from their life-giving connection with the apostles.[3] This chopping at the root of apostolic teaching and authority led many people within the church to question the content of the faith and its connection with the apostles. *Whom* are we to believe? *What* are we to believe?

John's letters were written, in part, to answer such concerns. To the question "Whom were they to believe—these new teachers or the old apostles?" John emphatically answers, "*The apostles*—only those witnesses who have seen, heard, and touched Jesus." To the question "What are they to believe?" John confidently asserts, "*The apostolic message*—'concerning the word of life'—the appearance of the eternal Son of God in the flesh."

Therefore, John had two main purposes for writing these epistles. His first purpose was pastoral. Some scholars have argued that John's central purpose is the final imperative in 1 John ("Keep yourselves from idols," 1 John 5:21) or the first indicative ("God is light," 1:5). But John explicitly states four purposes for writing (1:3, 4; 2:1; 5:13), and my view is that the last summarizes the overall message best. The authorial intent involves knowledge. It is not some secret, Gnostic-like knowledge, but knowledge of "eternal life" for those "who believe in the name of the Son of God" (5:13). It is the assurance of faith. John is writing, as James Montgomery Boice summarizes, "to lead those who already believe to a deeper understanding of the faith and to confidence in that which they already possess."[4]

He also writes, as mentioned, with a polemical purpose.[5] As he states in 1 John 2:26, "I write these things to you about those who are trying to deceive you" (cf. Acts 20:28–30). Throughout the three letters, these twin

3. According to Revelation, there were two groups of leaders in Ephesus: those who called themselves apostles and truly were apostles and "those who call[ed] themselves *apostles* and [were] not" (Rev. 2:2). Throughout John's epistles, the true apostle addresses these "apostles" who are "not." He calls them "antichrists" (1 John 2:18), "false prophets" (4:1), and "deceivers" (2 John 7).

4. James Montgomery Boice, *The Epistles of John: An Expositional Commentary* (Grand Rapids: Baker, 1979), 12.

5. As John R. W. Stott notes: "It is not a theological treatise written in the academic peace of a library, but a tract for the times, called forth by a particular and urgent situation in the Church. This situation concerns the insidious propaganda of certain false teachers." *The Epistles of John: An Introduction and Commentary*, Tyndale New Testament Commentaries (Downers Grove, IL: InterVarsity Press, 1976), 41.

purposes intertwine. From his polemical concerns (i.e., the content of the false teaching) arises John's pastoral counsel (i.e., his corrective message). For example, to the impostors' "gospel" that is contrary to what the Ephesians received (see Gal. 1:9), John upheld the necessity of belief in Jesus' incarnation and obedience to his commandments, especially that of brotherly love. True Christian disciples "live in the light ([1 John] 1:5–2:29) as children of God (3:1–5:13)."[6]

Following many commentators before me, I will explain John's letters by agreeing with Robert Law's classic thesis that John presents us with "three cardinal tests" by which we may judge whether we possess eternal life or not.[7] The first test is theological: we must believe that Jesus is the Son of God (1 John 3:23; 5:5, 10, 13; 2 John 3, 9; cf. 3 John 1–4), the Christ come in the flesh (1 John 4:2; 2 John 7). The second test is moral: we must obey God's commandments (e.g., 1 John 2:1–6; 2 John 6). The third test is social: we must love others (e.g., 1 John 2:10; 2 John 5; 3 John 5).

Moreover, in line with the healthy balance contained in the Westminster Standards, I will approach John's letters by acknowledging both that "no mere man since the fall is able in this life perfectly to keep the commandments of God, but doth daily break them in thought, word, and deed" (Westminster Shorter Catechism [WSC] A. 82) *and* that obedience marks the Christian life:

> They, who are once effectually called, and regenerated, having a new heart, and a new spirit created in them, are further sanctified, really and personally, through the virtue of Christ's death and resurrection, by his Word and Spirit dwelling in them: the dominion of the whole body of sin is destroyed, and the several lusts thereof are more and more weakened and mortified; and they more and more quickened and strengthened in all saving graces, to the practice of true holiness, without which no man shall see the Lord. (Westminster Confession of Faith [WCF] 13.1)

Boice summarizes the balance in this way: "The life of God within makes obedience to the commands possible, and the love the Christian has for God and for other Christians makes this obedience desirable."[8]

6. Stephen S. Smalley, *1, 2, 3 John*, rev. ed., Word Biblical Commentary (Nashville: Thomas Nelson, 2007), 16.

7. *The Tests of Life* (1909).

8. Boice, *The Epistles of John*, 127.

These sermons were originally preached at New Covenant Church in Naperville, Illinois. Because I have accepted a call to lecture at Queensland Theological College in Brisbane, Australia, 1–3 John was my last sermon series at the church I planted nearly a decade ago. Thank you, NCC, for allowing me to serve you. Thank you for your persistent eagerness to have the Bible opened, explained, and applied. May you continue in "the practice of true holiness."

1–3 *John*

A Gospel-Transformed Life

1

Apostolic Fellowship

1 John 1:1–4

That which we have seen and heard we proclaim also to you, so that you too may have fellowship with us; and indeed our fellowship is with the Father and with his Son Jesus Christ. (1 John 1:3)

Tongue twisters are my archenemy. I cannot say, and I no longer attempt to say, phrases such as "Peter Piper picked a peck of pickled peppers," "How can a clam cram in a clean cream can?," "Send toast to ten tense stouts' ten tall tents," and "Unique New York, unique New York, you know you need unique New York."

While the opening verses in 1 John are not tongue twisters, they do present us with an "abrupt," "exceedingly complex," "syntactically convoluted," "frequently ambiguous," "complicated interweaving" of "stammer[ing]," "infuriatingly obscure" "'insider' language," as a compilation of commentators puts it,[1] or, more plainly, "a grammatical tangle," as C. H. Dodd

1. "Abrupt" comes from John Calvin (quoted in Robert W. Yarbrough, *1–3 John*, Baker Exegetical Commentary on the New Testament [Grand Rapids: Baker, 2008], 31); "exceedingly complex" from C. H. Dodd, *The Johannine Epistles*, Moffatt New Testament Commentary (New York: Harper & Brothers, 1946), 1; "syntactically convoluted" from Yarbrough, *1–3 John*, 31; "frequently ambiguous" from John Painter, *1, 2, and 3 John*, Sacra Pagina (Collegeville, MN: Liturgical Press, 2002), 126; "complicated interweaving" from H. J. Holtzmann (quoted in Yarbrough, *1–3 John*, 31n1); "stammer[ing]" from Martin Luther's phrase "language [that] is altogether childlike; it stammers rather than speaks" ("Lectures on the First Epistle of St. John," in *The Catholic Epistles*, vol. 30 of *Luther's Works*, trans. and ed. Jaroslav Pelikan and W. A. Hansen [St. Louis: Concordia, 1972], 221); "infuriatingly obscure" from Raymond E. Brown (quoted in Yarbrough, *1–3 John*, 31); and "'insider' language" from Painter, *1, 2, and 3 John*, 126.

bemoaned.[2] We wonder: *What is "which,"* and *who is "we,"* and *what does "we" have to say about "which" to "you"?* We wonder whether we have jumped into a Dr. Seuss book.

Admittedly, the pronouns can be perplexing in this opening sentence that runs rhythmically for nearly three verses and includes a parenthesis.[3] Yet the message itself is plain enough: divine fellowship demands apostolic fellowship. Put metaphorically, if we want to hold the hand of God (stay in fellowship with him), we must hold the apostles' hands (stay in fellowship with their God-appointed and God-approved testimony concerning Jesus Christ).

With that message in mind, I want to untangle this strange but straightforward text by implementing the odd but accurate questions I presented above, the first of which is "What is 'which'?"

What Is "Which"?

First John is a letter. Or is it a short sermon, an encyclical, a tractate, or some sort of theological manifesto? Whatever its precise genre, it is a short writing that begins without a beginning (i.e., there is no "from John to Gaius in Ephesus, grace and peace in Christ") by beginning, "That which was from the beginning" (1 John 1:1). Some Bible translations hide this initial ambiguity by starting verse 1 with the verb found in verses 2 and 3, "we proclaim." Thus, it is rendered "We proclaim to you" (NLT) or "We declare to you" (NRSV). The English Standard Version (ESV) wisely left the original alone, since the ambiguity is likely intentional. Like the reader of a good mystery novel, we have to wait until the end, or nearly the end (the very end of verse 3!), to solve the riddle. Who or what, then, is the "that which"? Five times in verses 1–3 we find the Greek word *ho*, rendered "which" in the ESV.[4] "That *which* was from the beginning, *which* we have heard, *which* we have seen . . . , *which* we looked upon . . . [,] *which* we have seen and heard" (vv. 1, 3).

The word *which* is a neuter singular relative pronoun, thus pointing us to the Father's Son, Jesus Christ (1 John 1:3), as the answer to the ques-

2. Dodd, quoted in John R. W. Stott, *The Epistles of John: An Introduction and Commentary*, Tyndale New Testament Commentaries (Downers Grove, IL: InterVarsity Press, 1976), 61.

3. Painter, *1, 2, and 3 John*, 127.

4. The "which" in verse 2 is a different Greek word, one that, nevertheless, modifies the same reality or person.

tion "what is 'what'?" or "who is '*ho*'?" That deduction was reached not directly from the grammar but by common sense and a basic grasp of John's style and vocabulary. Grammatically, the neuter word *which* (*ho*) cannot connect with the masculine word *word* (*logos*) or the feminine word *life* (*zōē*). It can, however, connect with the neuter word *message* (*angelia*) in verse 5 (cf. 3:11). But in verses 1–2, it is surely not the gospel message that was "seen" and "touched." It might be, as some have suggested,[5] that John uses the neuter for Jesus to encompass both the divine man (Jesus) and the divine message (about Jesus). Whatever the case may be, it is certainly true that in John's Gospel the words *word* and *life* are used to represent Jesus. Moreover, it is not uncommon for John to use the neuter for the masculine gender (e.g., John 3:5a with 5b; 1 John 5:4 with 5).[6] Thus, the "which" is God incarnate. Or perhaps it is better to say: he who "was from the beginning" and is "the word of life" is God's Son, the man Jesus.

With this mystery solved, let us delve into it deeper. Why call Jesus "that which was from the beginning" and "the word of life" (1 John 1:1)? Both phrases are brimming with theological significance. The phrase "from the beginning" is used eight times in 1 John (cf. 2 John 5–6), and it has a few different connotations based on its context. For example, in 3:8 we read that "the devil has been sinning from the beginning." This means something like "he has always sinned and continues to do so."[7] Or "from the beginning" refers back to Genesis 3. In 1 John 2:7, 24, and 3:11, we read of Jesus' love command as being "from the beginning," namely, from the time that Jesus gave it or the time that John's recipients first received it. The way "from the beginning" is used in 1:1 could speak of the event of the incarnation, Jesus' ministry after his baptism, the apostolic proclamation of his teachings, the absolute beginning of the universe (as in 2:13–14), or the time before creation when Jesus was the preincarnate *logos*. I take the last reference to be correct, namely, that John's "from the beginning" is essentially the same as his declaration: "In the beginning was the Word, and the Word was with God,

5. For example, "The term *that* [*which*, ESV] is broader than the word *who*, for it includes the person and message of Jesus Christ." Simon J. Kistemaker, "Exposition of the Epistles of John," in *James, Epistles of John, Peter, and Jude* (Grand Rapids: Baker, 2002), 234.

6. As noted by Rudolf Schnackenburg, *The Johannine Epistles: Introduction and Commentary*, trans. R. Fuller and I. Fuller (New York: Crossroad, 1992), 57. For further examples, see ibid., 57n26.

7. Painter, *1, 2, and 3 John*, 120.

and the Word was God. He was in the beginning with God" (John 1:1–2).[8] In terms of Habakkuk's question to Yahweh in Habakkuk 1:12 (NIV), "O LORD, are you not *from everlasting*?" (LXX,[9] *ap' archēs*), Jesus replies, "Yes, *I am*!" Jesus existed before creation and enjoyed (as he now continues to enjoy; see 1 John 1:3) an eternally intimate fellowship with the Father.

The phrase "word of life" is in tune with this high Christological note, teaching that the eternal, preexistent, fully divine Son came into the world as the "*definitive revelation* of God."[10] He is the voice, image, and embodiment of God. Through him, God is made audible (cf. Heb. 1:2–3), visible (cf. Col. 1:15), and touchable (cf. Mark 3:10). Also through him, we are given "life" (1 John 1:1), even "eternal life" (v. 2; cf. John 17:3). Rudolf Schnackenburg says it beautifully: the incarnation is "the descent of the life eternal into the world of humankind alienated from God, the invasion of the absolute, indestructible power of life into this transitory cosmos, destined as it was to perdition (1 John 2:17)."[11] Are you concerned about death and damnation? You should be. We are all doomed to die and then face the judgment. So, then, how can anyone escape? Is there deliverance? Where? How? Who? Come hear, see, and touch Jesus.

Who Is "We"?

But how are we to hear, see, and touch Jesus when he no longer lives on earth? How can we behold the eternal and ascended Lord? John answers through the "we" of verses 1–3. Here our attention turns to our second question, "Who is 'we'?"

The English pronoun "we" is used six times in the first three verses ("we," "our," and "us" are used eleven times!): "That . . . which *we* have heard, which *we* have seen with our eyes, which *we* looked upon and have touched

8. Clement of Alexandria summarizes the Christian consensus: "For when he says 'which was from the beginning' he is referring to the generation of the Son which has no beginning, because he exists coeternal with the Father. Therefore the word *was* signifies eternity, just as the Word himself, that is, the Son, which is one with the Father in equality of substance, is eternal and unmade." "Adumbrations," in *James, 1–2 Peter, 1–3 John, Jude*, ed. Gerald Bray, Ancient Christian Commentary on Scripture, New Testament 11 (Downers Grove, IL: InterVarsity Press, 2000), 166.

9. *LXX* is shorthand for the Septuagint, an early Greek translation of the Old Testament.

10. Gary M. Burge, *Letters of John*, NIV Application Commentary (Grand Rapids: Zondervan, 1996), 58.

11. Schnackenburg, *The Johannine Epistles*, 60.

with our hands" (1 John 1:1); "And *we* have seen it" (v. 2); "that which *we* have seen and [we] heard *we* proclaim also to you" (v. 3). This "we" can be inclusive: it means the writer along with his readers. John uses "we" like that in verses 6–10, such as in verse 9, "If we confess our sins."[12] But in verses 1–3, as well as verse 5, John uses "we" exclusively, as in "we" and not "you" the readers. The emphasis and shift are obvious. There is something or someone (namely, "that which was from the beginning," v. 1) that a certain group of people (the "we") have heard, seen, and touched that is now being proclaimed to others (the "you" of verse 3). Think of it this way. Our text covers three periods: first, the timeless preexistence of Christ; second, the era of eyewitness testimony; third, the occasion when John wrote the letter and its intended audience received it.[13] The "we" is the key to the second and third eras.

While we can identify the "we" as generically "the authorized teachers of the Church"[14] or "the authoritative bearers of tradition,"[15] it is simplest to call them "the apostles." Here is where the matter of authorship comes to bear. If the apostle John, the son of Zebedee, was not the author, we have a small problem,[16] for the person writing verses 1–4 claims apostolic authority. In some ways, this prologue announces the same authority with which Paul opened his letter to the Galatians: "Paul, an apostle—*not from* men nor through man, *but through* Jesus Christ and God the Father" (Gal. 1:1). The author of 1 John presents himself not only as one of the few people who saw Jesus (there were more than five hundred people who witnessed the resurrected Jesus, 1 Cor. 15:6), but as someone especially commissioned to

12. Also note that only in 1:4 does John write "we are writing." "From here on reference is in the first person singular, 'I write' (2:1, 7, 12, 13 [2×], all in the present tense . . . ; then 'I wrote' (2:14 [3×], 21, 26; 5:13), all in the aorist." Painter, *1, 2, and 3 John*, 123.

13. Yarbrough, *1–3 John*, 31. Cf. Schnackenburg, *The Johannine Epistles*, 49.

14. Dodd, *The Johannine Epistles*, 11.

15. Painter, *1, 2, and 3 John*, 123, 128.

16. For an excellent defense of Johannine authorship, see Andreas Köstenberger, L. Scott Kellum, and Charles Quarles, *The Cradle, the Cross, and the Crown: An Introduction to the New Testament* (Nashville: Broadman & Holman, 2009), 783–90. Also note Yarbrough's and D. A. Carson's summaries of their findings: "There is ample reason to suppose that he [the author] was John son of Zebedee." Yarbrough, *1–3 John*, 32. "In line with the majority view among Christian students during the past two thousand years (though out of step with today's majority), I think it highly probable that John the apostle wrote the Fourth Gospel and the three letters that traditionally bear his name." D. A. Carson, "The Johannine Writings," in *New Dictionary of Biblical Theology*, ed. T. Desmond Alexander and Brian S. Rosner (Downers Grove, IL: InterVarsity Press, 2000), 132.

proclaim the message about Jesus: "that which we have seen and heard [and "touched"! 1 John 1:1] we proclaim also to you" (1 John 1:3). He aligns himself with those few men who qualify to be apostles because they witnessed "all that he [Jesus] did" (Acts 10:39; cf. 1:21–22; Luke 1:2) and were "chosen by God as witnesses" (Acts 10:41). So, then, in sum, the "we" representing the "apostolic we," as it is sometimes called, best explains the language of ear, eye, and hand testimony, as well as the whole authoritative tone of the letter.

What Does "We" Say about "Which" to "You"?

This introductory study to John's first epistle has centered on small words with big ideas behind them. Having looked at "which" and "we," we come now to "you." Our final question is: "What does 'we' have to say about 'which' to 'you'?" The answers are found by finding another small word—*hina* in Greek, "so that" in English. Each "so that" of 1 John 1:3 and 4 is joined to a subjective verb (highlighted in bold below), that is, a verb that expresses purpose or intent:

> that which we have seen and heard we proclaim also to you, *so that* **you too may have fellowship with us**; and indeed our fellowship is with the Father and with his Son Jesus Christ. And we are writing these things *so that* **our joy may be complete**. (1 John 1:3–4)

The medieval historian and exegete Venerable Bede wrote of 1 John 1:3: "John shows quite clearly that those who want to have fellowship with God must first of all be joined to the church."[17] That is part of the first answer to our third question. The point, however, is even more specific. John teaches that whoever wants to have fellowship with God must first be joined to the apostolic testimony about God incarnate. Thus, verse 3 can be amplified to read as follows: "That which we apostles have seen and heard we apostles proclaim also to you—those who have not seen and heard—so that you too may have fellowship with us; and indeed our fellowship is with the Father and with his Son Jesus Christ." The Jewish philosopher Martin Buber wrote of the "I" and "Thou" relationship between man and God. Man is the "I," God the "Thou." The text before us shows that the "we" and "you" relationship—"we"

17. Bede, "On 1 John," in Bray, *James, 1–2 Peter, 1–3 John, Jude*, 168.

being the apostles and "you" being all who believe in Christ on account of their message—must come before the "I" and "Thou." I will put it this way: "You" are in Christ because of the apostolic "we." Without this apostolic "we," there is no you and me. Without the "holy, catholic, and *apostolic* church" (Nicene Creed),[18] there is no "communion of the saints" (Apostles' Creed). The good news of 1 John is that we have *koinōnia* ("fellowship") with God through our *koinōnia* with one another (4:7–8, 11–12; 4:20–21; 5:1–3), a relationship that starts by aligning ourselves with the apostolic testimony. We align ourselves by holding to the New Testament as God's authorized witness and faithfully participating in a local church that sits under the apostles' teachings. Are we trusting God's Word? Are we sitting under its teaching? Are we believing and doing what it says? Are we rejoicing with other believers in the salvation that it proclaims?

In Ephesians 2:19–21, Paul pours some concrete imagery around this idea of apostolic fellowship. He writes:

> So then you are no longer strangers and aliens, but you are fellow citizens with the saints and members of the household of God, built on *the foundation of the apostles* and prophets, Christ Jesus himself being the cornerstone, in whom the whole structure, being joined together, grows into a holy temple in the Lord. (Cf. Eph. 3:4–5; Rev. 21:14)

As in Ephesians 2, so in 1 John 1 the image for Christian *koinōnia* ("fellowship" or "what we hold in common with each other") is not sharing calories and caffeine after the service. Neither is it pie-in-the-sky pietism, sentimental spiritualism, or ecstasy for a few elite enthusiasts that is detached from apostolic testimony and teaching. Rather, the image is as hard as a rock but as soft and as warm as a human body, with its various indispensable members—its eyes and ears, its feet and hands (cf. 1 Cor. 12).

Apostolic Fellowship

Speaking of the human hand, perhaps you noticed how tactile this text is. Here John stresses not merely the material manifestation of the eternal God

18. I use the term *apostolic* not in the sense of succession but submission to the apostles' oral and then written witness. The universal church at all times everywhere is to be "devoted . . . to the apostles' teaching" (Acts 2:42).

incarnate but also the material testimony of the apostles. He adds "heard" and "touched" (which could be rendered as the very expressive "handled") to his Gospel prologue—"The Word became flesh and dwelt among us, and we have seen his glory" (John 1:14). In this way, he reminds us of his Gospel, where the apostolic ear-, eye-, and hand-testimony was on full display.

Envision 1 John 1:1–3 as a courtroom scene. As the defendant, John takes the stand. The prosecuting attorney asks, "You claim that Jesus was a real man. Is that right?" "Yes, I affirm the historical Jesus," John replies. "Are there any other witnesses to validate your claim?" "Certainly," John smiles. "There are ten more than two" (cf. Deut. 19:15; Matt. 18:16). Soon the Twelve are put in the dock. "Did any of you *hear* this Jesus teach?" They all nod their heads. James says, "I sat through his Sermon on the Mount, his parables of the kingdom, his Olivet Discourse, his . . ." Simon the Zealot zealously interjects, "And I heard him say of *lawyers*, 'Woe to you lawyers! For you have taken away the key of knowledge. You did not enter yourselves, and you hindered those who were entering'" (Luke 11:52). Matthias quips, "Sure, but I heard his seven woes to the scribes and Pharisees. Quite the sermon that was!" The lawyer shakes his head in dismay. "Enough! Let's up the ante, shall we?" He continues, "But who has seen him? Did any of you *see* Jesus in the flesh?" They all nod again. "I saw him open a blind man's eyes," says Bartholomew. "I saw him turn over the tables in the temple," Andrew adds. "Oh, yeah," Philip interjects, "I saw him turn water into wine!" At this point, the prosecuting attorney shuffles a few papers, sits down, and utters, "No further questions, Your Honor."

Then the Twelve's attorney, Barrister Paraclete by name, walks over to the witnesses, folds his arms, winks, and begins his cross-examination: "I have only one question. We have heard testimony about hearing. But let's be honest: we all know that hearing is not the surest sense. We have also heard testimony about seeing, but again, while more compelling, it is not enough to convince me. My question, then, is this: Did any of you *touch* this Jesus of Nazareth?" The heretics in the balcony, whom we will meet soon enough in our study of 1 John, shudder. James the son of Alphaeus says, "He washed my feet." Matthew and Thaddeus say in unison, "Me, too." They all say, "Me, too." Peter says, "I touched his hand when he pulled me out of the stormy sea." John says, "I laid my head against his chest at the Last Supper." Then Thomas moves to the microphone.

The crowd mumbles beneath their breath, "Doubting Thomas, doubting Thomas, doubting Thomas." But the other Eleven are filled with excitement. "They all touched," Thomas begins, "his resurrected body." The courtroom quiets. "And . . . I did, too."

He then retells the dramatic story (now on official court record in John 20:24–28):

> "When the others told me, 'We have seen the Lord,' I said to them, 'Unless I see in his hands the mark of the nails, and place my finger into the mark of the nails, and place my hand into his side, I will never believe.' You see, I wanted not only to see and hear, but also to touch, to place my finger into Christ's wounds. Well, what happened? I got my wish. Eight days later, Jesus appeared to us. He stood among us and said, 'Peace be with you.' Then he approached me and said, 'Thomas, put your finger here, and see my hands; and put out your hand, and *place it in* my side. Do not disbelieve, but believe.' I complied with Jesus' finger-into-the flesh request, and needless to say, I doubted no more. My hesitancy turned into a hallelujah. I declared, 'My Lord and my God!'
>
> "Your Honor, ladies and gentlemen of the jury—along with these Eleven, I am an eye-, ear-, and hand-witness that the eternal and transcendent God became immanent and palpable!"
>
> "I have no further questions," Mr. Paraclete concludes.

The courtroom is abuzz. The judge pounds his gavel! He pounds it again. The verdict is clear. The apostolic victory cheer echoes throughout the chambers.

The prologue of 1 John instructs us that without the Twelve's testimony, we are left groping in the dark about Jesus. Don't underestimate their unique position and privilege. Before his resurrection, Jesus declared to them, "Blessed are your eyes, for they see, and your ears, for they hear. For truly, I say to you, many prophets and righteous people longed to see what you see, and did not see it, and to hear what you hear, and did not hear it" (Matt. 13:16–17). After his resurrection, in all his appearances, our Lord stressed the necessity of their tangible witness. In Luke 24:38–39, for example, he said to them, "Why are you troubled, and why do doubts arise in your hearts? See my hands and my feet, that it is I myself. *Touch me*, and see." Again, we stay in "touch" with the divine testimony concerning Jesus by staying in fellowship with the apostolic witness. Let us never let go of this God-appointed and God-approved hand! Let us hold on to it against all opposition to the truth.

Many summers ago, two Mormon missionaries knocked on my front door. On two successive Wednesday afternoons, we discussed the differences between the Church of Latter-day Saints and the apostolic church of Jesus Christ (historic orthodox Christianity). One of the issues I challenged them on was the historical viability of Mormonism. Namely, I questioned a few of the persons and places in the Book of Mormon that have no ancient or modern account to affirm their existence.

My fact-finding mission quickly frustrated them. In haste and apparent disgust, one of the young men replied, "Listen, I am a Mormon because I have faith." He paused, wiped his brow, and continued, "And I hope you would still believe in Christianity even if there was no historical evidence to support it." What do you make of that reply? It certainly fits the current postmodern mentality, and it does have a ring of piety to it. But since I am neither postmodern nor overly pietistic, I would have none of it. I immediately and emphatically stated that I would not believe in Christianity if there were no historical evidences to support its claims. I would not believe in Jericho and Jerusalem if there were no historical verification that such cities ever existed. I would not believe that Jesus walked on this earth and died on a cross unless there was proof. I would not believe that he rose from the dead unless eyewitnesses had actually heard his voice, seen his face, and touched his body.

The point I made to the Mormon missionaries still stands: Christian faith is not a leap in the dark. Our faith is factual. It is based on the facts of eyewitness testimony. So while it might sound super-spiritual to sing, "He lives, he lives, Christ Jesus lives today! He walks with *me* and talks with *me* along life's narrow way. . . . You ask me how *I know* he lives? He lives within *my heart*,"[19] apostolic piety sings a different tune. It sings of the fact of the living Christ on the basis of the testimony of those he walked with and talked with along life's narrow way. I know that he lives because of them.

Apostles' Joy

With his first "so that" phrase (1 John 1:3), John answers the question *what does "we" have to say about "which" to "you"?* by teaching that who-

19. Homer A. Rodeheaver, "He Lives" (1933).

ever wants to have fellowship with God must first be joined to the apostolic testimony concerning God incarnate. With his second "so that" phrase, he writes about the motive of joy: "And we are writing these things so that our joy may be complete" (1 John 1:4).

At first glance, two details about this fourth verse strike me as odd. First, why does John use the first-person plural "we" ("we are writing") when elsewhere in the letter he uses only the first-person singular (e.g., "I am writing," 1 John 2:1, and "I write to you," 2:21)? Did the Twelve sit down together and write chapter 1, and then John took it from there? That is highly unlikely, especially since at this time (A.D. 85–95), John might be the only surviving apostle. The answer can be seen in the three different ways in which John uses "we" in 1 John:

1. John uses "the *dissociative* 'we'" in 1 John 1:1–3 as well as verse 5: "we apostles," not "you nonapostles."
2. Then in verse 4, he uses "'we' as a substitute for 'I'" (close to "the royal we" in English): "we [John on behalf of the other apostles] write to you."
3. Finally, in verses 6–10, he uses "the *associative* 'we.'"[20] This "we" includes us (e.g., "If we say we [author(s) and reader(s)] have fellowship with him while we walk in darkness, we lie and do not practice the truth," v. 6).

Next we turn our attention to the second oddity. I did not expect the "our"! I expected John to write: "And we are writing these things so that *your* [not *our*] joy may be complete." It is strange enough that John would end his rooted-in-history prologue with a plea for an unfulfilled emotion. What does joy have to do with eyewitness testimony and apostolic fellowship? The oddity is enhanced when we ask, "What is John on about with his own *personal* joy?" That sounds self-centered. It was so off-putting a purpose statement that some scribe along the way, as he was copying the New Testament, deleted "our" and inserted "your." This is called a *textual variant* or a *variant reading*. The variant reading is wrong (note especially

20. These three ways of talking about "the 'we' of authoritative testimony" come from Richard Bauckham, *Jesus and the Eyewitnesses: The Gospels as Eyewitness Testimony* (Grand Rapids: Eerdmans, 2006), 371–72.

2 John 12; cf. 1 Thess. 3:9), not only because our oldest and best manuscripts of the New Testament do not have it, but also because it is thematically off.

I'll illustrate. My joy as a parent is "full" (KJV) or fuller—brought "into a state of completeness"[21]—when my children obey the Lord. I am full of joy when I obey the Lord. My joy is fuller when they also obey the Lord. Similarly, when John thinks of the Christians in or around Ephesus—whom he calls "my children" throughout this epistle (e.g., "my little children," 2:1)—his joy is perfected when they are walking hand in hand with the apostolic testimony and teaching. That is his pastoral goal in this overtly pastoral love letter.

Yet there is a dark side to this end stress on joy. It "also constitutes a certain sober foreshadowing, like sunshine bathing a picnic while thunderheads boil up on the horizon."[22] John speaks of joy, knowing that the church or churches that he was writing to were on the verge of losing their theological, ethical, and social bearings, or had already lost them, because of "false prophets" (1 John 4:1), "antichrists" (2:18), and "deceivers" (2 John 7). These impostors were denying that Jesus had come in the flesh—that he had even had a human body to hear, see, and touch.

We will encounter these proto-Gnostics soon enough. For now, we are reminded that the incarnation is the foundation of our salvation. Rejoice in that! We are also reminded that, as Hilary of Arles summarized: "The fullness of joy comes when we are in *fellowship with the apostles*, as well as of the Father, Son and Holy Spirit."[23] Let us also rejoice in that, as we continue to live and share our apostolic faith.

The Foundation of Christian Fellowship

In the prologue of John's first epistle, we have learned about apostolic fellowship: namely, that the unique and eternal fellowship between the Father and the Son that was manifested in the once-for-all, exclusive event of the incarnation, observed by the apostles at a particular point in history, has been through them extended to the universal church. Today when some-

21. Colin G. Kruse, *The Letters of John*, Pillar New Testament Commentary (Grand Rapids: Eerdmans, 2000), 58–59.

22. Yarbrough, *1–3 John*, 43.

23. Hilary of Arles, "Introductory Commentary on 1 John," in Bray, *James, 1–2 Peter, 1–3 John, Jude*, 168 (emphasis added).

one becomes a Christian, he or she "enters into this one ageless, universal fellowship—a fellowship springing from the Godhead, coursing through the apostles, and flowing through every genuine believer who has ever been or will ever be."[24] We are now and eternally in living fellowship with the One who was "from the beginning." That is a *koinōnia* worth celebrating! It is also a *koinōnia* worth living out. Let us not grow weary of holding on to Christ through holding on to the apostles and holding out to the world the joyful good news of our gospel.

24. Philip W. Comfort and Wendell C. Hawley, *1–3 John*, Cornerstone Biblical Commentary (Carol Stream, IL: Tyndale, 2007), 332.

2

Live in the Light

1 John 1:5–10

This is the message we have heard from him and proclaim to you, that God is light, and in him is no darkness at all. If we say we have fellowship with him while we walk in darkness, we lie and do not practice the truth. But if we walk in the light, as he is in the light, we have fellowship with one another, and the blood of Jesus his Son cleanses us from all sin. (1 John 1:5–7)

Have you ever stared directly at the sun? That is one of those strange activities that your mother warned you not to do—and yet, drawn by curiosity, sinful tendencies, or even unavoidable innocence, at some time or another you have stared into the sun. Then what happened? Immediately your eyes began to burn, and the intense burning compelled you to turn your face. Then, when you turned from looking into the sun back to the world around you, your eyes had trouble refocusing. You also experienced—because your retina's cells kicked into overdrive—a brief eclipse and then what seemed like black blotches bouncing around you.

In 1 John 1:5–10, the apostle John intends to provide a similar experience. He sets before us the vision of God as absolute light, a light far greater and purer than that spotted sun above. In so doing, he wants his readers to experience and recognize the blackness that is all around us and within us. He wants us to see the blackness of sin, the great darkness that is exposed only when we gaze intently on the perfect light of God. He also wants us to live in light of that light—to grasp that as "children of the light" (1 Thess. 5:5), we have a living bond with God (1 John 1:3), which means a life of lawfulness (2:1–6) and love (2:7–11).

God Is Light

In the fourth century, a scribe copying what we now call *Revelation* wrote atop the first page, "A Revelation of John." He also wrote in the margin the Greek words *tou theologou* ("the theologian"). Eugene Peterson notes the appropriateness of this title for John:

> St. John is a theologian whose entire mind is saturated with thoughts of God, his whole being staggered by a vision of [*theos*] God. The world-making, salvation-shaping word of God is heard and pondered and expressed. He is God-intoxicated, God-possessed, God-articulate.[1]

Along this same line of commendation, Robert Yarbrough adds the following observation concerning John's letters:

> If 1–3 John leaves the disciple who studies them with any single lasting impression, it is the grandeur and centrality of God . . . . Part of this is the sheer volume of references to him. There is hardly a verse or even clause anywhere that does not name a person of the Godhead (Trinity), a divine attribute, or a divine work (like a command that has come from God). These letters are not simply theological, as one might say ale is alcoholic; they are rather theology distillate, analogous to highest-proof grain alcohol that is highly flammable and intoxicating in even small amounts. God—mainly Father and Son, but occasionally also Holy Spirit—suffuses every situation John envisions, each piece of counsel he issues, every sentiment he conveys, each affirmation he sets forth. No OT psalmist is any more God saturated in awareness than the writer of these letters.[2]

1. Eugene H. Peterson, *Reversed Thunder: The Revelation of John and the Praying Imagination* (New York: HarperOne, 1991), 3.

2. Robert W. Yarbrough, *1–3 John*, Baker Exegetical Commentary on the New Testament (Grand Rapids: Baker, 2008), 27–28.

After the prologue (1 John 1:1–4), the body of the letter begins with a proclamation. It is a heralding of a royal decree defining the divinity! Who is God?

People answer this question in a variety of ways. An atheist claims that the notion of God is fictitious or delusional, while an agnostic believes that God is an unknowable possibility. Other views range from God's being seen as cosmic Santa Claus to God's being hailed as the divine feminine. The Westminster divines answered this question, stating that "God is a Spirit, infinite, eternal, and unchangeable, in his being, wisdom, power, holiness, justice, goodness, and truth" (WSC A. 4). John gives a shorter definition than the catechism, but it is no less accurate: "This is the message we have heard from him and proclaim to you, that God is light, and in him is no darkness at all" (1 John 1:5).

Perhaps John earned the designation "the theologian" not only because he is God-focused but also because he is able to bring clear definition to difficult concepts, as he does here. Instead of compiling a list of all the single, compound, and descriptive names for God (there are 192 in the Bible),[3] or laying out all the designations and descriptive and metaphorical titles for God (there are 152),[4] John simply goes with "light," an image and word that even a child can picture and say.

But in what sense is God light? Light enables vision, produces growth, reveals beauty, exposes blemishes, guides travelers, and warms the earth. Is one, some, or every one of those characteristics characteristic of God's character? The Bible sheds some light on what John likely means by "light." In the Old Testament, when referencing God, light symbolizes communication (what God reveals) and character (who God is). In Exodus, for example, God reveals himself to Moses in the burning bush and to Israel as a cloud of fire illuminating the people's way. When the tabernacle is erected, God's presence is signaled with fire present in the golden lampstands. In the Psalms, we read lines such as "The Lord is my light and my salvation" (Ps. 27:1) and "You are clothed with splendor and majesty, covering yourself with light as with a garment" (104:1–2). Interestingly (and Christologically significant!), this Old Testament imagery is echoed in the New Testament by and for Jesus.

3. From Walter W. Elwell, *Topical Analysis of the Bible* (Grand Rapids: Baker, 1991), 10–34, cited in Yarbrough, *1–3 John*, 48n7.

4. Ibid.

For example, Jesus announced, "I am the light of the world" (John 8:12; cf. 9:5). He also claimed, "I have come into the world as light, so that whoever believes in me may not remain in darkness" (John 12:46). Similarly, Simeon described Jesus' mission as "a light for revelation" (Luke 2:32), while Paul spoke of the resurrected and exalted Lord as "the blessed and only Sovereign, the King of kings and Lord of lords, who alone has immortality, *who dwells in unapproachable light*" (1 Tim. 6:15–16). Perhaps the biggest light show concerning Jesus was his transfiguration, when his face was "like the sun" and his clothes "white as [the] light" (Matt. 17:2). Jesus' self-producing, self-sustaining, and self-projecting light reflects only one other person on the scene: the Father, who shows up with or within "a *bright* cloud" (v. 5).[5] So while God the Father is the "light" that John has in view in 1 John 1:5, who am I to say that Jesus—who "has made [the Father] known" to us (John 1:18; cf. 14:9)—doesn't shed some light on the communicative and character dimensions of God? And after all, it is Jesus who has given the apostles this precise message to announce: "This is the message we have heard *from him* [Jesus] and proclaim to you" (1 John 1:5). While this message is not a complete summary of Jesus' earthly teachings, it certainly is an excellent summary of the divine nature, the starting point of the gospel, and the antidote for the community John addresses that is "beset by darkness of a doctrinal, ethical, and relational nature."[6]

Jesus' light on the Father centers on the Father's character, namely, that "God is light" in the sense that he is perfectly pure both morally (no evil/all good) and intellectually (no error/all truth). As 1 John 1:9 clarifies, "light" equals "faithful[ness]" (God does what he says he will do) and "just[ice]" (and he does so in absolute righteousness). That perfect purity is emphasized in the synthetic parallelism below (in which the first idea in the first line is expanded on or further explained in the second line):

God	is	light,
in him	is	no darkness at all

5. Also compare Jesus Christ super*star* with Moses and Elijah (Matt. 17:3), who are stars in their own right, but seemingly not shining. Jesus' brightness is about Jesus' divine glory. The *shekinah* glory that led Israel in the wilderness (Ex. 13:21), came upon Moses at Sinai (24:15–18), and filled the tabernacle (40:34–35) and temple (2 Chron. 7:1–3) is embodied in Jesus.

6. Yarbrough, *1–3 John*, 50.

The double negative in Greek—"no darkness . . . none" (author's translation)—highlights God's positive perfections. "In him is no shade, speck, or stain of moral imperfection."[7]

> My God, how wonderful thou art, thy majesty how bright!
> How beautiful thy mercy-seat, in depths of burning light!
> How wonderful, how beautiful, the sight of thee must be,
> Thine endless wisdom, boundless pow'r, and aweful purity![8]

This "aweful purity," as the poet Faber called it, must be our starting point. To John, God is both "love" (1 John 4:16) and "light" (1:5). But the apostolic ordering is significant. To the issues in ancient Ephesus as well as to our evangelistic presentations in the contemporary world, it matters that light comes before love. God's holiness (he is light) shows our unholiness (we are stained black with sin) and thus the need of an incarnate and crucified Christ to wash us in his holy blood.

If We Say We Have Fellowship

In 1 John 1:6–10, John moves us from the acknowledgment that "God is light" to what it means to live in that light. These personal implications are the logical extension of the preceding verses. If we are to have fellowship with God (v. 3), who is holy (v. 5), then we are to be holy as he is holy. This is a call not to obtain equality with God but rather to share a quality with him. John warns, exhorts, and instructs in this way:

> If we say we have fellowship with [God] while we walk in darkness, we lie and do not practice [literally, "do"] the truth. But if we walk in the light, as he is in the light, we have fellowship with one another, and the blood of Jesus his Son cleanses us from all sin. (1 John 1:6–7)

These verses are the first two of five terse conditional clauses (*if*, etc.). As table 1 below shows, the ordering of the phrases goes this way: negative,

7. David L. Allen, *1–3 John: Fellowship in God's Family*, Preaching the Word (Wheaton, IL: Crossway, 2013), 34.

8. Frederick W. Faber, "My God, How Wonderful Thou Art" (1848).

positive, negative, positive, negative.[9] Note also that the phrase "if we say" occurs three times followed by a corrective phrase that starts "we" (1 John 1:6, 8, 10), with the last clause—"We make [God] a liar"—an intentionally shocking end stress. Those negative *if*-clauses contrast the positive phrases that speak of the Father and the Son's cleansing actions (the Father "cleanses us," v. 7, and Jesus' blood "cleanse[s] us," v. 9).

Verse 6	Negative (-)	If we *say*	We lie and do **not** practice the *truth*
Verse 7	Positive (+)	If we *walk*	He [God] *cleanses* us from all sin
Verse 8	Negative (-)	If we *say*	We deceive ourselves, and the *truth* is **not** in us
Verse 9	Positive (+)	If we *confess*	[God] *cleanse*[s] us from all unrighteousness
Verse 10	Negative (-)	If we *say*	We make him [God] a liar [**un***truthful*]

Table 1. John's Symmetric Structure

While it is clear that the phrase "if we say" introduces some aspect of false belief within the church followed by a denial and correction, it is uncertain that these are popular slogans from the false teachers we will meet in 1 John chapters 2–5. I do not deny that the spiritual adultery that happened in Jeremiah's day is witnessed by John in his own: "the prophets prophesy falsely, and the priests [leaders] rule at their direction; [and!] my [God's] people love to have it so" (Jer. 5:31). Yet it is also quite possible that Christians—false teachers or no false teachers—are tempted to think and act in the way laid out in 1 John 1:6.

In 1 John 1:6, the apostle teaches that a person claiming closeness with God while walking in the world's darkness (see John 3:19–21) has broken fellowship with God, or never had it in the first place. Yarbrough contrasts "cheap talk"

9. There are various ways to divide the beginning of 1 John into preaching units. First John 1:5–2:11 could form a unit because of the theme of light and darkness, including the inclusio where light and darkness are mentioned five times in 1:5–7 and six times in 2:9–11. First John 1:6–2:2 could also form a unit because of the theme of sin ("sin" is mentioned in nearly every verse, seven times in 1:8–2:2!). But I chose 1:5–10 based on John's symmetric structure, as noted in table 1.

(1 John 1:6) with "authentic living" (v. 7).[10] Envision the cheap talk in this way. Picture the popular gospel drawing in which God in his holiness is on one side of the chasm and man in his sinfulness is on the other side. The cross is then drawn in the middle to show the only way to get to God. In verse 6, John gives an ironic twist to that image. In the chasm, he draws a man yelling up to God and boasting to the world, "I'm in fellowship with God." Like Talkative in John Bunyan's *The Pilgrim's Progress*, "He talketh of Prayer, of Repentance, of Faith, and of the New-birth: but he knows but only to *talk* of them. . . . Religion hath no place in his heart . . . . All he hath lieth in his *tongue*."[11] He thinks he is "on moral high ground when from God's viewpoint we languish in some [dark] pit."[12] What a grim and gross sight of human arrogance!

John teaches that we cannot claim to have fellowship with God and still continue to "walk" in "darkness." He tells us that we are not to be hypocrites, pledging allegiance to God with our lips but trampling on his law with our lives. Those who profess to know God are to be distinguishable from the rest of the world—as distinguishable as light is from darkness. We are to be different especially, as we will see in 1 John 1:8–10, in both our attitude toward sin and our actions against it. Before we look at the final verses, however, notice first John's correction in verse 7, "But if we walk in the light, as he [God, 1:5] is in the light, we have fellowship with one another, and the blood of Jesus his Son cleanses us from all sin." To walk in the light is to live a life that reflects the holiness of God. As we will explore in the next chapter, it is to imitate Christ's lovingly obedient example.

There are two results of walking in the light. The first result is fellowship with other believers. We saw in 1 John 1:1–4 how John sees an intrinsic connection between our relationship with God and our relationship to the apostolic eyewitnesses. Here we see that if we are rightly connected to God, then we will be rightly connected with other Christians. What a curse-crushing truth! Christian *koinōnia* walks upon the communal enmity caused by the fall and walks across all ethical and cultural divides created by human sin. How wonderful it is to think and *act* on this truth. Our local churches should celebrate this reality when we gather for worship, share meals, reach out to the lost, provide for the poor, comfort the oppressed,

10. Yarbrough, *1–3 John*, 56.

11. *The Pilgrim's Progress*, World's Classics (Oxford: Oxford University Press, 1984), 63–65.

12. Yarbrough, *1–3 John*, 55.

support and encourage missionaries, and join hands with gospel-centered churches in our cities and around the world.

The second result is that "the blood of Jesus . . . cleanses us from all sin" (1 John 1:7). Rudolf Bultmann claimed that this phrase was an artificial editorial edition, and that the "content" of the verse "is disturbing."[13] Bultmann missed the whole point. He failed to see the logical connection that when one walks in God's light, that light shows us who we are—sinners! As a result, the only way forward is to cling to the cross, or, to follow the metaphor here, to be washed in the blood. As Christians, we need the ongoing benefits ("cleanses" is in the present tense) of Jesus' atoning death ("the blood"). We also need to know and remember that "all sin"—or perhaps translated "every sin" or "any you please"[14]—is continually covered.

Does John mean the sin of adultery, bearing false witness, coarse joking, deceit, envy, fraud, gossip, holding a grudge, idleness, judgmentalism, killing the innocent, lying, malice, not keeping oaths, oppressing the poor, prayerlessness, quarrelling, returning insult for insult, slander, trusting in riches, unlawful divorce, violence, and witchcraft? Yes. Does he mean the sin of loving the world, loving yourself, not loving your neighbor or enemy or fellow Christian or God? Yes. They are "all" covered! Every single sin that stains us and makes us too defiled to commune with a holy God has been cleansed by Christ's propitiation. His atoning sacrifice for our sin has made fellowship with God possible. Amazing! While Bultmann found Jesus' blood disturbing, we are to find it preserving. It preserves our fellowship with each other on earth and with our Father in heaven.

If We Say We Have No Sin

With our eyes open to the awesome effects of Christ's atonement, let us not be blind, as some of John's opponents were, to the reality of our ongoing struggle with sin. In 1 John 1:8–9, John moves from his first claim and correction (vv. 6–7) to his second. The second claim is saying that "we have no sin." The correction follows: "we deceive ourselves, and the truth is not

13. Rudolf Bultmann, *The Johannine Epistles*, trans. R. Philip O'Hara, Hermeneia (Philadelphia: Fortress, 1973), 20.

14. "Every sin" is from Daniel Wallace, and "any you please" is from Nigel Turner, quoted in Yarbrough, *1–3 John*, 58.

in us. If we confess our sins, he is faithful and just to forgive us our sins and to cleanse us from all unrighteousness."

This false claim sounds quite contemporary. We have come up with creative names for *sin* (*mistake*, *flaw*, *slip-up*, *my bad*). We have reinterpreted our wickedness through very sophisticated psychological and social lenses (e.g., if a woman pregnant out of wedlock will likely suffer economic and emotional hardships, then abortion is acceptable). Still, the irony is that *sin* isn't dropped from our vocabulary in the common heartfelt confession, "I am not a *sinner*!" "We have no sin" is the ancient version of it. Here John is dealing either with someone who denies that there is something fundamentally wrong with human nature brought about by Adam's sin or with a Christian who believes he is now sinless by virtue of some mystical fellowship with Christ. I take it to mean the second. I say that because the verb is in the present tense (an ongoing action) and because each time the expression *echō hamartian* ("to have sin") is used in the New Testament (John 9:41; 15:22, 24; 19:11), it addresses the guilt related to actual sins. Yet whether it is the denial of the existence of original sin in all humans or actual sin in the believer, the thought is heretical.

John replies to this old but still-alive heresy by saying that such people are untruthful and self-deceptive. Those who deny their sinful nature ("we are not sinners") deceive no one around them and certainly not God. When Adam, as our representative, first sinned, God regarded that sin to be ours as well. We inherited sin from Adam! And the guilt of Adam's sin imputed, as well as the continuing effects of that imputation even in the regenerate, should be obvious (cf. WCF 6.3.6). The only people they deceive are themselves. Note for emphasis the parallelism:

we deceive	ourselves, and
the truth is not in	us.

Such liars are "doubly damned—guilty before God objectively and sinning again by being oblivious to the fact."[15] No one lives like those prisoners described in Plato's *Allegory of the Cave*. Life on earth is no illusion. Sin is no shadow on the wall. For example, like every other parent in the world, I am teaching my young children not to hit, bite, lie, and steal. I am teaching them not to be selfish. Why?

15. Ibid., 62.

I do so because those sins come so naturally to them. It is not just my kids. Why is it that we have never had to spend one instant telling our children how to love themselves, but that we battle daily to make them consider others better than themselves? Those who deny original sin deny the very noses on their faces. Yet the sad fact is that we live in a world where people have Pinocchio-sized noses but they simply ignore the obvious. The Russian novelist Ivan Turgenev gives a contrary perspective. Wisely, he writes, "I do not know what the heart of a bad man is like, but I do know what the heart of a good man is like, and it is terrible."[16] Or you might be more familiar with Jesus' version of that truth: "If you then, who are evil, know how to give good gifts to your children . . ." (Matt. 7:11). According to our sinless Savior, even gift-giving fathers are not free from the radical fallenness of the human condition.

Both Scripture and experience teach that man is both majestic and monstrous. We indeed are *majestic*, for among all creation we alone have a capacity for rational thought, moral choice, artistic creativity, covenantal relationships, and humble worship of the divine. But we are also *monstrous*. As Jesus said elsewhere, "For from within, out of the heart of man come evil thoughts, sexual immorality, theft, murder, adultery, coveting, wickedness, deceit, sensuality, envy, slander, pride, foolishness" (Mark 7:21–22). It is out of the heart—the very core of our being—that sin sprouts. Our sinful nature cannot be explained away by the social sciences as a surface problem!

What, then, is the way forward? Part of the solution that John gives to the denial of sin is the confession of sin: "If we confess our sins, [God] is faithful and just to forgive us our sins and to cleanse us from all unrighteousness" (1 John 1:9). If there is anything we are to "say," it is not that we have "no sin," but rather that we are "full of sin"—from head to heart and tail to toes—and therefore, "I'm sorry; please forgive me."

Confession can be public (Luke 18:13) and private (Ps. 32:5), individual (Ezra 10:1) and corporate (Neh. 9:3). We can confess personal sins (Matt. 3:6) and even the sins of others (Dan. 9:20). Confession can be made to others (Josh. 7:19–21), to those offended (James 5:16), and always to God (Ps. 51:1–4). The confession that John speaks of in 1 John 1:9 is to God.[17] Following the

16. Turgenev, quoted in R. Kent Hughes, *The Sermon on the Mount: The Message of the Kingdom*, Preaching the Word (Wheaton, IL: Crossway, 2001), 145.

17. "The conditional clause 'if we confess our sins' carries the force of a mitigated command: 'we should confess our sins.' Instead of a direct imperative telling us to confess our sins, John chooses a

biblical pattern for confession, we are to present our "transgressions to the LORD" (Ps. 32:5; cf. Dan. 9:20), knowing that whoever confesses will obtain his mercy (Prov. 28:13–14).

In *The Way of a Pilgrim*, a classic book in Russian Orthodox spirituality, the author combines the publican's prayer, "Lord, have mercy on me, a sinner," with Paul's admonition to "pray without ceasing." He calls this combination the *Jesus Prayer.* This is modeled by Franny in J. D. Salinger's *Franny and Zooey.* The Jesus Prayer consists of repeatedly saying, "Lord Jesus Christ, Son of God, have mercy on me." Although this is called the *Jesus Prayer,* in reality it is far from how Jesus taught us to pray (Matt. 6:5–15). Especially if you increase the speed and number of repetitions, it resembles more a pagan mantra than a Christian prayer. Yet this Jesus Prayer certainly highlights the necessity of a life of continuous confession, which is the point that John is making. Our confession is not merely the sinner's prayer (the confession made when we first came to Christ) but the sinner-simultaneous-saint's prayers (our continual confession of sins as we grow in God's lightness and thus likeness). To borrow from two traditional Presbyterian prayers for corporate worship, we should pray privately and publicly:

> Almighty God, you love us, but we have not loved you.
> You call, but we have not listened.
> We walk away from neighbors in need,
> wrapped in our own concerns.
> We condone evil, prejudice, warfare, and greed.
> God of grace, help us to admit our sin, so that as you come to us in mercy,
> we may repent, turn to you, and receive forgiveness;
> through Jesus Christ our Redeemer. Amen.[18]

Followed by:

> O LORD our God, Thou art holy and we are sinful; Thou art strong and we are weak; Thou art ever in the light and we walk in darkness. Give us of Thy Spirit; That in penitence and trust we may grow in grace and in the

less direct method of pressing on us the necessity of confession of sin to God when we as Christians sin." Allen, *1–3 John*, 46.

18. Composed for the *Presbyterian Worshipbook* (Philadelphia: Westminster Press, 1970) and slightly altered for the *Book of Common Worship* (Louisville: Westminster John Knox, 1993), 89.

knowledge of our Lord and Saviour. Enlighten our minds; Purify our hearts; Renew our wills; And may we give ourselves wholly to Thee; For the sake of Jesus Christ our Lord. Amen.[19]

Throughout Scripture, we find warnings about the danger of concealing our sins as well as the blessings of confessing them (e.g., "Whoever conceals his transgressions will not prosper, but he who confesses and forsakes them will obtain mercy," Prov. 28:13). Indeed, genuine repentance does lead to mercy, or to forgiveness and cleansing, as John words it, because God is "faithful and just."[20] We are often faithless and unjust. We sin against God and others. God is always faithful and just. He keeps his promised punishments for sin and does so through the cross. So again on the basis of Christ's blood, God *forgives* and *cleanses*. He cancels the debt and brings restoration, and he removes the stain of sin, making us holy and thus renewing our fellowship with him.

IF WE SAY WE HAVE NOT SINNED

As we will see in the chapters ahead, John will continue some of these same themes as he moves into chapter 2. But before he gets there, he adds one final thought, dealing with a final false claim: "If we say we have not sinned, we make him [God] a liar, and his word is not in us" (1 John 1:10).

Once a woman confided in the hymn-writer Charles Wesley, "I am a great sinner. I am a Christian, but I sometimes fail so dreadfully. Please pray for me." Wesley looked at her rather sternly and replied, "Yes, Madam, I will pray for you; for truly you are a great sinner." Taken aback by Wesley's demeanor and straightforward reply, she answered, "What do you mean? I have never done anything very wrong."[21] In verse 10, John is dealing with someone similar to this woman, namely, a person who acknowledges original sin but fails to see the depth of her depravity—or, worse, someone who thinks

19. *Book of Common Worship* (Philadelphia: Board of Christian Education of the Presbyterian Church in the United States of America, 1946), 89.

20. Note the Old Testament link of God's attributes—"faithful" and "just" (Ex. 34:6–7; Deut. 32:4; Pss. (LXX) 18:8–9; 32:4–5; 84:12; 88:15; 95:13; 118:160)—with his forgiveness (Isa. 1:18; Jer. 31:34; 33:8; 50:20; Ezek. 18:21–23; 33:11, 14–16; cf. Pss. 33:5; 51:4; 119:64; Mic. 7:18–20). See John Painter, *1, 2, and 3 John*, Sacra Pagina (Collegeville, MN: Liturgical Press, 2002), 155–56.

21. For the Wesley illustration, see James Montgomery Boice, *The Epistles of John: An Expositional Commentary* (Grand Rapids: Baker, 1979), 34.

she has become perfectly sanctified.[22] And while we might chuckle upon hearing that Wesley story, this attitude toward sin is no laughing matter. In fact, this third false claim might be the most serious of the three mistakes in moral judgment.

In Proverbs 30:20 we find one of those poignant proverbs: "This is the way of an adulteress: she eats and wipes her mouth and says, 'I have done no wrong.'" That is not just the ancient adulteress's mentality. From the Oval Office to death row, we have become experts in eating from the forbidden tree, wiping our mouths, and then turning to the world and saying, "I have not sinned. I have done nothing wrong. What do I need to confess?" But God's Word tells us here that God hates such denial. Why? He hates it because to say that we have never sinned is to call God "a liar." What sacrilege! To lump God who is "light" (1 John 1:5) in with the dark world's darkest characters—the devil (John 8:44) and false teachers (1 John 2:22; 4:20; 5:10)—is a grave offense. This claim of sinlessness stemming from whatever it might be called today—"a complete surrender," "second blessing," "double portion of the Spirit"—makes God a liar because God makes the opposite claim. He claims that "all have sinned" (Rom. 3:23). He claims, "Surely there is not a righteous man on earth who does good and never sins" (Eccl. 7:20).[23] He claims that we are in need of ongoing forgiveness because we continue to sin (1 John 2:1). So who is right and who is wrong? Who is lying? Is it the man, claiming that he has never sinned, or is it God, who claims that all have sinned? There is only one right answer: "Let God be true, and every man a liar" (Rom. 3:4 NIV).

It is said that a man who claimed to be without sin once confronted Charles Spurgeon, the great Baptist preacher. Intrigued, the preacher invited this man home for dinner. After hearing the claims through, Spurgeon arose from his chair, picked up his glass of water, and threw it across the man's face. Immediately and understandably, this "perfect" man showed his imperfections, causing quite a scene, allowing his anger and language to cross the line of courtesy. To which Spurgeon (with a

22. Is 1 John 1:10 a restatement of verse 8, a summary of verses 6–9, or a progressive expansion of the preceding verses? I take it as the latter, as Philip W. Comfort and Wendell C. Hawley summarize: "the focus is on the actual acts of sin emanating from the sinful nature." *1–3 John*, Cornerstone Biblical Commentary (Carol Stream, IL: Tyndale, 2007), 333.

23. Cf. Job 15:14–16; Prov. 20:9; Isa. 53:6.

twinkle in his eye, I imagine) replied, "Ah, you see, the old man within is not as dead as you claim. He had simply fainted and I have revived him with but a glass of water!"[24]

That story might or might not be true. But it does help to illustrate the point: there may be a few "perfect" people who need a perfectly good splash of water to awaken them to their imperfections. For, you see, no one in the kingdom of God on earth "has been so transformed by God that they have reached a level of spiritual maturity that excludes the need for ongoing forgiveness."[25] No one has reached "sinless perfection." We are all still sinners in need of God's constant cleansing.

Forgive Us Our Daily Debts

At almost exactly the center of the Sermon on the Mount (with 116 lines before and 114 after it) is a perfect masterpiece on prayer—the Lord's Prayer (Matt. 6:9–13). It is perfect in both structure and substance. Structurally, Jesus gives six petitions in two symmetrical parts. The first part, with its three petitions, focuses on God, and thus all the petitions contain the word *your* (referring to God)—"hallowed be *your* name," "*your* kingdom come," "*your* will be done." These are what we might call the *divine petitions*. The second part, with its three petitions, focuses on human needs; hence the *our* and *us* in the petitions—"give *us* this day *our* daily bread," and "forgive *us our* debts,"[26] and "lead *us* not into temptation, but deliver *us* from evil." These are the *human petitions*. These final three petitions focus, in some way or another, on our struggle with sin. We live "in the land of debts," and "we are up to our ears" in debt.[27] We war against daily temptations. We fight against the cosmic evil forces without and common evil forces within. And yet we pray to our holy, heavenly God—"Our Father in heaven, hallowed be your name" (Matt. 6:9).

24. The Spurgeon illustration, with slight changes, was taken from David Jackman, *The Message of John's Letters*, The Bible Speaks Today (Downers Grove, IL: InterVarsity Press, 1988), 36.

25. Gary M. Burge, *Letters of John*, NIV Application Commentary (Grand Rapids: Zondervan, 1996), 92.

26. The verb *to forgive* (*aphiēmi*) in the phrase "forgive us our debts" is the same word used in 1 John 1:9.

27. Martin Luther, quoted in Frederick Dale Bruner, *The Christbook: Matthew 1–12*, 2nd rev. ed. (Grand Rapids: Eerdmans, 2004), 308.

"God is light" is the message of 1 John 1:5–10. If we are to walk in the light, as we are called to do, our first step is to recognize the darkness within. A proper assessment of self and sin—in which we say neither "we have no sin" nor "we have not sinned" but rather "we have sin" and "we still sin"—should lead to a life of consistent contrite confessions whereby the Father's forgiveness is given and our fellowship with God and others, through the blood of Christ, is renewed. It should also lead to a life that reflects the light of God—a theme that we will explore further in the rest of the epistle.

3

Advocacy and Example

1 John 2:1–6

My little children, I am writing these things to you so that you may not sin. But if anyone does sin, we have an advocate with the Father, Jesus Christ the righteous. (1 John 2:1)

Adolf Schlatter was a world-class Bible scholar. He was born in St. Gallen, Switzerland, in 1852 and died in Tübingen, Germany, in 1938. During his lifetime, he wrote on theology, ethics, and philosophy and published nine commentaries, including one of the world's best on the Gospel of John. His last book was a devotional that centered on knowing Jesus through the Gospels and other New Testament texts. It is entitled *Do We Know Jesus?* Historically, Schlatter's final quest "to know Jesus more deeply and fully" coincided with the rise of Nazi Germany. He did not live to see the atrocities, but he wrote as one who saw them coming. "Against the ominous backdrop of Adolf Hitler, the self-styled *Führer* (leader), who rallied the German masses in a quest for worldwide domination that would entail the extermination of millions of Jews,"[1] Schlatter presents Jesus as the ultimate Leader and Lord. For example, he begins his January 10, 1937, devotional on 1 John 1:8, 10:

1. From the "translators' preface" to Adolf Schlatter, *Do We Know Jesus? Daily Insights for the Mind and Soul*, trans. Andreas Köstenberger and Robert Yarbrough (Grand Rapids: Kregel, 2005), 17.

> If our *Führer* commanded me, "You must not acknowledge that you are a sinner. You are a useful member of the nation only if you are honorable," this is how I would respond: "This command cannot be obeyed. For if I obeyed it, I would be dishonorable. In that case I would be a liar."

Later he adds, "We are not spinning yarns when we acknowledge that we have sinned: we do, in fact, sin, and when we deny it we sin once again, with completely disastrous and shameful results. The apostle confronts us with God's testimony in order that we may not be cowards and resort to lies."[2]

In the previous chapter, we saw the blackness of human sin as exposed by the perfect divine light. In view of God's holiness, we should admit our sinfulness. We are not to say that "we have no sin" or "we have not sinned" but rather that "we have sin" and "we still sin." Through such heartfelt confessions, the Father's forgiveness is given afresh, and our fellowship with God and others, through the blood of Christ, is renewed. In 1 John 2:1–6, John picks up on the theme of reflecting God's light (1 John 1:7) through Jesus' advocacy and example. Because Jesus is our righteous Advocate who offered an expiatory propitiation for our sins, we can know that we have come to know him if we follow his lovingly obedient example. Put differently, because of the living fellowship we have with "Jesus Christ" (1:3), who is our Advocate and example (2:1b–6), we have the living hope of being delivered from the control and consequences of sin (v. 1a).

A Christ-Possible Hope

With a mix of fatherly tenderness, pastoral comfort, and apostolic authority, the aged elder wants those under his oversight—his spiritual "children"—to avoid sin: "My little children, I am writing these things to you so that you may not sin" (1 John 2:1). Yet John recognizes the sinfulness of humankind, even Christians. And so he balances that opening admonition with God's ongoing mercy in Christ: "But if anyone does sin, we have an advocate with the Father, Jesus Christ the righteous" (v. 1). Sin is inevitable but not excusable. Sin is inevitable, not excusable, and yet forgivable! It is forgivable because of Jesus' constant advocacy.

2. Ibid., 46–47.

But before we discuss that advocacy, let's not overlook John's hope. After what John said about sin in 1 John 1:8 and 10, does he genuinely believe that Christians can transcend their transgressions? Is John hopelessly idealistic or realistically serious? Oh, he is serious, and he is realistic. He doesn't believe in "sinless perfection," but he does believe in lives transformed by the power of the gospel. He does believe that "there is no room for sin in the Christian life."[3]

In his commentary on 1 John, Robert Yarbrough writes:

> In popular Christian religion of modern times, the impression is sometimes given that sin is in the end not intrinsic to the person ("God hates the sin but loves the sinner"), or that sin is compulsory by God's design ("that's just the way God made me"), or that salvation alters the destiny of the soul *someday* but not necessarily the behavior of the body *today* ("Christians aren't perfect, just forgiven" . . .), or that tolerance mandated by Scripture forbids ethical distinctions of any kind ("judge not lest you be judged"). While John would no doubt recognize the element of truth in some of these slogans in appropriate contexts, he would also decry their misuse. He writes to commend a higher road: liberation from the compulsion to believe, behave, and love in ways that fall short of God's glorious and transforming light. He writes to commend a full, satisfying, and efficacious knowledge of God.[4]

For John, in 1 John, to know God transcends intellectual understanding. It involves believing the right truths about Jesus, but also obeying Christ's commands, especially living out his law of love. Thus, when John writes, "I am writing these things to you so that you may not sin" (1 John 2:1), *sin* is broad enough to include disobeying God's revealed will concerning Jesus, as well as disregarding his ethical and social demands. Unbelief, disobedience, and lack of love are inseparably intertwined in John's definition of *sin*. In John's language, to "not sin" is nearly synonymous with "knowing God," for the person who knows God demonstrates the "pistic" (faith, 5:10–13), "ethical" (obedience, 3:3–4, 10a), and "agapic" (love, 4:20–21) characteristics of redemption.[5]

3. Rudolf Schnackenburg, *The Johannine Epistles: Introduction and Commentary*, trans. R. Fuller and I. Fuller (New York: Crossroad, 1992), 85.

4. Robert W. Yarbrough, *1–3 John*, Baker Exegetical Commentary on the New Testament (Grand Rapids: Baker, 2008), 71.

5. Ibid., 73. See especially figures 1–4 on pages 72–74. Martin Luther summarized this traditional Protestant view: "If the true knowledge of Christ is present, it will not be without fruit or without

Pistic (faith)	We cannot say that we know God and not believe in Jesus.
Ethical (obedience)	We cannot say that we know God and disobey his Word.
Agapic (love)	We cannot say that we know God and hate our neighbor.

Throughout 1 John, orthodoxy and orthopraxy are lawfully wed.

Thus, John's view of sin moves us beyond superficial stereotypes—that the nose-pierced, tattooed teenager is a sinner while the old lady with a long skirt and her hair in a bun is not. Moreover, it moves us to a deeper understanding of the challenge of Christian discipleship. We struggle not only against obvious evils, but also against the multicolored complexities of possible wickedness. Denying the desires of the flesh, the lusts of the eyes, and the pride in life is not checking off a list of *do*s and crossing out a list of *don'ts*. Overcoming the world and the devil isn't avoiding R-rated movies and smoking. Knowing God by saying "no" to sin is hard work. But it is work that God's Word calls us to. It is work, however, that is grounded in the finished work of Christ, the topic that John turns our attention to next.

His Advocacy, Our Security

Admittedly, knowing God by not sinning is a goal as lofty as climbing Mount Everest without food, shoes, gloves, and an oxygen supply. Yet it is obtainable through Mount Calvary. How do we prevent sin, which once controlled our lives, from ruling our lives? We cling to the finished (but ever-working) work of Jesus. The answer is Jesus' advocacy and example.

John starts with Jesus' role as our Advocate. Before the imperative to keep Christ's commandments (1 John 2:3–6), we are given the indicative of Christ's cross (2:1b–2): "But if anyone does sin, we have an advocate with the Father, Jesus Christ the righteous. He is the propitiation for our sins, and not for ours only but also for the sins of the whole world."

---

works that are truly good." He also wrote that "true believers . . . prove their faith with good works. For true knowledge does not consist in speculation but moves forward to performance." "Lectures on the First Epistle of St. John," in *The Catholic Epistles*, vol. 30 of *Luther's Works*, trans. and ed. Jaroslav Pelikan and W. A. Hansen (St. Louis: Concordia, 1972), 238.

The Lawyer

Nearly two hundred different names are used for Jesus in the Bible, such as *Immanuel, King of kings, Bread of Life, Alpha and Omega, Man of Sorrows, Root of David, Prince of Peace, Second Adam, Word of Life, Son of Man*, and *Son of God*. In 1 John 2:1, John calls Jesus *paraklēton*, translated "helper," "comforter," "intercessor," or, as the English Standard Version has it, "advocate." "Advocate" is an excellent translation because it highlights the legal sense of the word. The New Living Translation and New International Version also capture the sense of the word with their paraphrases, "someone to plead for you" (NLT) and "one who speaks . . . in our defense" (NIV 1984). Just as the Holy Spirit testifies "in favor of Jesus over against a hostile world,"[6] Jesus testifies before the throne of God in favor of us over against our sin and its due punishment. We have been assigned the greatest defense attorney in the universe, an Advocate who, every time we commit a crime against the divine, selflessly and justly "pleads" (Rom. 8:34) our case: "Father, I have suffered for this sinner. My righteousness is his now and forever."

Jesus is a willing and inexpensive defense attorney. For all his cases, he works pro bono. Moreover, he breaks the stereotype: he is not a greedy crook but a generous champion of our otherwise lost cause. In fact, he is a "righteous" Mediator who reflects the very holiness or "light" of God (1 John 1:5). As "the righteous" died "for the unrighteous" (1 Peter 3:18), so now he lives for the unrighteous (cf. Heb. 7:25ff.). It is a tremendous thought to think that Jesus—because of his love for us—died for our sins. But it is also a tremendous thought to know that Jesus has never stopped loving us or lost interest in our situation, that when on the cross he cried, "It is finished" (John 19:30), he was not yet finished with us. He will never be finished interceding for our sins. What comfort! What joy! It makes you want to sing that old Wesleyan tune:

> Arise, my soul, arise; shake off thy guilty fears;
> The bleeding Sacrifice in my behalf appears.
> Before the throne my Surety stands;
> My name is written on his hands.[7]

6. Colin G. Kruse, *The Letters of John*, Pillar New Testament Commentary (Grand Rapids: Eerdmans, 2000), 72. For this term as applied to the Holy Spirit, see John 14:16, 26; 15:26; 16:7.

7. Charles Wesley, "Arise, My Soul, Arise" (1742).

The Lamb

Christ's everlasting and ever-living intercession, of course, is made possible only by his sacrificial death. There is no intercession without first propitiation! As John writes of Jesus in 1 John 2:2: "He is the propitiation for our sins, and not for ours only but also for the sins of the whole world." Here the scene has changed. We have moved from the courtroom into the temple, from Christ's being our Advocate, "who speaks in our favor in the presence of God despite our sins,"[8] to Christ's being the atoning sacrifice itself for those same sins. He is the Lamb who was slaughtered on the temple altar.

The Greek word here translated as "propitiation" is used only four times in the New Testament (Rom. 3:25; Heb. 2:17), twice in 1 John (here in 2:2 and then again in 4:10). This word, as used in other ancient Greek literature, usually indicates the removal of God's wrath by an acceptable offering. J. E. Alsup's work on the LXX lexicography of *hilasmos* ("propitiation")—"citing Gen. 32:30 (32:21 MT); Num. 16:47–48 (17:12–13 MT); 25:11; 1 Sam. 26:19; 2 Sam. 21:3–4; 24:25; Prov. 16:14"—and Yarbrough's view that John's theology of "God's wrath (John 3:16, 36; cf. 8:24; 1 John 3:14; 5:16) and of Jesus' suffering of it in place of sinners (John 3:14; 10:11; 11:51; 1 John 3:16)" make the propitiatory notion in 1 John valid.[9] Thus, with 1 John 2:2 in mind, it is appropriate to say that on the cross Jesus turned away God's righteous anger, satisfied the demands of divine justice, and averted our punishment in a substitutionary manner. But "propitiation" as used in 1 John is used in the sense not only of turning away God's wrath but also of wiping away all sin. The "sins" mentioned in 2:2 and 4:10 are expiated through Jesus' sacrifice. The Lamb of God takes away our sins.

Moreover, this Lamb of God takes away "the sin of the world" (John 1:29), as John the Baptist proclaimed, or "the sins of the whole world," as the apostle John announces (1 John 2:2). By using the phrase "the whole world," the apostle has not embraced universalism. He is not advocating that everyone will be saved on the basis of Jesus' death. John has also not embraced antinomianism, namely, that everyone can do whatever one wants to do.[10]

8. Kruse, *The Letters of John*, 73.

9. Yarbrough, *1–3 John*, 78.

10. Moreover, this verse does not deny the Reformed doctrine of limited atonement (see Yarbrough's excellent argument, *1–3 John*, 80–81), summarized in the following sentence: "Amid the wideness of the atonement's scope . . . there is at the same time an undeniable particularity." Ibid., 80.

Just as John the Baptist followed his proclamation of the world's salvation with his word of warning, "Every tree . . . that does not bear good fruit is cut down and thrown into the fire" (Matt. 3:10), so John's announcement about the universal scope of Christ's death is followed by a dozen or so cautions about the damnable dangers of presumption and compliancy (e.g., read 1 John 2:19–23!). Therefore, as in John 3:16 ("For God so loved the world, that he gave his only Son"), so here in 1 John 2:2, the apostle again has "the . . . world" in view not in a universalistic sense. Rather, he speaks of it in a sufficiency sense, namely, that Jesus' death is sufficient to deal with every Christian's sin. His sacrifice covered the sins ("our sins") of the apostolic era, as well as the sins of believers "scattered everywhere and in all times."[11] Jesus' sufficient death "provides the basis throughout all human history for God the Father to extend . . . [his] divine longsuffering."[12]

How wonderful to contemplate "the far-reaching scope of Christ's redeeming work."[13] Think of it this way: "Christ's death is as cosmic in *time* (B.C., A.D.; past, future) as it is cosmic in *space*. . . . The death of Jesus reaches out as far horizontally into history as it reaches up vertically into eternity."[14] And it reaches out to all of us even now. The universal scope provides a universal offer. The cross is great enough to cover everyone, and its benefits can be enjoyed by all who embrace the saving work of Jesus.[15] So let us embrace it, perhaps for the first time, or maybe for the millionth time. We all need Christ's propitiation always! Let us acknowledge our sins, confess them, and be washed anew in the blood of the cross.

His Example, Our Assurance

First John 2:1b–2 contains words of comfort. It is comforting to know that Jesus stands in our place, that through his death and intercession he is our Advocate. Building on Christ's advocacy, verses 3–6 call us to conformity with Christ's example. Such a call might be discomforting at first,

11. Following Calvin and Turretin, this is Yarbrough's view as well. Ibid.

12. Ibid., 79.

13. Schnackenburg, *The Johannine Epistles*, 88.

14. Frederick Dale Bruner, *The Churchbook: Matthew 13–28*, 2nd rev. ed. (Grand Rapids: Eerdmans, 2004), 763.

15. John R. W. Stott, *The Epistles of John: An Introduction and Commentary*, Tyndale New Testament Commentaries (Downers Grove, IL: InterVarsity Press, 1976), 74.

and perhaps even surprising to some. For if we expected the test of genuine Christianity to lie merely in our confession of faith in the objective work of Christ—"We cling to the cross"—we are confronted, and perhaps chastened, with the call to "keep his commandments" and the necessity of compliance to that call as the basis for our assurance.

> And *by this we know* that we have come to know him [Jesus],[16] if we keep his commandments. Whoever says "I know him" but does not keep his commandments is a liar, and the truth is not in him, but whoever keeps his word, in him truly the love of God is perfected. *By this we may know* that we are in him: whoever says he abides in him ought to walk in the same way in which he walked. (1 John 2:3–6)

Only 303 vocabulary words are used in 1 John. With five chapters comprising 2,134 words, this means that John often reuses the same words. This is certainly the case in 1 John 2:3–6. The word *know* (as in "by this we know") is used four times; *in him* (as in "abides in him") four times; and *keep* (as in "keep his commandments" or "word")[17] three times. If we take those key words and put them together, we come up with the point of verses 3–6: We *know* that we are *in Christ* if we *keep his commandments*. Put simply, the one who knows the true God walks like Christ.

What That Walk Looks Like

What does that walk look like? It obviously does not mean that we live in Palestine, wear a tunic, choose twelve apostles, saunter across a stormy sea, cast out demons, die on a cross, and the like. We cannot walk in exactly the same way, for exactly the same purpose, or with the same results. Even if we could heal the blind and raise the dead, our miracles would have no messianic significance. Moreover, when we die, our deaths will save no one from his sins. Jesus is uniquely different from us; our feet cannot fit precisely

16. While *him* and *his* in 1 John 2:3–6 could refer to the Father or the Son (perhaps John is intentionally ambiguous), I take those pronouns to refer to Jesus because verses 2 and 6 make it clear that Jesus is the subject. With that observation in mind, note not merely the Christian stamp on the text but also the high Christology. It is Christ's commandments that we are called to keep; and it is not God generically whom we are to imitate, but Jesus. The literal walking of Jesus and earth-given commandments also contrasts the Gnostic notion of a purely spiritual connection with a heavenly Jesus.

17. While *word* has a broader connotation than *commandments*, the terms are practically synonymous.

into his footprints. Therefore, as Calvin noted, our walk is marked not by an "exact reduplication of the details of his outward life," but rather by "acting according to the Spirit that moved Jesus."[18] So walking like Christ is not mimicking his Galilean accent but "'living the whole of life' *coram Deo*, as in God's presence" and for God's purposes, as Jesus did.[19]

A Spirit-filled life or a *coram Deo* lifestyle is one of union with and imitation of Christ that is especially characterized by faithfulness to Christ's commandments. As Jesus stated in the Great Commission, we are to "observe all" that he commanded (Matt. 28:20), which certainly includes his ethical imperatives (there are nearly fifty in the Sermon on the Mount alone!). But John is most concerned with Jesus' own summary of the comprehensive, all-embracing aspect of imitation—the ethic of love. Like Paul, he wants us, as "imitators of God" (Eph. 5:1) in Christ, to "walk as children of light" (v. 8), namely, to "walk in love, as Christ loved us and gave himself up for us" (v. 2).

This command to love is clear from the immediate context (1 John 2:7–11), as well as the rest of the epistle, where the command "to love" is given fourteen times. So while 2:5 is the first appearance of *love*, it will not be the last. It will be used—as a noun or verb—sixty more times in 1, 2, and 3 John. That is a lot of love for three little books! To walk as Jesus walked is to walk in love for God and others. Jesus obeyed the will of the Father, followed the Bible's ethical commands, and sacrificed his life even for his enemies. "By this we know love, that he laid down his life for us, and we ought to lay down our lives for the brothers" (3:16); "In this is love, . . . that he [God] loved us and sent his Son to be the propitiation for our sins. Beloved, if God so loved us, we also ought to love one another" (4:10–11). That 1960s tune "They Will Know We Are Christians by Our Love" is not far off John's point; he simply adds to it, in effect, "And so will we." Love is not a condition for our salvation, but it is a sign of it. As Martin Luther wrote:

> This should be the sign by which they should know whether they are true Christians or not. Where Christ dwells through faith, there He makes that person conform to Him; that is, He makes him humble, gentle, and ready to help his neighbor in any need.[20]

18. Calvin, quoted in Jason B. Hood, *Imitating God in Christ: Recapturing a Biblical Pattern* (Downers Grove, IL: InterVarsity Press, 2013), 205.
19. Yarbrough, *1–3 John*, 88.
20. Luther, "Lectures on the First Epistle of St. John," 240.

Why That Walk Is the Surest Proof

Why is walking as Jesus walked the surest proof that we know God? It shows that God is at work! When someone claims to be a Christian based merely on some experience, there is nothing remarkable about that. (Even the irreligious sometimes admit to having religious experiences.) But when we see the dead alive in the Spirit, lives transformed from dark living to light living, the loveless becoming lovers of God and man, the disobedient become obedient, our only right reaction is to admit, "Truly this is the work of God!"

In 1 John 2:5, John writes that "whoever keeps his word, in him truly the love of God is perfected." This term *perfected* (*teteleiōken*) does not carry the idea of sinless perfection, for it is clear that Christians sin (1:8, 10; 2:1; 5:16) and must continually confess and repent of sin. *Perfected* is also not to be viewed in some medieval monastic sense—as the final mystical encounter with God. Rather, the love of God is "perfected" in us (2:5; 4:12, 16–21) if we obey his commands, particularly loving others (cf. Matt. 5:44–48). There is an emphasis on our obedience. But don't miss the other action in the sentence! The verb—"is perfected"—is passive, which indicates that some actor—"God"—took the initiative. The sense, then, is this: "Only as one born of God and beloved by him is a human being able to reciprocate this love and keep God's commandments."[21] When we faithfully follow Christ, it is then that "the divine love is realized to the full."[22]

So while personal holiness is not the basis of our salvation, it is the clearest assurance of our salvation. The converted slave trader John Newton said of himself, "I am not what I ought to be; but I am not what I once was. And it is by the grace of God that I am what I am."[23] The cross of Christ is powerful to save *and sanctify*. And knowing God, according to John, is to know something of that power. Power that is personal and practical, experiential and active; power that is given not once at conversion but consistently throughout our arduous journey through the valleys of doubt, across the torrents of temptation, and out of the caverns of our habitual sins. "To know God is to experience his love in Christ, and to return that

21. Schnackenburg, *The Johannine Epistles*, 98.

22. Ibid.

23. Newton, quoted in David Jackman, *The Message of John's Letters*, The Bible Speaks Today (Downers Grove, IL: InterVarsity Press, 1988), 43.

love in obedience."[24] To know God is to hate sin and do everything in our power and through God's power to be killing it before it kills us. As Luther vowed, "I, wretched Christian that I am, am protected by Christ, the eternal Righteousness, and I will not permit sin to reign in me."[25] Christ's life (and death!) is "both a model to be imitated, and . . . the means for that imitation to become a possibility."[26]

Written with Golden Letters

When I was a senior at Driscoll Catholic High School, my religion class studied the Gospels. Our teacher was earning her Ph.D. at DePaul University, studying under John Dominic Crossan, best known in the public sphere as a prominent member of the Jesus Seminar. Under his tutelage, my teacher walked us through the life and teachings of Jesus, often commenting on what was historical and what was not. The ironic thing (truly amazing thing) is that the Spirit of God also showed up to class and, as he is known to do, used the words of the Gospels to work on my heart, despite my teacher's false teaching. I started to wonder why so many self-professed Christians I knew didn't know the commandments of Christ or, if they knew them, didn't make much attempt to obey them (me included).

The summer after I graduated, I was invited to try out for the Illinois Prairie State Games, a statewide version of the Olympics. Out of hundreds of players, I made the team! On that team was the Illinois basketball player of the year, Marc Davidson. Marc was strong and fast, could jump out of the gym, and shot like he was from Indiana. He was also a Christian. I knew he was a Christian by the way he talked and walked. Marc knew the Lord's commandments and obeyed them. As important as he was, he genuinely considered others more important than himself. As strong as he was, he looked out for the weak. As fast as he was, he was quick to listen and slow to speak. As popular as he was, he was unashamed to proselytize even the unpopular claims of Christ. Marc demonstrated a knowledge of God that was pistic, ethical, and agapic.

24. C. H. Dodd, *The Johannine Epistles*, Moffatt New Testament Commentary (New York: Harper & Brothers, 1946), 32.

25. Luther, "Lectures on the First Epistle of St. John," 240.

26. Stephen S. Smalley, *1, 2, 3 John*, Word Biblical Commentary (Nashville: Thomas Nelson, 1984), 53.

He believed in Jesus, obeyed Christ's commands, and loved others. His authentic Christianity was obvious to all.

Authentic Christianity is always obvious to all, isn't it? We are not playing games here. We all know the difference. We all know that a saving relationship with God expresses itself "not in sentimental language or mystical experience but in moral obedience"[27]—a Christlike walk . . . with a limp, of course.

God has brought us into his classroom today to sit under instructor John in order to remind us that while we might lapse into sin, our lives are not to be characterized by disobedience but by a striving after Christlikeness and a growth in godliness. We have an Advocate and an example who, through his powerful cross, saves and sanctifies. Let us take this text, which Luther said "should be written with golden letters . . . and painted in the heart,"[28] and color our chests accordingly.

27. Stott, *The Epistles of John*, 91. Schnackenburg adds that John's writings are "eminently practical and down to earth in their moral concern. This leads to a practical Christianity diametrically opposed to a mysticism divorced from action." *The Johannine Epistles*, 96.

28. Luther, "Lectures on the First Epistle of St. John," 236.

4

Why Love Matters

1 John 2:7–11

Whoever loves his brother abides in the light, and in him there is no cause for stumbling. (1 John 2:10)

Math has always been difficult for me. So when I was assigned to the honors algebra class, which was very much over my head, I persuaded my friend Joe to help. He tutored me, but he also tempted me. For example, one day Joe finished his exam quickly, as he always did. He then proceeded to hand-copy all his work on a separate sheet of paper, which he then dropped on my desk while he walked up to hand in his test. Can you imagine? What was I to do? What would you do? Without much hesitation and only a slight pang of conscience, I gave in. I copied 80 percent of his 100 percent correct work. I passed the test.

When I became a Christian a year after graduating from high school, everything changed on the inside, and eventually on the outside. So when I transferred to Wheaton College to major in Bible/theology, I vowed never again to cheat. This vow, however, was quickly tested. In my second semester of New Testament Greek (which I'm convinced uses the same mental muscles as math), I missed the midterm exam because I'd caught the flu. My professor graciously allowed me to take the test on my own time. He told me that he would leave a copy of it in his mailbox outside his office. I could pick it up and take it whenever I felt better.

A few days later, in good health, I stood before the mailbox. I saw the test and grabbed it. Yet as I looked down in the mailbox again, I noticed another exam, completed by one of the class's best students. What was I to do? What would you do? I looked around. The hallway was empty. I cautiously lifted the other exam. It felt heavy, as though a thousand fat devils were dancing on it. Yet as heavy as it felt, it was as though a calm, angelic voice whispered from it, "Take and copy. Take and copy." I began to heed that advice. I placed both exams in my backpack and hurried across the street to the library. I opened the backpack, placed the blank test on the right, and then slowly lifted the other exam.

Then . . . I stopped. I didn't place it down on the left. Instead, convicted by the Spirit that God sees all, that cheating is a sin, and that such a sin would be offensive to God, my teacher, and my classmate, I placed the completed exam in my backpack again. I walked back across the street and placed it back in the professor's mailbox. I returned to the library and took the test on my own. I passed the test—both the Greek test and the temptation!

In 1909, Robert Law gave the Kerr Lectures at the University of Glasgow, entitled *The Tests of Life: A Study of the First Epistle of St. John*. In those talks, he argued that 1 John presents us with three cardinal tests by which we may discern whether we know God or not.

The first test is theological. Do we believe that Jesus is "the Son of God" (1 John 5:5, 10, 13; cf. 3:23), the Christ "come in the flesh" (4:2; cf. 2 John 7)?[1] According to John, those who deny Jesus' preexistent divinity and his historical incarnation deny "the Father" (1 John 2:23). They fail the test! We have already seen a hint of this test in our study of 1:1–3, where John speaks of Jesus as being from "the beginning" and yet "made manifest"—made manifest in such a way as to be "heard," "seen," and "touched." The second test is moral. Are we obeying God's commandments? This is the test we saw in 2:1–6. There we looked at the fact that a saving relationship with God expresses itself not primarily in a sentimental confession or some ecstatic experience but in moral obedience. It is not the one who says he knows God

1. John R. W. Stott, *The Letters of John: An Introduction and Commentary*, 2nd ed., Tyndale New Testament Commentaries (Downers Grove, IL: InterVarsity Press, 2009), 57.

who knows God, but the one who keeps his Word. The third test is social: whether or not we love others. "Since God is love and all love comes from God, it is clear that a loveless person does not know him (4:7–8)."[2] Do we keep Christ's commandment to love our neighbor or, as John has it in 2:10, our "brother"?[3] This is the test question that God gives in 2:7–11.

Knowing the Commandment

How do we know whether we pass or fail the test? This test is not like a Greek exam that asks us to translate a sentence and parse the vowels; and it is unlike a math quiz that asks us to answer a few equations and solve a word problem. Rather, this test involves knowing and keeping an old, yet new commandment—or, as Robert Yarbrough put it, a message that is "old yet current (2:7)" and "new yet true (2:8)."[4] We begin with *knowledge*, and the question, "Do you know the old-yet-current, new-yet-true commandment?" In 1 John 2:7–8, John writes:

> Beloved, I am writing you no new commandment, but an old commandment that you had from the beginning. The old commandment is the word that you have heard. At the same time, it is a new commandment that I am writing to you, which is true in him and in you, because the darkness is passing away and the true light is already shining.

Note four important details. First, note that John repeats a number of the same words and phrases. The phrase "I am writing to you" is repeated twice, as is "new commandment" and "old commandment"; thus, the word *commandment* tallies a total of four repetitions. The word *true* is repeated (2×), *hates* (2×), *brother* (3×), *whoever* (3×), *light* (3×), and *darkness* (5×). Why the repetition? Is it to aid the reader's memory? Is it to express some artistic sensibility—to paint a minimalist picture with a few strokes of the brush? N. T. Wright admits his frustration with John's repetition:

2. Ibid.

3. Just as in the parable of the Good Samaritan Jesus expanded the definition of *neighbor* beyond racial and religious lines, so I take *brother* in 1 John (and *brothers* in 3 John) to be an elastic metaphor for believers that can be stretched out to include all human beings (e.g., 1 John 3:15).

4. Robert W. Yarbrough, *1–3 John*, Baker Exegetical Commentary on the New Testament (Grand Rapids: Baker, 2008), 95.

> If someone (like myself) has spent a long time studying Paul and then suddenly moves across to John, and particularly to 1 John, one is tempted to be a bit frustrated. Surely John should get on with it, say what he means and move on to the next point.[5]

Thankfully, Wright acknowledges that John's style is intentional—that the apostle, through a repetition that is "on the move," is "mulling it all over and wants his readers to do so too."[6] So for example, when the word *commandment* is repeated four times, it sticks in the reader's mind. This commandment must be important.

Speaking of the *commandment*, note, second, that its content is assumed. As I said, four times in 1 John 2:7–9 John talks about the *commandment*, yet in those verses he never defines it. What commandment? The answer does come by deduction in verse 10. It is Jesus' brotherly-love commandment, stated elsewhere as: "This is my commandment, that you love one another as I have loved you" (John 15:12; cf. 15:17) and "You shall love your neighbor as yourself" (Matt. 22:39). Yet the sense seems to be that John's audience, without his clearly stating it, knew precisely what command he was talking about. It would be like my saying to a group of Chicagoans, "I went to the Taste." They would all know that I was referring to Taste of Chicago—"the nation's premier outdoor food festival," at least according to the city's website.[7]

Third, note that the love commandment is old and new. It is perhaps old in the sense that this commandment is nearly as old as the creation of the world;[8] or it is at least as old as human beings, for in 1 John 3:11–12 John echoes this command to love and then illustrates the rejection of it by referring to Cain's murder of Abel. So as early as Adam's first sons, humans are taught to love our brother. With the adjective *old*, however, John could also mean that the command is as old as the Old Testament law, for this command is apparent in the second half of the Ten Commandments (see

5. N. T. Wright, *The Letter of John: 9 Studies for Individuals and Groups* (Downers Grove, IL: InterVarsity Press, 2012), 14.

6. Ibid.

7. See http://www.cityofchicago.org/city/en/depts/dca/supp_info/taste_of_chicago.html.

8. E.g., Robert Law argues for this wider sense of "old" and "from the beginning" in speaking of God's eternal law that "God has impressed upon all creature-life; which is seen in the self-sacrificing care of the tigress for her whelps, of the mother-bird for her nestlings." *The Tests of Life: A Study of the First Epistle of St. John*, 3rd ed. (Grand Rapids: Baker, 1968), 223.

Matt. 22:37–40), and then clearly and simply stated in Leviticus 19:18, "You shall love your neighbor as yourself."

Yet I think the oldness of this command is not as old as those two possibilities. Rather, it simply goes back to the beginning of the gospel proclamation to the church in Ephesus, or "from the moment they became Christians."[9] I say this because the apostle speaks of this old commandment as being that which they "have heard" (1 John 2:7b) "from the beginning" (v. 7a), namely, the first time they learned about Christ's "commandments" (note the plural in vv. 3–6), which includes his key "commandment" (singular in vv. 7–8) to love.[10] Unlike John's progressive opponents, who are introducing unauthorized and "new"—nonapostolic and nonhistorical Jesus—ideas, the apostle's instructions go back to Jesus of Nazareth's now decades-old teachings (cf. 3:23) and that particular church's time of conversion.[11]

This command is ancient and contemporary. And John speaks of that newness in 1 John 2:8: "At the same time, it is a new commandment that I am writing to you, which is true in him and in you, because the darkness is passing away and the true light is already shining." The important phrase in understanding the nature of this newness is "which is true in him and in you." This command to love is true "in him" in that it finds its ultimate definition and illustration in Jesus. In John 13:34, Jesus said this to his disciples: "A *new* commandment I give to you, that you love one another: *just as I have loved you*, you also are to love one another." Therefore, what is new about this command is the part about Jesus' model of love—a newness of quality, emphasis, and extent.

Jesus' message was exclusive (e.g., enter by the narrow gate, Matt. 7:14), but his love inclusive. Jesus loved everyone! He loved his "friends like Martha, Mary, and Lazarus (John 11:5); lost souls like the rich young

9. Rudolf Schnackenburg, *The Johannine Epistles: Introduction and Commentary*, trans. R. Fuller and I. Fuller (New York: Crossroad, 1992), 104.

10. Ulrich Luz comments on Matthew 22:40 that "*love* is the foremost commandment, and hence the *guiding precept* by which Jesus' other commandments are to be interpreted." *The Theology of the Gospel of Matthew*, trans. J. Bradford Robinson, New Testament Theology (Cambridge: Cambridge University Press, 2008), 52.

11. As Philip W. Comfort and Wendell C. Hawley summarize: "the apostles had been faithful to teach others what they had heard from Jesus from the very beginning of his ministry so that their beginning could be as close to the apostles' as possible. Since a lot of new and strange doctrines were circulating in those days, John was encouraging the believers to stay with the primary, fundamental teachings of the apostles." *1–3 John*, Cornerstone Biblical Commentary (Carol Stream, IL: Tyndale, 2007), 338.

ruler (Mark 10:21); his close disciples (John 13:1); his mother at the hour of his own execution (19:26–27); a largely hostile city over which he wept (Luke 19:41); [and] those who carried out the crucifixion (23:34)."[12] In love, he cried out, "Father, forgive them" (Luke 23:34). Jesus so loved his neighbor, and even his enemies, that he gave his life for them. In the cross of Christ, the love of God is perfected (see Matt. 5:43–48) and supremely demonstrated. As Paul wrote, "For while we were still weak, at the right time Christ died for the ungodly. For one will scarcely die for a righteous person—though perhaps for a good person one would dare even to die—but God shows his love for us in that while we were still sinners, Christ died for us" (Rom. 5:6–8).

So this commandment is new in that it relates directly to Jesus and his example of love. It is a commandment "which is true in him." But it is also a commandment, as John says, "which is true . . . in you [plural]"—in the attitudes and actions of the Christian community. In Jeremiah 31:33, the prophet promised that there would be a day when God would write his law on his people's hearts. In Christ and under the new covenant, that day has been inaugurated—a time when "the darkness is passing away and the true light is already shining" (1 John 2:8). Here John shouts, "Victory!" as he speaks of the escalating triumph of Christian love and light. In the end, God's love triumphs! The darkness dispels and the ever-bright day dawns. Love will reign at last. Hatred will be crushed under *agapē*'s heel, if I can create an odd but appropriate image of charity's conquest.

And *now*, while the war between love and hate and light and darkness pervades the world, those who believe in Christ do "not remain in darkness" (John 12:46). Put differently, we live in the light of love. Why? Because Christ commanded us. How? Because we are "in him." Because we "abide in the light" (1 John 2:10). Jesus is not only the revelation of love, but also the source of love! Within every believer—through spiritual regeneration or the new birth (3:9)—there is the Christ-controlled compass of brotherly love. Paul refers to this in 1 Thessalonians 4:9, where he writes, "Now concerning brotherly love you have no need for anyone to write to you, for you yourselves have been taught by God to love one another." This explains why John is not commanding Christians to love. He is not "recapitulating

12. Yarbrough, *1–3 John*, 100.

a familiar imperative but explicating and evoking a living truth."[13] That living truth is that "Christ is on location as promised (John 16:10, 28) in his mediatorial role (1 John 2:1) to enable such love."[14] Christians love because what is true in Jesus is now true in us. Christ is the Vine; we are the branches (John 15:4–5). If we truly abide in him, we will bear fruit, especially the fruit of love (Gal. 5:22). In and through Christ—who was the fulfillment of the law (Matt. 5:17)—we fulfill the law of love, which is: "You shall love your neighbor as yourself" (Matt. 19:19; cf. Rom. 13:8–10). As John Cotton said, "Never look to fulfill this commandment to imitate Christ until you become a new man; for it is a new commandment, and a new commandment requires new obedience, and new obedience requires a new spirit."[15]

We have noted, first, that John repeats a number of the same words and phrases; second, that the content of the commandment is assumed; and third, that the commandment is old and new. Fourth and finally, note that John calls his readers "beloved." This is the first time he will use this title for Christians (but not the last; see 1 John 3:2, 21; 4:1, 7, 11). He uses this expression to reinforce the idea that the beloved of God are to be lovers of the brothers, but also simply to remind Christians of God's love for them. Because we are elected and adopted in Christ—the "beloved" (Matt. 3:17; 12:18; 17:5)—the overflow of God's love for Jesus flows into our lives. Let it roll "as a mighty ocean in its fullness over" us; let "the current of [God's] love" flow "underneath" and "all around" us.[16] Let us dive into the deep, deep love of Jesus! For, you see, in him we are "God's chosen ones, holy and *beloved*" (Col. 3:12); and because we are his beloved, we should "put on . . . compassionate hearts, kindness, humility, meekness, and patience" (v. 12), we should bear "with one another" and forgive one another (v. 13), and "above all" we should "put on love, which binds everything together in perfect harmony" (v. 14). The quality, emphasis, and extent of our love should emulate the quality, emphasis, and extent of Christ's love.

13. Ibid., 101. And "the commandment is the message of Christ, whose saving death (2:2) makes possible the perfection of divine love (2:5) in those who hear the gospel message." Ibid., 98.

14. Ibid., 101.

15. John Cotton, *An Exposition of First John* (Evansville, IN: Sovereign Grace, 1962), 128.

16. S. Trevor Francis, "O the Deep, Deep Love of Jesus" (1875).

Keeping the Commandment

John next turns to that common Christian calling. Or, to return to the test-language of the introduction, we might say it this way: In 1 John 2:7–8, like a generous teacher who preps his class minutes before he hands out the final exam, John gives us a brief lecture on the oldness and newness of the brotherly-love commandment. Then, in verses 9–11, the test is laid before our eyes. On paper, it looks simple enough. There is only one question! Are you *keeping* this commandment or not? That is, do you love or hate your brother? Prosaically and poetically, it looks like this:

A. *Whoever* says he is in the light and <u>hates his brother</u> is still in **darkness**.

B. *Whoever* <u>loves his brother</u> abides **in the light**, and in him
there is no cause for
stumbling. But

A'. *Whoever* <u>hates his brother</u> is in the **darkness** and walks in the **darkness**,
and does not know where he is going, because the **darkness** has blinded his eyes.

In the previous chapter, we saw John's portrait of the "talker" versus the "walker." Here we have the "hater" versus the "lover." In 1 John 2:9 and 11, John describes the person who hates his brother. What is said of him? First, he is one of those talkers. He "*says* he is in the light." He confesses faith in Christ ("the light of the world," John 9:5), and he is part of the local church ("the light of the world," Matt. 5:14). But second, he "hates." The verb is present tense, which implies a settled and ongoing attitude and action. Thus, his continual hatred of his brother proves that whatever outward illumination he has, it is an illusion. His light is not only under a bushel, but also buried under a millstone at the bottom of the deep, dark sea. For, as said in both 1 John 2:9 and 11, he "is still in darkness" and he "walks in the darkness," and thus he "does not know where he is going."[17] He is spiritually blind, and therefore he stumbles in the dark.

17. Note the similarities to the end of Jesus' saying in John 12:35, "The light is among you for a little while longer. Walk while you have the light, lest darkness overtake you. The one who *walks in the*

When discussing the phrase "God is light" (1 John 1:5), I talked about being blinded by the light of God's holiness, blinded as when we look into the sun. That was a good blindness, a temporary blindness with a benefit to it. But the blindness in 2:11 is a bad blindness, a blindness that leads not to a recognition of sin but to a continued ignorance of it. Hatred has so blinded this person that he cannot see what is in front of him. This so-called Christian cannot see that he is acting opposite of Christ. He is like the elder in a California church who committed adultery, was confronted by the elders, admitted to the act, refused to repent, was excommunicated, and then sued the senior pastor and elders' board for defamation of character. How unlovely! He is like a high-powered businessman in an Illinois church who so disliked the pastoral search committee's nominee that he wrote an all-church e-mail slandering his new shepherd and, more foundationally, "his brother." How diabolically blind! There are many more church horror stories. Those are two samples of "Christian" hatred of Christians. They are appalling pictures of what it looks like for a professing believer to be cut off from fellowship with God (cf. 1:6). The ultimate consequence of insistent hatred of others is God's condemnation to eternal darkness (see Matt. 8:12; 22:13; 25:30).

Opposite the one who hates his brother is the one who loves him. Sandwiched between the *hate*-verses (1 John 2:9, 11), we find the key verse, both structurally and theologically (v. 10): "Whoever loves his brother abides in the light, and in him there is no cause for stumbling."[18] Notice that this man says nothing. His actions speak louder than his words. He doesn't claim to be in the light; he *is* in the light. John records it this way: he "abides in the light." And because he abides in the light, when he walks he does not stumble. He does not stumble into wrong thinking (i.e., Jesus didn't come in the flesh) and wrong living (i.e., it is acceptable to hate my brother because love for Christ transcends love for Christians). And he does not cause others to stumble.

Recently when I was traveling back to Chicago from Brisbane, I had a layover in Los Angeles. When I went into the men's room to wash my face

---

darkness does not know where he is going." The phrase "does not *know* where he is going" is perhaps a rebuke of the Gnostic-like claim of special *knowledge*, as Schnackenburg claims: "It is like an insult flung in their faces." *The Johannine Epistles*, 109.

18. In 1 John, the noun *love* is used eighteen times, *beloved* ten times, and the verb *to love* twenty-eight times, 2:10 being the first occurrence of the verb.

and brush my teeth, I overheard the conversation of the two custodians cleaning the bathroom. The one was telling the other about a woman they both knew who needed physical help. He was walking through the various people in this woman's life who were possible options for offering aid. When the other man asked about a certain family member, this reply came: "Oh, you would think she would help. She's the Christian. She *should* help, but she is so selfish and lazy." He quickly crossed her off the list. My face was dripping water. I wanted to cry, and I wanted to cry out for the glory of Christ's name.

Would your neighbors cross you off their brotherly-love list? Would your friends? Would your family? Would your church? In John 13:34, Jesus declared: "A new commandment I give to you, that you love one another: just as I have loved you, you also are to love one another." In verse 35, he added: "By this all people will know that you are my disciples, if you have love for one another." If love is lost in the church, the lost stay lost. Without Christian love, the light to the world is eclipsed!

Christian love is not the absolute embodiment of Jesus' love. We cannot be our sinless Savior. Yet Christians are mirrors of his love. We might be cracked and dimly lit mirrors, but we are mirrors. The likeness to Jesus is obvious to all who look at us. And just as "if you love your neighbor, all of the other commandments fall into place"[19]—you won't steal, commit adultery, murder, bear false witness, covet his goods, and so on—likewise, if you love your Christian brother, our witness to the world falls into place. Eyes, ears, and hearts open to the gospel. "See how they love one another! What kind of love is this? Where does it come from? How can I get it?"

Nonarrogant Assurance

Are you a Christian? According to 1 John, there are three tests of life. Do you pass the theological, moral, and social tests? The social test is given in 1 John 2:7–11, and the results of this final test are obvious to all, as obvious as the difference between light and darkness. Are you living in the darkness—are you controlled by the unholy habit of hatred? Are you envious, arrogant, rude, irritable, resentful, and insistent on your own way (1 Cor. 13:4–5)? Do

19. David L. Allen, *1–3 John: Fellowship in God's Family*, Preaching the Word (Wheaton, IL: Crossway, 2013), 76.

you rejoice when others stumble (v. 6)? Or are you living in the light—does the love of Christ compel you to love others? Are you kind and patient with everyone (v. 4)? Have you forgiven those who have trespassed against you (Matt. 6:12)? Do you serve "the least of these my brothers" as you would Jesus himself (25:40)? Do you bear all things, believe all things, hope all things, and endure all things (1 Cor. 13:7)?

If so, you can be assured that you know God and that you share eternal life with him. You have passed from life to death, from the darkness to the light, from the devil's domain into Christ's kingdom. This is not self-confidence or some arrogant or ungrounded assurance. Neither is it overly introspective navel-gazing. Rather, this is what the Word teaches in our text and throughout 1 John. Consider 3:10: "By this it is evident who are the children of God, and who are the children of the devil: whoever does not practice righteousness is not of God, nor is the one who does not love his brother" (cf. 4:20); also 4:7: "Beloved, let us love one another, for love is from God, and whoever loves has been born of God and knows God." Since we have been born of God, the proof of his saving power is in our brotherly love (cf. 1 Peter 1:22–23), something that can be witnessed by everyone, including us. We all lapse in love, but those who live a consistent life of a "faith working through love" (Gal. 5:6) can know their standing before God. They are in good standing! God's eternal life and love is theirs (yours?) to keep. It is what I call a nonarrogant assurance. Do you have it?

5

Knowing Christ and Overcoming the Devil

1 John 2:12–14

I am writing to you, fathers, because you know him who is from the beginning. I am writing to you, young men, because you have overcome the evil one. (1 John 2:13)

Maximus of Turin preached in northern Italy, serving sometime between the years 390 and 408/423. In what is listed as his third sermon, his introduction caught my attention, especially as it relates to our study of 1 John. He began, "Beloved brethren, I think that it is sufficient reproof to you that on the previous Sunday, when I was about to depart, I dispensed no spiritual gifts to you from the sacred Scriptures but upbraided and accused you because of sin, dismissing you without any consoling preaching."[1]

We do not have the previous sermon he mentions. (That would have been a most interesting read.) But it is interesting enough to note that in the sermon we do have (the third sermon), Maximus tells us how he scolded his congregation for their sin, and how he disciplined them by withholding

1. St. Maximus of Turin, *The Sermons of St. Maximus of Turin*, trans. Boniface Ramsey, Ancient Christian Writers 50 (New York: Newman, 1989), 19.

Bible teaching—what he calls in another place "the sacraments of the heavenly Scripture."[2] So he preached to them, but he preached only *his* words of rebuke and reproof. He gave them no "consoling preaching."

As we think through 1 John 1:1–2:11, we notice that the apostle John was likewise hard on his congregation. He was not hard in the sense that he was scolding them by withholding God's Word, but hard in the way in which he was challenging them with it. Along with his first readers, we have been taking his tests of life—the theological, moral, and social. And if we are honest, we admit that our Christian faith has been challenged. Do we really know God? Do we affirm that Jesus, who is fully God, came in the flesh? Do we walk in the light as he is in the light? Do we keep his commandments? Do we exemplify brotherly love? Or does the devil still have a hold on our hearts? Do we deny Jesus as the Son of God incarnate? Do we walk in darkness? Do we hate our brothers? Have our sins truly been forgiven? Who is our Father—the good One or the evil one?

In 1 John 2:12–14, in "a kind of parenthesis in the series of appeals and exhortations,"[3] sincere seekers finally find some "consoling preaching." In 2:15–17, John puts Christians back in the hot seat with his first stringent imperative ("Do not love the world"). But for now, enjoy these three verses of comfort and encouragement.

Who Is Addressed?

In much of his letter thus far, John has been challenging the confessing Christian who is a phony follower—the talker but not walker. Now his attention shifts solely to the authentic believer who may be struggling with assurance. The shift comes in the content (you are "forgiven," "you know him," "you have overcome the evil one," etc.) and in the structure (in words that are "certainly poetical and strongly rhythmical"[4]). It also comes in the way in which he addresses his readers. Each sentence starts either with "I am writing [*graphō*] to you" or with "I write [*egrapsa*] to you." While *graphō* is present tense and *egrapsa* is aorist tense, the

2. Ibid.

3. Martyn Lloyd-Jones, *Life in Christ: Studies in 1 John* (Wheaton, IL: Crossway, 2002), 201.

4. William Barclay, *The Letters of John and Jude*, Daily Bible Study Series (Philadelphia: Westminster, 1976), 50.

slight difference is not "the result of misplaced scribal creativity"[5] or a reflection of John after having been interrupted in the middle of verse 13 and later returning to the letter ("Now, where was I? 'I wrote to you . . .' "). Rather, the repetition is "intended for emphasis."[6] It is an "attention-getting device."[7] It would be like my saying to my children (for the millionth time!):

> I am telling you that you need to listen.
>   I am telling you that you need to sit up.
>   I am telling you to buckle your seat belt.
> I told you to listen.
>   I told you to sit up.
>   I told you to buckle your seat belt.

Beyond the six phrases intended to grab the reader's attention, John addresses these Christians with terms of endearment. To his typical Johannine title *little children* and *children* he adds *fathers* and *young men*. What does he mean? Is he speaking literally or metaphorically? In other words, is he addressing three different ages of people within the church—literally children, young men, and fathers (i.e., older men)? Or is he addressing different stages of spiritual maturity? John Stott takes this second position and summarizes it in this way: "The little children are those newborn in Christ. The young men are more developed Christians, strong and victorious in spiritual warfare; while the fathers possess the depth and stability of ripe Christian experience."[8] Stott provides little support for this interpretation. Others, however, such as F. F. Bruce, have suggested that this threefold division based on spiritual maturity makes best sense of the specific reassurance given to each group. For example, Bruce writes:

5. John Calvin, as summarized in Robert W. Yarbrough, *1–3 John*, Baker Exegetical Commentary on the New Testament (Grand Rapids: Baker, 2008), 121.

6. John R. W. Stott, *The Epistles of John: An Introduction and Commentary*, Tyndale New Testament Commentaries (Downers Grove, IL: InterVarsity Press, 1976), 96.

7. David L. Allen, *1–3 John: Fellowship in God's Family*, Preaching the Word (Wheaton, IL: Crossway, 2013), 87.

8. Stott, *The Epistles of John*, 96. Following this view, the NLT translates "fathers" as "who are mature."

> The younger believers have made a beginning by knowing their sins forgiven for Christ's sake. They have also started to appreciate their new status as children of God (cf. 3.1) in that they have come to "know the Father."[9]

Another view takes the titles *little children* (*teknia*, 1 John 2:12) and *children* (*paidia*, v. 13) to be essentially synonymous. Those words express Christians in general, not new or immature believers. This is supported by 2:1, 28; 3:4, 18; 4:4; and 5:21, where John addresses those under his pastoral care as *little children* or *children* (note also Jesus' use of the two terms for his disciples in John 13:33 [*teknia*] and 21:5 [*paidia*]). Therefore, by *little children* and *children* John means "children of God" (1 John 3:1, 10; 5:2). Then with the titles *fathers* and *young men*, he subdivides the Christian community into two age groups—the old and the young.

A final view, which is based on part of the previous view, is more viable. Since the term *children* is used metaphorically, it follows that the terms *fathers* and *young men* function symbolically as well. *Fathers* does not mean "men who have fathered offspring," and *young men* does not mean "teenage boys" or "the twenty-somethings with the XY chromosome." Rather, both terms, similar to the term *children*, relate to all Christians and two key aspects of their union with Christ and fellowship with the Father.[10] To be sure, there are people in the church who function as fathers to the church. They are experienced and established leaders who instruct and emulate the ways of Christ. Further, there are some Christians who do battle with the devil with what seems like the strength of young men. We sometimes call them *spiritual warriors*. What John says about these three groups (*children* included) is said of all Christians in his writings—notably in the subsequent context (1 John 2:15–18).[11] There it is true of all believers that God is our Father, our sins are forgiven, and we stand strong against Satan.

9. F. F. Bruce, "The Epistles of John," in *The Gospel and Epistles of John* (Grand Rapids: Eerdmans, 2004), 59.

10. My reading aligns with C. H. Dodd, *The Johannine Epistles*, Moffatt New Testament Commentary (New York: Harper & Brothers, 1946), 37–39, and I. Howard Marshall, *The Epistles of John*, New International Commentary on the New Testament (Grand Rapids: Eerdmans, 1978), 138.

11. My reading of the three terms to be representative of all Christians also fits the succeeding context in the following ways. First, the verb *love* in 1 John 2:15 is technically *you love*, and the *you* is plural. With this plural pronoun John seemingly groups the three designations into one—i.e., fathers, young men, and children are to refuse to love the world. Second, in verse 18 the "you [all]" are called "children." Third, the "you [all]/children" all share the characteristics of the "fathers," "young men,"

Therefore, in trying to make best sense of the poetic structure, language, and logic, my take is that John's pair of triplets in 1 John 2:12–14 are to be applied to Christians in general. Using six announcements, he gives five uplifting encouragements about three dimensions of our life in Christ (as *children*, *young men*, and *fathers*). As *children*, (1) our sins have been forgiven in Christ and (2) we have a saving knowledge of God the Father. As *fathers*, (3) we know Christ. Finally, as *young men*, (4) we are strong in the Lord, and thus (5) we are victorious over the devil.

As Children

As Christians, we are like *little children*. In 1 John 2:12 and the end of verse 13, we read:

> I am writing to you, little children,
> because your sins are forgiven for his name's sake.
> . . . .
> I write to you, children,
> because you know the Father.

John calls the Christians here *children* both because he is much older than they[12] and because it is a gospel-term that emphasizes both the freshness and humility of their faith and the utter dependence that they now have on their Lord. So to these "newborns" (or, better, "born-agains") John gives the pure milk of the gospel, from one side the forgiveness of sins and from the other side the fatherhood of God.

When I pastored at Christ the King Church in Batavia, a family adopted a boy from Guatemala. His name was Brandon. He was eleven months old when he arrived. He came right before Christmas, the perfect gift from God! The first Sunday he came to church, I was overjoyed to see him. I lifted him up in my arms, ran my fingers through his dark curly hair, made a joke about the boy's hair resembling his new father's bald dome, and asked his

---

and "children" of verses 12–14, namely, they have a relationship with the "Father" (vv. 15, 16), and they are called to fight evil (those "antichrists" who deny that Jesus came in the flesh or was "from the beginning," vv. 18, 24).

12. Taking into account the approximate date of the apostle's birth (A.D. 1–6) and composition of 1 John (A.D. 85–95), it is safe to estimate that John is at least in his eighties.

new mom whether he had said any words yet. She replied, "No, not really. He is just saying, 'Da Da.'" "Well," I said, "you know that that will soon turn into 'Daddy.'" The couple smiled in agreement.

For those in Christ, what happened to Brandon physically has happened to us spiritually. We have been adopted into God's family. It is as John Calvin wrote: "We are all like orphans until we reach the grace of adoption by the Gospel."[13] While we were once distant from God, now, through faith in Jesus, we have been brought near to God. We have been brought into a saving relationship with our heavenly Father (Matt. 6:9). And like most children, our first words of faith are "Abba! Father!" (Rom. 8:15; cf. Gal. 4:6),[14] which reflects the shared family intimacy.

We "know the Father" (1 John 2:13). That is no small claim and consolation. For we know that, like a good earthly father, our heavenly Father will provide and protect; he will nourish and nurture. He will never stop loving us. He cannot disown his own. He will not abandon his adopted. In his classic book *Knowing God*, J. I. Packer writes:

> If you want to judge how well a person understands Christianity, find out how much he makes of the thought of being God's child and having God as his Father. If this is not the thought that prompts and controls his worship and prayers and his whole outlook on life, it means that he does not understand Christianity very well. For everything that Christ taught, everything that makes the New Testament new and better than the Old, everything that is distinctively Christian, is summed up in the knowledge of the Fatherhood of God the Father.[15]

Along with the fatherhood of God, John adds another wonderful encouragement: the forgiveness of sins—our "sins are forgiven for his name's sake" (1 John 2:12). What a glorious statement! The verb here—*they are forgiven*—is in the perfect passive, the sense being: "'They have been forgiven' and are therefore forgiven,"[16] or our "sins have been once and for all forgiven and

13. John Calvin, "1 John," in John Calvin and Matthew Henry, *1, 2, 3 John*, Crossway Classic Commentaries (Wheaton, IL: Crossway, 1998), 38.

14. While James Barr correctly argues that "Abba" does not mean "daddy" or "papa," he also notes that the expression was used by small children and "belonged to a familiar or colloquial register of language." "Abba Isn't Daddy," *Journal of Theological Studies* 39 (1988): 46.

15. J. I. Packer, *Knowing God* (Downers Grove, IL: InterVarsity Press, 1973), 19–20.

16. John Painter, *1, 2, and 3 John*, Sacra Pagina (Collegeville, MN: Liturgical Press, 2002), 187.

will never be brought up before God again."[17] This can be called *forensic forgiveness*. Based on Christ's finished work on the cross, we are rendered "not guilty" before God—for past, present, and future sins. This is good news!

The early church certainly thought so. As Brooke Foss Westcott wrote, "The proclamation of the forgiveness of sin was the message of the Gospel."[18] After Christ's resurrection, Jesus opened the Scriptures and said to his disciples, "Thus it is written, that the Christ should suffer and on the third day rise from the dead, and that repentance and forgiveness of sins should be proclaimed in his name to all nations" (Luke 24:46–47). In nearly every sermon represented in the Acts of the Apostles, we find that message. For example, in Peter's Pentecost sermon he preached, "Repent and be baptized every one of you in the name of Jesus Christ for the forgiveness of your sins" (Acts 2:38). Later he preached, "To him all the prophets bear witness that everyone who believes in him receives forgiveness of sins through his name" (10:43).

Notice the "name," not only in Acts but also in 1 John. In 1 John, Jesus has been called our "propitiation" (2:2), "advocate" (2:1), and he who "was from the beginning" (1:1). Jesus' name is redolent with his divine person and saving purpose. So when John says that our sins are forgiven "for his name's sake" (2:12), he is reminding us that we are forgiven not because our character and reputation are pleasing before God, but rather because Christ's name is pleasing and acceptable before the Father. Our sins are not forgiven for anything that we have "done or deserved"—that is, our contrition, repentance, faith, good works, or merit—"but because of what Christ had done and earned" for us.[19] As Martyn Lloyd-Jones wrote, "Christians know that their sins are forgiven, not because they bank loosely and vaguely upon the love of God, still less because they rest upon the hope of their own good lives and merits or their own good works." Rather, we know that we are forgiven "because of the perfect, the finished, the full work of the Lord Jesus Christ on our behalf."[20]

17. Allen, *1–3 John*, 87.

18. Brooke Foss Westcott, *The Epistles of St. John: The Greek Text with Notes and Essays* (Cambridge and London: Macmillan, 1892), 59. Yarbrough summarizes: "'Forgiveness of sins' in Christ and him alone was apparently at the very center of the apostolic proclamation across the three decades spanned by Acts (e.g., 2:38; 5:31; 10:43; 13:38; 26:19)." *1–3 John*, 119.

19. Allen, *1–3 John*, 87.

20. Lloyd-Jones, *Life in Christ*, 206.

So when we place our trust in Jesus, like a newly married bride, we take on our Bridegroom's name—the name of Jesus—the only "name under heaven given among men by which we must be saved" (Acts 4:12). God can be known as "Father" (1 John 2:13) only through the forgiveness of sins offered in Jesus' name (v. 12). We cannot have the fatherhood of God without the atonement of the Son. Jesus is "the way, and the truth, and the life," and "no one comes to the Father" except through him (John 14:6).

As Fathers

From Christians as *children* whose sins have been forgiven in Christ and who share a saving knowledge of God the Father, we move to our role as *fathers*. Verses 13 and 14 of 1 John 2 both begin by expressing our knowledge of Christ:

> I am writing to you, fathers,
> because you know him who is from the beginning. (v. 13a)

> I write to you, fathers,
> because you know him who is from the beginning. (v. 14a)

The second halves of the sentences above are identical, and the thought is simple but profound. "Him who is from the beginning" is a reference to Jesus as the incarnate *logos* ("that the Son had always existed"[21]). There are two reasons to believe that it alludes to Jesus specifically and not just God as Trinity or God the Father. First, this is what Jesus is called in 1 John 1:1. Second, the *his* in the phrase "for his name's sake" (2:12) certainly references Jesus' name; in John's writings, that designation is commonplace.[22]

The simple but profound thought, then, is that we "know" this very Jesus—"him who existed from the very beginning."[23] All Christians know Jesus at that

21. Clement of Alexandria, "Adumbrations," in *James, 1–2 Peter, 1–3 John, Jude*, ed. Gerald Bray, Ancient Christian Commentary on Scripture, New Testament 11 (Downers Grove, IL: InterVarsity Press, 2000), 182.

22. "In John and 1 John references to 'the name' generally refer to Jesus and in doing so identify him with the name of God. Jesus as the incarnate *logos* is God revealed. In him God's name has been made known. In him the name of God is revealed in the work of forgiveness. Consequently the author affirms: 'your sins are forgiven, on account of his name.'" Painter, *1, 2, and 3 John*, 188.

23. Heinz W. Cassirer's translation, quoted in Yarbrough, *1–3 John*, 119.

foundational but deep level. It is not merely the bishops who defended the deity of Christ at the Council of Nicea (A.D. 325) who deserve the distinguished title *fathers* of the church, but everyone who "abides . . . in him" (1 John 2:10). All Christians know Jesus; that is, they are in an intimate saving relationship with him. It is not merely a mark of Christian maturity. The day-old convert and the sixty-year Bible scholar and saint know Jesus equally. The scholar-saint might know more intellectually and experientially about Jesus, but both truly know him.

Perhaps an illustration will illuminate the point. Dave Helm is a pastor at Holy Trinity Church in Chicago. Along with my wife and thirty-five other adults, I helped to plant that church. That was nearly twenty years ago. I have known Dave and his family for a long time. Dave's father, Dick Helm, coached for fifteen years in the NBA alongside the legendary Lenny Wilkens. Years ago, when I was in Toronto for the annual meeting of the Evangelical Theological Society, I thought I would try to get a ticket for a game. Dick was then the assistant coach of the Toronto Raptors. I called Dave and Dave called his dad. Hours before the game, Coach Helm called to tell me that everything had been arranged. All I needed to do was to go to the ticket booth at the stadium and say his name, and I would be handed a ticket. That is precisely what I did. I went up to the ticket booth and said, "My name is Doug O'Donnell. There is a ticket set aside for me under the name Dick Helm." The attendant immediately grabbed an envelope and handed me the ticket. On the envelope was written "Dick Helm." Because I *knew* that name, I was allowed in for free. I sat in the players' family section. Needless to say, the view of the game was first-class.

The point of that illustration is not to demonstrate the truth that we will get into heaven because we know the name above all names. Rather, it is to show that different levels of knowledge exist in different relationships. Because I know Dick Helm, I gained easy access to a basketball game. Do I know Dick Helm as his son Dave does? Of course not. But my relationship with him is as real as the relationship of a father and son; it is simply at a different level. As Christians, *we all* know Christ—which, when you think about it, is a beautiful, beautiful thing.

As Young Men

As Christians, we are like *little children*, *fathers*, and finally *young men*. At the middle of 1 John 2:13 and end of verse 14, we read:

I am writing to you, young men,
 because you have overcome the evil one.

. . . .

I write to you, young men,
 because you are strong,
 and the word of God abides in you,
 and you have overcome the evil one.

Note three details. First, this is the longest commendation. Perhaps its length is due to the end stress of the poem/hymn, or due to its function as an emphatic and thematic transition to the imperative of 1 John 2:15. Second, three characteristics are recounted—their strength, God's Word abiding in them, and their victory over Satan.[24] Third, their victory over Satan is mentioned twice—"because you have overcome the evil one." Perhaps this repetition is for emphasis, with the logic being that (1) because God's Word abides in you, (2) you are strong in the Lord, and (3) therefore, you have successfully conquered the forces of darkness. In this way, the theological flow of the text is similar to that of the Lord's Prayer. That model prayer opens with divine praises ("hallowed be your name") and petitions ("your kingdom come") and ends with a plea for divine help ("deliver us from evil") (Matt. 6:9–10, 13). Or perhaps the ordering is spelled out more simply by stating that John says three things of these *young men*: (1) they are strong, (2) that power is *derived* from the Word that abides in them, and (3) it is *displayed* in their victory over the evil one. Whatever the possible logical flow, the theological truth is plain. In Christ, Christians have victory over the powers of the devil. Sin, death, and a guilty conscience have all been conquered![25]

Therefore, we can "be of good cheer," for Jesus has "overcome the world" (John 16:33 KJV). We can take heart, for "he who is in you is greater than he who is in the world" (1 John 4:4), namely, Satan, who is called "the ruler of this world."[26] This, however, does not mean that Satan is not our most formidable opponent or that his influence is not everywhere in "the world" (2:15): "The whole world lies in the power of the evil one" (5:19). Spiritual warfare is no illusion. We war against Satan every day. This is why James

24. In 1 John, the "evil one" is Satan (2:14; 3:12 [linked to "devil" in v. 10]; 5:18–19).

25. See Martin Luther, "Lectures on the First Epistle of St. John," in *The Catholic Epistles*, vol. 30 of *Luther's Works*, trans. and ed. Jaroslav Pelikan and W. A. Hansen (St. Louis: Concordia, 1972), 242–43.

26. John 12:31; 14:30; 16:11; cf. Eph. 2:2.

teaches, "Submit yourselves therefore to God. Resist the devil, and he will flee from you. Draw near to God, and he will draw near to you" (James 4:7–8). This is why Peter pleads with the church: "Be sober-minded; be watchful. Your adversary the devil prowls around like a roaring lion, seeking someone to devour. Resist him" (1 Peter 5:8–9).

In order to resist Satan, we need strength—the strength of young men! We need their strength in a spiritual sense.[27] The strategy is simple: we are to be "strong" (1 John 2:14) in the Mighty One (Ps. 50:1) and in the strength of his might (Eph. 6:10). We need the strength that comes from "the word of God" that abides in us; that is, we need both the saving message of God and the Savior himself. God's Word, in both senses, is the fount of our "strength and the ground of [our] victory."[28] We are victorious through his divine strength and it alone! This is why Paul writes in Ephesians 6:10–12:

> Finally, be strong in the Lord and in the strength of his might. Put on the whole armor of God, that you may be able to stand against the schemes of the devil. For we do not wrestle against flesh and blood, but against the rulers, against the authorities, against the cosmic powers over this present darkness, against the spiritual forces of evil in the heavenly places.

The war is real, but the victory is certain. "The reason the Son of God appeared was to destroy the works of the devil" (1 John 3:8). In his life, death, resurrection, and ascension, Jesus has taken "the teeth out of the roaring lion" and "the fangs out of the serpent."[29] We are protected from the overwhelming onslaughts of evil. And we are free to fight. Like young men on the front line of God's army, we have conquered and we will conquer "by the blood of the Lamb" (Rev. 12:11). Rest assured of it. Take comfort in Christ's conquering. We are marching on to victory.

A Fivefold Encouragement

Perhaps you arrived at this text a bit downcast. Perhaps reading and applying 1 John 1:1–2:11 has greatly troubled your soul. Perhaps you were

27. "The biblical concept of strength is not purely physical." Raymond E. Brown, *The Epistles of John*, Anchor Bible (Garden City, NY: Doubleday, 1982), 305. This is certainly the case in 1 John 2:14.

28. Painter, *1, 2, and 3 John*, 189.

29. Allen, *1–3 John*, 91.

questioning your faith or questioning the goodness of God. Perhaps the darkness of doubt is still clouding your vision. In this chapter, I have sought to bring you, in the words of Maximus of Turin, some "consoling preaching"—words of comfort and encouragement. F. F. Bruce called our text "a threefold encouragement."[30] As I have stated, however, there are actually *five* uplifting encouragements. Recall them. Apply them. Take comfort in them. Share them with others. Here they are again: As *children*, (1) we have our sins forgiven in Christ and (2) we have a saving knowledge of God the Father. As *fathers*, (3) we know Christ. And as *young men*, (4) we are strong in the Lord, and thus (5) we are victorious over the devil.

In the next few chapters, we return to the fight. We are up against the devil, the antichrists, and the world. For now, however, we prepare ourselves for the imperative to fight with the indicatives of forgiveness and fellowship. Our sins have been forgiven in Christ. We are in eternal fellowship with the Father. So, then, let us wield the sword of the Spirit and return to the holy war!

30. Bruce, "The Epistles of John," 57.

6

What Not to Love

1 John 2:15–17

Do not love the world or the things in the world. If anyone loves the world, the love of the Father is not in him. (1 John 2:15)

"She loves me, she loves me not. She loves me, she loves me not. She loves me, she loves me not." We all know the words and cadence of that familiar lover's game in which the petals of a flower fall to the ground until there remains but one. That one providential petal supposedly reveals whether the affections of the person desired are mutual or not.

The theme of love is addressed throughout the Bible, but nowhere more than in 1 John. In this little letter, the word *love* (with its derivatives) is used fifty-one times, and all those uses are positive except one. The only place we are told to "love not" is in 1 John 2:15.[1] Here, and only here, we hear that "great negative exhortation"[2] to "not love the world or the things in the world." This chapter will examine that negative imperative—what it is and why we should heed it—so that we might apply it positively to our lives.

1. John does use *not* with *love* (such as in 1 John 3:10, 14, 18), but it is not in a prohibitive sense (i.e., saying what not to love).

2. Martyn Lloyd-Jones, *Life in Christ: Studies in 1 John* (Wheaton, IL: Crossway, 2002), 213.

Context and Command

When my son Sean was a freshman in high school, he played on the freshman basketball team. At that same time, I helped to coach the varsity team. For practices, we were often in the same large gym. At the start of each practice, all the teams would do some basic drills. Sometimes I would wander down to the freshman squad, jump in the line, and do the drills with them. One day Sean told me that a number of the boys on his team were intimidated by me. I asked him, "Why? Is it because of my basketball prowess?" He said, "No, it's because you always have a serious look on your face."

The members of John's congregation, as they read the first twenty-one verses of his epistle, might have sensed some apostolic intimidation. Perhaps they felt that his presentation of their calling in Christ was too hard and too high. That is why John penned that pastoral poem in 1 John 2:12–14, where he said in essence, "My children, let me reassure you that you are in a state of grace. Beloved, you are loved by me and, more importantly, loved by God in Christ." He gave them a fivefold encouragement. Here John returns to his old countenance. Because of the dangers that the beloved encounter in this often-unlovely world, he puts on his serious and intimidating game face. He moves from affirmation to exhortation and admonition. Like any good coach, he goes from saying, "Good job," to shouting, "Let's go!" For here in 1 John 2:15–17, we begin with his sternest warning and most stringent demand yet: "Do not love the world or the things in the world" (v. 15).

This categorical and comprehensive command appears to be fairly straightforward. Yet the more we look at this command, the more questions arise: What does John mean when he says that we are not to love the world? What's wrong with the world? Genesis teaches that God created the world—the mountains, trees, rivers, animals, and people in it. John's Gospel adds that God so loved the world that he sent his Son to save the world (John 3:16; cf. 1 John 4:19) and that Jesus is "the Savior of the world" (John 4:42; cf. 1 John 2:2). First John reiterates Jesus' own teaching that Christians are to love other people in the world (see 1 John 3:11). So what in the world does John mean by "do not love the world"? If he doesn't mean avoiding people, snubbing social action, discarding political involvement, resisting medical treatment, rejecting the invention of the automobile, refusing to believe in the law of gravity, and leaving planet Earth posthaste, what does he mean?

In John's writings, the word *world* has a wide range of meaning.[3] To summarize the data: on one hand, the world was made by God through Christ and is loved by God through Christ. On the other hand, the world lies in the grip of Satan and comprises people on earth who oppose and ignore God and seek to live independent of him. It is obvious that it is this second "world" that John has in mind. Robert Yarbrough's summary of "the world" is worth quoting in full:

> As a whole it is a realm that does not (or will not) recognize Christ (3:1) and that despises people who follow Christ (3:13). It is shot through with the influence of dangerous deceivers like false prophets (4:1) and antichrist himself (4:3), the evil one "who is in the world" (4:4). "The world" is conceived of as the stronghold of those who ignore the apostolic testimony (4:5; cf. 4:6). While "the Father has sent his Son to be the Savior of the world" (4:14 NIV), this saving work consists in equipping believers to "overcome the world" (5:4–5), not benignly acquiesce to its ways. In the end, in a sense "the whole world is under the control of the evil one" (5:19 NIV). In the light of such numerous and pervasive negative associations, the κόσμος is a sinister sphere indeed; it is an image "of life where God does not rule" (Loader 1992:24).[4]

Therefore, "the world" in this passage does not mean the world in general; rather, it means the world that has abandoned its Creator and lives apart from his rule. It is the godless world that is totally "at variance with God" and his will.[5] It is the Babylon described in Revelation, "the sensual, materialistic pagan society that Christianity had to overcome."[6] It is a group of people who are part of a system that is "organized on wrong principles, and characterized by base desires, false values, and egotism."[7] Quite simply, "the world" means "worldliness," and quite sadly, it means "the typical kind of life that is being lived by the average person today."[8]

3. See F. F. Bruce, "The Epistles of John," in *The Gospel and Epistles of John* (Grand Rapids: Eerdmans, 2004), 60.

4. Robert W. Yarbrough, *1–3 John*, Baker Exegetical Commentary on the New Testament (Grand Rapids: Baker, 2008), 127.

5. John Calvin, "1 John," in John Calvin and Matthew Henry, *1, 2, 3 John*, Crossway Classic Commentaries (Wheaton, IL: Crossway, 1998), 39.

6. Raymond E. Brown, *The Epistles of John*, Anchor Bible (Garden City, NY: Doubleday, 1982), 113.

7. C. H. Dodd, quoted in William Barclay, *The Letters of John and Jude*, Daily Bible Study Series (Philadelphia: Westminster, 1976), 56.

8. Lloyd-Jones, *Life in Christ*, 216.

In the book *Worldliness*, C. J. Mahaney defines the term *worldliness* as "a love for this fallen world." He clarifies: "It's loving the values and pursuits of the world that stand opposed to God. More specifically, it is to *gratify and exalt oneself to the exclusion of God*. It rejects God's rule and replaces it with our own." To that definition he adds self-evaluating questions, such as:

> Does outward prosperity appeal to you more than growth in godliness?
> Do you esteem and crave the approval of those around you?
> Do you go to great lengths to avoid looking foolish or being rejected for your Christian faith?
> Do you consider present and material results more important than eternal reward?
> Have you departed from God and adopted idols instead?[9]

Do you love the world? We must not! As Christians, we must *continually* refuse to let worldliness "squeeze [us] into its mold."[10]

The Three Things

If we must avoid worldliness, what are the characteristics of such worldliness? First John 2:15 says that we are not to love the godless world and the "things" of that world. But what exactly are these "things" that we are to avoid? Should we avoid reading muscle magazines, buying designer jeans, playing video games, gambling at casinos, listening to rap music, showing cleavage, watching sitcoms, getting a second home, upgrading to a luxury sedan, downloading an R-rated movie and then ignoring the violence, talking over the obscenities, and fast-forwarding through the sex scene? Maybe. Let's find out.

While Hollywood is commonly a cesspool whose films desensitize us to sin, the glow of the idiot box dulls our brains, and the world outside us beckons with an omnipresent seduction, John takes us inside *ourselves*.

9. C. J. Mahaney, "Is This Verse in Your Bible?," in *Worldliness: Resisting the Seduction of a Fallen World*, ed. C. J. Mahaney (Wheaton, IL: Crossway, 2008), 27–28.

10. On the nature of the command, John Painter notes that the meaning of the verb "is not 'stop this instant' but 'do not love the world,' a command with continuing effect." *1, 2, and 3 John*, Sacra Pagina (Collegeville, MN: Liturgical Press, 2002), 190. Painter quotes J. B. Phillips's paraphrase of Romans 12:1 on page 193.

The beast is within! In 1 John 2:16, John writes of our "desires of the flesh," our "desires of the eyes," and our "pride of life" (KJV). Those are the three "things"—or inordinate attitudes, interests, ambitions, affections, or actions—that we also must not love. And while these three are not a comprehensive catalogue of every vice, they do embody "every kind of wickedness which exists"[11] and characterize what we all know is natural to everyone (see Mark 7:20–23; John 2:24–25). Thus, they exemplify the core of what we daily struggle against.

The first thing is "the desires of the flesh" (1 John 2:16). We might use the word *desire* in a positive sense, such as "I desire to be a better husband" or "I desire to honor God." But the word used here is almost always used in the Bible in a negative way. It has a morally negative connotation. That is why the NLT translates it "a craving for physical pleasure" and the NIV "the cravings of sinful man." Perhaps "sinful bodily cravings" gets the point across best.

When the Bible speaks about *the flesh*, it does at times refer to sexual sin. Here, however, the term is as broad as our bodies. It is all the evil lusts that we might have or do have for physical pleasure, and all the accompanying aims and ambitions. Martin Luther defined it this way: "The lust of the flesh is that pleasure with which I desire to indulge my flesh, such as adultery, fornication, gluttony, ease, and sleep."[12] William Barclay gives a fuller summary:

> To be subject to the flesh's desire is to judge everything by purely material standards. It is to live a life dominated by the senses. It is to be gluttonous in food; [overindulgent] in luxury; slavish in pleasure; lustful and lax in morals; selfish in the use of possessions[;] . . . extravagant in the gratification of material desires. The flesh's desire [disregards] the commandments of God, the judgment of God, the standards of God and the very existence of God.[13]

So the "desires of the flesh" are like a lasso that tightens around our chests, seeking to turn our attention from the eternal, invisible, and holy God to that which is merely material, transitory, and evil.

11. Bede, "On 1 John," in *James, 1–2 Peter, 1–3 John, Jude*, ed. Gerald Bray, Ancient Christian Commentary on Scripture, New Testament 11 (Downers Grove, IL: InterVarsity Press, 2000), 184.

12. Martin Luther, "Lectures on the First Epistle of St. John," in *The Catholic Epistles*, vol. 30 of *Luther's Works*, trans. and ed. Jaroslav Pelikan and W. A. Hansen (St. Louis: Concordia, 1972), 250.

13. Barclay, *The Letters of John and Jude*, 57.

In Genesis 4:7, the Lord said to Cain, "Sin is crouching at the door. Its *desire* is for you, but you must rule over it." The same is true for us. Sin is crouching at the door, and its desire is to push its way through in order that it may rule over us. But unlike Cain, we must succeed in keeping that door to sin shut. The apostle John has already told us that we have "overcome the evil one" (1 John 2:13–14)—the devil himself! Here he is simply telling us that we need also to overcome ourselves and those internal desires that seek to choke the life of faith. In Romans 13:14, Paul tells us to "put on the Lord Jesus Christ, and make no provision for the flesh, to gratify its desires." John's intention is the same. Because, through faith, we have put on Jesus, we must put aside all bodily desires that are opposed to God.

"The desires of the flesh" are the first thing that we must avoid. The second thing is "the desires of the eyes." Here we move from the temptations within—our flesh—to the temptations without, those cravings that come through those two little crevices that we call our *eyes*. Of our whole body, these two one-inch-wide openings are the parts most susceptible to sin. The devil wants our eyeballs wide open to all that is worldly on this terrestrial ball. He wants us to *covet* all that is opposed to God, whether it is ungodly status, success, pursuits, possessions, or people. The lustful look, the greedy gaze, and the being dressed to impress (or seduce or tempt) are three of three thousand sins that fall under this expansive root vice.

Here is the same temptation that Eve experienced in the garden of Eden and Jesus in the wilderness. Eve listened to the crafty snake and thus allowed sin to enter into her heart through her eyes. Genesis 3:6 says that she "*saw* that the tree was good for food, and that it was *a delight to the eyes*, and that the tree was to be desired to make one wise." So she disobeyed God's one command, and "she took of its fruit and ate" (3:6). Our Lord Jesus experienced a similar temptation. He was tempted by the same tempter and through the same means. In Matthew 4:8–9, we are told that that same serpent tried to get to Jesus' heart through his eyes. In the third temptation, "the devil took [Jesus] to a very high mountain and *showed* him all the kingdoms of the world and their glory. And he said to him, 'All these I will give you, if you will fall down and worship me.'" But what did our Lord do? He closed his eyes to this strong seduction. He refused to desire those delights dangled before him. He resisted: "Be gone, Satan! For it is written, 'You shall worship the Lord your God and him only shall you serve'" (4:10).

We live in a world of images. We cannot drive the highway, turn on the television, walk through the mall, or check out at the supermarket without being surrounded by seductive images. And our fallen eyes, being so vulnerable to the wiles of this world, are greatly tempted to be lifted up to view such worldliness. It is hard to avert our eyes. It is hard to turn away from these attractive icons. Yet we must not indulge our eyes. We must not follow the first Eve but rather the "last Adam" (1 Cor. 15:45). Resist the devil. Overcome his allurements. Close our eyes to those attitudes and ambitions that take us from our vision of God. Worship the Lord and him alone. Long for and *look* to God, in whose presence there is "fullness of joy" and there are "pleasures forevermore" (Ps. 16:11).

There is one final member of the unholy trinity of temptations, perhaps "the most serious and terrible of the three,"[14] and that is the "pride of life" (1 John 2:16 KJV). The word translated "life" (*biou*) can refer to "possessions" (thus the ESV translation, "pride in possessions"), or simply "everyday life" or "livelihood."[15] The idea here, then, is something like this: "pride of life" speaks of the attitude of someone who refuses to rely on God as Father while he boasts in what he has seemingly gained by himself. It is self-dependence and self-glorification. It is unholy conceit in viewing God's gifts as human achievements. It is "boastful self-confidence in the ability to secure one's own life."[16] It is Jesus' parable of the rich fool in fullest form. It is pride in *your life*, rather than the life you could have *in the Son* as a child of the Father.

Some Christians talk like the fools atop the fourth floor of the Tower of Babel. They talk with their heads near the heavens, about making "a name" for themselves (Gen. 11:4)—be it through their elite education, elevated erudition, ecclesial honors, or even extravagant almsgiving. We must abandon such self-promotion. We must reject all boasting, lest the bricks of our vanity crumble down upon us. We cannot let a hint of the "pride of life" creep into the church. God is not impressed by what family we are from, how we look, what we own, whom we know, what we know, where we went to school, what club memberships we hold, or how we have supposedly changed the world. What God loves is when his children look like his beloved Son. He has fatherly pride when we "do nothing from rivalry or conceit, but in humil-

14. Lloyd-Jones, *Life in Christ*, 219.
15. Yarbrough, *1–3 John*, 133.
16. Painter, *1, 2, and 3 John*, 192.

ity count others more significant than [ourselves]" (Phil. 2:3). He rejoices when we share the humble mind of Christ, the One who taught: "Blessed are the poor in spirit, for theirs is the kingdom of heaven" (Matt. 5:3) and "whoever would be great among you must be your servant, and whoever would be first among you must be your slave" (20:26–27). He is glorified when we follow the Savior's path to greatness—the path of the One born in a cave and crucified on a cross, the One who "came not to be served but to serve, and to give his life as a ransom for many" (v. 28).

Far be it from us that we boast in anything "except in the cross of our Lord Jesus Christ" (Gal. 6:14)—not our birth or appearance or knowledge or wealth or status or accomplishments. For hasn't the "world . . . been crucified" to us and we "to the world"? In Christ and him crucified, our birth is now rebirth, our wealth is the riches of heaven, our loftiest associations are the communion of the lowly saints, and our honor will be to hear those blessed words on the last day, "Well done, good and faithful servant. . . . Enter into the joy of your master" (Matt. 25:21).[17]

Love Not! Why Not?

"The desires of the flesh," "the desires of the eyes," and "the pride of life" are the three things of the world that we must not love. "But why?" we might ask. We must love not, but why not? Thankfully, John handles that very question next by providing us with two sensible reasons why having these worldly interests is wrongheaded.

The first reason is that such attitudes and actions are *incompatible with God's nature*. Two verses touch on this. First, at the end of 1 John 2:15 we read, "If anyone loves the world, the love of the Father is not in him." While love for the Father must be preceded by the Father's love for the sinner—"In this is love, . . . that he [God] loved us and sent his Son to be the propitiation for our sins" (4:10)—here in 2:15, God is the object of our love (or lack of love, as the case may be). Second, in verse 16, this is followed by "all that is in the world . . . is not from the Father," namely, that in the world which does not accord with God's will. The fallen world and the things of that world are incompatible with "the Father."[18] If you love the world, you forfeit the

17. Lloyd-Jones, *Life in Christ*, 221.
18. Cf. 1 John 1:2–3; 2:1, 13, 15.

Father! There is a famous saying by Cyprian on ecclesiology: "You cannot have God for your Father if you have not the Church for your mother."[19] John's version on ethics goes: "You cannot have God as your spouse and still have the world as your mistress." You cannot be in an intimate relationship with both God and the world. You cannot love all that God is and has to offer and still love this world and all that it has to offer.

I once watched a sermon in which an immensely popular health/wealth preacher from Houston shared this awful illustration: Years ago, he and his wife were walking through a refurbished neighborhood in their city. He was a young pastor and was living in a small and simple apartment a few blocks away from this old neighborhood with its now new, beautiful, large, expensive homes. Each time they walked by these homes, they dreamed of how wonderful it would be to own one. Well, one day the Lord (so he claimed) spoke to his wife and told her that soon they would own one of those grand houses. He laughed at her prophecy. He didn't have faith. But she did! And sure enough, as time went on and his ministry blossomed and as his salary quadrupled, they were able to buy that house of their dreams. Now, the point of this preacher's multimillion-dollar-house illustration was that God can and will do the same for you *if* you will just let him. Through your faith, God will fulfill all your wildest (or should we add *worldliest*?) dreams.

What rubbish! Do not listen to such lies! Do not think you can have your best worldly life now and your best heavenly life later. You cannot have all that the world has to offer and all that God has to offer. As Jesus made clear: "No one can serve two masters, for either he will hate the one and love the other, or he will be devoted to the one and despise the other. You cannot serve God and money" (Matt. 6:24). Here John says much the same thing: you cannot love God and love the world. You cannot love that which the world loves most and then also try to put God first. If God is tied for first place in your heart, he is in fact placed last. God demands that you love him with heart, soul, and strength (Deut. 6:5). "To attempt to love God in multitasking fashion, dedicating a portion of one's love worldward and then the remaining godward, is fruitless because it fails to acknowledge God as he truly is: sole, unique, sovereign, alone deserving one's core allegiance."[20]

19. St. Cyprian, *The Lapsed; the Unity of the Catholic Church*, trans. Maurice Bévenot, Ancient Christian Writers (New York: Newman, 1956), 48–49.

20. Yarbrough, *1–3 John*, 130.

"I am the Lord your God, who brought you out of the land of Egypt, out of the house of slavery. You shall have no other gods before me" (Ex. 20:2–3).

The first reason that we should not love the world and the things of the world is that such a love is incompatible with God's nature. The second reason is that *this world and its values are transient.* They are temporary and thus headed for destruction. That is what we are told at the beginning of 1 John 2:17. We should not love the world because "the world is passing away along with its desires." As David Jackman notes, "there is no future in worldliness."[21] There is literally no future to clinging to that which this fallen, fading, and soon-to-be-forgotten world has to offer.

Once the richest American, the industrialist J. Paul Getty famously said, "The best things in life . . . are things."[22] That might be true if "the present form of this world" weren't "passing away" (1 Cor. 7:31) and if everything under its shelter were not soon to prove bankrupt. I wonder how Getty's final audit went when he died, stood before his Maker, and found his portfolio completely bare. "Riches, learning, knowledge, social status and all these things, they are vanishing, they have the seeds of death in them."[23] Loving this present world is disastrous (2 Tim. 4:10); having "living affections for dying things" is foolish.[24] Saying "my precious" to Gollum's golden ring or to Getty's mansion in Malibu is simply silly. And this should be obvious to any observer.

In China, France, Greece, India, Italy, Cambodia, the Americas, and Egypt, we have unearthed pyramids, those elaborate tombs for royalty. The oldest and largest of the Egyptian pyramids, the Great Pyramid of Giza, is called one of the seven wonders of the ancient world. And yes, architecturally, it is indeed a wonder. But theologically, it is quite a blunder. We will never find even a footnote in a journal article saying, "Ancient Egyptian leaders such as Pharaoh Khufu and King Tutankhamen were among the world's biggest fools." But such a footnote would be quite accurate. For what an absolute waste of thought, strength, and time it was to build an elaborate burial tomb and fill it with priceless treasures that never made it into the afterlife. The golden chariots, gilded figures, fine jewelry, and heavy

21. David Jackman, *The Message of John's Letters*, The Bible Speaks Today (Downers Grove, IL: InterVarsity Press, 1988), 96.

22. Getty, quoted in Dave Harvey, "God, My Heart, and Stuff," in Mahaney, *Worldliness*, 93.

23. Lloyd-Jones, *Life in Christ*, 222.

24. John Owen, quoted in C. J. Mahaney, "Is This Verse in Your Bible?," 32.

thrones are all still there, if not long since stolen. While we may enjoy them, the pyramids never served their original purpose. They illustrate how true 1 John 2:17 reads.

"The world is passing away along with its desires" (1 John 2:17a). Yet there is an alternative to loving and living for this world. Notice the conjunction *but*—an amazing contrast is coming! "But whoever does the will of God abides forever" (v. 17b). What a climactic ending, as we have moved from that negative command to this positive plea and amazing incentive!

Why would we, as heirs of the eternal world, concentrate our interests and ambitions on what is passing away? Why would we who are on the winning side—the light that is steadily but surely overcoming the darkness (1 John 2:8)—want to live like a loser? Why not rather do "the will of God" (v. 17), which is to love God first, trust in his Son for our salvation, and live according to his Word? There is a future in that kind of thinking. There is a future in that kind of lifestyle! It is like building a house on rock rather than sand (Matt. 7:24–27). The one who does the will of God abides "forever." As missionary and martyr Jim Elliot put it, "He is no fool who gives what he cannot keep to gain that which he cannot lose."[25] Or as Jesus put it: Why lay up for ourselves "treasures on earth [that] moth and rust destroy" (Matt. 6:19–20), when we can lay up for ourselves "treasures in heaven" (v. 20) that are as permanent as God and his kingdom (v. 33)? As Luther asks, "What sort of god is it that is not even capable of defending himself against moths and rust?"[26] The choice is simple. Let us use our heads. Would we rather desire that which is "passing away" or that which "abides forever"? This last reason should be a good enough reason to love not this world.

Rivals for the Human Heart

We must admit that the world has great appeal. It takes our heartstrings and pulls at them each and every day. That is why we need to be reminded of what we are called to do and why we are called to do it. We need to be reminded of who we are and what we are to be about. We need to remember that question posed long ago by our Lord who still lives today: "For what does

25. Elisabeth Elliot, ed., *The Journals of Jim Elliot* (Old Tappan, NJ: Revell, 1978), 174.

26. Martin Luther, *The Sermon on the Mount and the Magnificat*, vol. 21 of *Luther's Works*, ed. Jaroslav Pelikan (St. Louis: Concordia, 1956), 173.

it profit a man to gain the whole world and forfeit his soul?" (Mark 8:36). And we need to remember Jesus, who was unworldly for the world so that he might save the world! Yes, we need to remember him—to know that our lifelong battle with worldliness cannot be won by sheer willpower or personal resolve, but only through replacing our love for the world with a love for someone far lovelier. The glory of Christ is the antidote for all that dazzles and sparkles but fades. The old song got it right:

> Turn your eyes upon Jesus,
> Look full in His wonderful face;
> And the things of earth will grow strangely dim
> In the light of His glory and grace.[27]

27. Helen H. Lemmel, "Turn Your Eyes upon Jesus" (1922).

7

Antichrist Is Coming!

1 John 2:18–27

I write these things to you about those who are trying to deceive you. (1 John 2:26)

When I was in college, I had a crush on a girl named Janet. *Crush* is the right word only because my infatuation was grounded in junior-high unreality. I was *totally* interested in her, but she wasn't *overly* interested in me. Yet the air I breathed as a college student was the air of everything-in-the-world-that-God-was-doing-revolved-around-my-life. I was certain that God was orchestrating events so that she would fall in love with me. The evidence was substantial. There were *two* signs! We both played varsity basketball. We both ended up living in campus houses next to each other.

But I needed a bigger and better sign than those two that God was indeed working to bring us together. So one day, I stood outside the dining hall and prayed, "Lord, let me know that Janet likes me. If she comes to eat in the next five minutes, I will know that you want me to continue pursuing her." A minute passed; then two more; finally, and sure enough, she ran by, waved, and said, "Hi." The God-ordained pursuit was on! The only detail that got in the way was her telling me months later, in passing, that she was engaged to a friend from home. Jeff something-or-another. I squeezed out the fleece and carried on.

The next girl about whom I wanted to know God's view was Anna. Anna and I actually dated for a year. But I was uncertain whether I should marry her. So I came up with quite the test for God. This is not a joke, and I wish I could eye the reader to help you refrain from laughing at me. Here was the test: If Anna made me zucchini bread, I would know that she was the one. There you have it. Get to work, God! Well, God did get to work through my sinister friend Erik. Erik was the only soul I told about the zucchini-bread divination. Afterward and when alone, Erik couldn't control his laughter. Or his tongue. He told Anna straight away. They both had a good laugh. And soon after—miraculously—the bread from heaven was sent. I learned months after Anna broke up with me about their devilish plot.

The church in Ephesus to which John was writing wasn't into *bad* theology—you discern God's will through waiting for freshly baked bread with a certain vegetable (or is it fruit?) in it—rather, the Ephesians were into *false* teaching. They were being lured into an anti-Messiah movement that was claiming something new and improved—"Jesus wasn't really God's last word to his people."[1] Those who had been "anointed" by the Holy Spirit were tempted to move from the Father's revealed will by denying Jesus as the heavenly anointed Son come in the flesh. They were tempted to move out of the true Trinitarian church and into what they knew deep down was a false fellowship. John sounds the warning bell. Don't listen to such lies!

Deceive, Deny, Depart

As we already know from our study of 1 John 1:1–2:17, John is a man of stark contrasts—light and darkness, love and hate. In 2:18–27 he adds *truth* and *lies*. Here he teaches the truth about the light of Jesus by setting before us a black backdrop of those who hate it. Here we encounter the apostate antichrists—those who deceive, deny, and depart.

In 1 John 2:26, John says, "I write these things to you about those who are trying to *deceive* you." These deceivers deceive through doctrinal denials. (We have arrived at the *truth test*.)

1. N. T. Wright, *Early Christian Letters for Everyone*, New Testament for Everyone (Louisville, KY: Westminster John Knox, 2011), 146.

> I write to you, not because you do not know the truth, but because you know it, and because no lie is of the truth. Who is the liar but he who *denies* that Jesus is the Christ? This is the antichrist, he who *denies* the Father and the Son. No one who *denies* the Son has the Father. Whoever confesses the Son has the Father also. (1 John 2:21–23)

They deny that Jesus is "the Christ" (1 John 2:22), the long-awaited, Scripture-prophesied, and God-anointed Messiah. They deny that Jesus is "the Son" (vv. 22–23), the divine Son of the Father. These two lies—or, better, one lie with two closely related parts—constitute their anti-confession! This is "the supreme lie,"[2] because, according to the apostolic account:

> The Son is the expression of the Father—God made visible, God made known. To see the Son is to see the Father (John 14:8–10). He is the image of the invisible God (Col 1:15), the express image of God's substance and radiance of his glory (Heb 1:2–3).[3]

Just as you cannot divide the human body vertically—slicing through the brain and leaving the heart on the left side—and live, so, too, you cannot divide the Father from the Son and the Son from the Father.[4] Father, Son, and Spirit (the humble member of the Trinity, least often mentioned in John's letters, whose job it is to lift up the Father and the Son) are one.

Now, while these deceivers weren't precisely spouting the modern maxim that "even though we don't believe the same things about Jesus, we still worship the same God," the root error was the same. And such tolerance is intolerable to John. We are to love our enemies, but love does not tolerate terrible teaching. John calls such a deceiver and denier "liar" and "antichrist" (1 John 2:22).

Who is the antichrist? John's antichrist is a Christological rebel. In 2 John 7, we read: "For many deceivers have gone out into the world, those who do not confess the coming of Jesus Christ in the flesh. Such a one is the deceiver and the antichrist." First John 4:2–3 states, "By this you know the

2. Bede, "On 1 John," in *James, 1–2 Peter, 1–3 John, Jude*, ed. Gerald Bray, Ancient Christian Commentary on Scripture, New Testament 11 (Downers Grove, IL: InterVarsity Press, 2000), 189.

3. Philip W. Comfort and Wendell C. Hawley, *1–3 John*, Cornerstone Biblical Commentary (Carol Stream, IL: Tyndale, 2007), 344.

4. See Irenaeus, *Against Heresies*, 3.15.5.

Spirit of God: every spirit that confesses that Jesus Christ has come in the flesh is from God, and every spirit that does not confess Jesus is not from God. This is the spirit of the antichrist, which you heard was coming and now is in the world already." Then in our passage we read in 1 John 2:22: "Who is the liar but he who denies that Jesus is the Christ? This is the antichrist, he who denies the Father and the Son," and in verse 18, "Children, it is the last hour, and as you have heard that antichrist is coming, so now many antichrists have come."

Do you know how many times the title *antichrist* is used in the Bible? You just read them all! It is not one hundred times or even ten times; it is only four times. To put that into perspective, the name *Silas* is mentioned three times as much (12 times) and the title *Christ* is used over a hundred times as much (524 times)! The small number of references, however, does not mean that the antichrists in the world are not a force to be reckoned with, or that the coming antichrist is not perhaps the same powerful and diabolical figure as "the beast" in Revelation 13:1–10 and "the man of lawlessness" in 2 Thessalonians 2:3. In "the last hour" (1 John 2:18)—the period between Pentecost and the Parousia[5]—the church is under siege. From Cerinthus in the second century to Joseph Smith in the nineteenth, from the earliest Arians to the Jehovah's Witnesses today, we fight the antichrists. Jews deny Jesus as the Christ, Muslims deny Jesus as the Son, and Christians should not be offended to see those two major religions under the *antichrist* category or to say that we must "fight" a real spiritual battle with them. The enemy is obvious (we are not on the lookout for an emerging secret society or mysterious political figure) but not easily overcome.

As John relays in 1 John 2:19, some have been captured and led away:

> They went out from us, but they were not of us; for if they had been of us, they would have continued with us. But they went out, that it might become plain that they all are not of us.

Here we are told about the false teachers' departure, which is our third *D*—deceive, deny, and *depart*. John speaks of a schism within the church. Any

5. John's "the last hour" is synonymous with other New Testament expressions, such as "the last days" (Acts 2:17), "the last time" (Jude 18), and "the last times" (1 Peter 1:20), which speak of the time between Jesus' death and the final judgment.

division within Christ's visible church is sad, but this one, John reassures those who remain, is necessary and even beneficial to the overall health of the body. The cancer has removed itself.[6] The rats have left the ship. For notice the contrast made with the words *they* (6×) and *us* (5×). "Believers belong; deniers depart" is how Simon Kistemaker summarizes this verse.[7] Believers (the *us*) belong (remain in the apostolic community); deniers (the *they*) depart (leave the communion of the saints). The apostate antichrists, who were once members of the visible church, seceded from it: "They went out from us." Their secession only revealed their true nature. They departed because they had never been united to Christ through a Spirit-wrought living and enduring faith.

We should be discouraged if people leave our fellowship after being with us for years because the church is not meeting their needs, because their favorite hymns are not sung often enough, because the sermons are too long, or because of some other superficial reason. And we should weep over gullible but genuine Christians who temporarily leave the apostolic fellowship because they are deceived. But we should not grieve for the church when wolves come in and steal wolves. True sheep abide in the Good Shepherd; true sheep stay safely within the gates of the apostolic testimony. Put differently, the anointed abide in *the* Anointed.

Those Anointed Abide in the Anointed

Set against the darkness of the antichrists—those who deceive, deny, and depart—we have the anointed who abide in *the* Anointed. As it happens, the *D*-words highlight the actions of the apostates who opposed Jesus as Christ, so the *A*-words illuminate the action of the remnant who acknowledge Jesus as Christ. These two *A*-words dominate John's call to Christians. The word *anoint* (*anointed*, *anointing*) is used three times, and the word *abide* is used five times (six times if we were to include 1 John 2:28). But it is not the word

6. "But there are . . . others who are malignant tumors, and when they are removed the body is spared." Bede, "On 1 John," 188. Cf. "This is deplorable and lamentable. Nevertheless, it is comforting. The wheat is not at fault when tares shoot forth. Nor is the truth the cause of so many evils." Martin Luther, "Lectures on the First Epistle of St. John," in *The Catholic Epistles*, vol. 30 of *Luther's Works*, trans. and ed. Jaroslav Pelikan and W. A. Hansen (St. Louis: Concordia, 197), 254.

7. Simon J. Kistemaker, "Exposition of the Epistles of John," in *James, Epistles of John, Peter, and Jude* (Grand Rapids: Baker, 2002), 277.

count that matters so much as the message, namely, that *Christians abide in the Anointed One by means of their anointing.*

The Greek word *Christos* means "anointed," also translated "Christ," as in "Jesus the Christ" or "Christians" (*Christianous*, Acts 11:26). In 1 John 2:20, when John is transitioning from those who are *antichristos* in verses 18–19, he uses this play on words. He writes, "But you have been anointed [*chrisma*]." Later in verse 27, he speaks of "the anointing [*chrisma*] that you received." Our God-given anointing (*chrisma*) enables our true confession of Jesus as the Christ (*Christos*). To be a Christian is to be christened into Christ. The Heidelberg Catechism, one of the great documents of the Protestant Reformation, answers question 32, "Why are you called a Christian?," by saying, "Because by faith I am a member of Christ and so share in his anointing. I am anointed to confess his name, to present myself to him as a living sacrifice of thanks, to strive with a free conscience against sin and the devil in this life, and afterwards to reign with Christ over all creation and all eternity."

It has become commonplace to use the word *anointed* in ways that are foreign to its usage in Scripture. For example, we might call preachers, sermons, songs, or worship services *anointed.* Popular usage speaks of a person or event in which there is an awareness of God's power or presence. In the Bible, however, to anoint someone has to do with setting a person apart for a special purpose. Such anointing was the privilege of the chosen few—priests, prophets, and kings. These offices were fulfilled by Christ, and now this priestly, prophetic, and kingly anointing has been bestowed on all who confess that Jesus is the Christ who "has come in the flesh" (1 John 4:2).

The ancient writer Tertullian wrote that Christians were anointed with holy oil during their baptism as a sign that the same Holy Spirit that descended upon Jesus at his baptism has now come upon Christ's disciples.[8] John is likely not referring to water baptism; he is speaking of Spirit-baptism. We have been "anointed by the Holy One" (1 John 2:20). God is called the "Holy One" in the Old Testament (e.g., Ps. 71:22), and Jesus receives the same title in the New Testament (e.g., Rev. 3:7).[9] It is most likely, however, that "the

8. See "Chrism," in *Cyclopaedia of Biblical, Theological, and Ecclesiastical Literature*, ed. John McClintock and James Strong (New York: Harper and Brothers, 1894), 2:259.

9. "John's Gospel is perhaps most helpful in delimiting the meaning of 'from the Holy One' in 1 John 2:20. The adjective 'holy' occurs there only five times. Three times it refers to the Holy Spirit (John 1:33; 14:26; 20:22), once to Jesus (6:69), and once to God the Father (17:11). These references, in light of the context of 1 John 2:20, suggest that John could have in mind Christ, God, the Spirit, or

Holy One" here references the Holy Spirit.[10] What John says here is similar to what Paul says in 2 Corinthians 1:21–22: "And it is God who establishes us with you in Christ, and has anointed us, and who has also put his seal on us and given us his Spirit in our hearts as a guarantee."

This "anointing," then, has little to do with whether or not the presence or power of God exudes from us. Rather, it has to do with the Spirit, who leads us into all truth. The anointing, in this context, is more cognitive than expressive. As 1 John 2:20 begins, "But you have been anointed by the Holy One," so it ends "and you all have knowledge." Verse 27 similarly ties the anointing to truth-thinking and -teaching: "But the anointing that you received from him abides in you, and you have no need that anyone should teach you. But as his anointing teaches you about everything, and is true, and is no lie—just as it has taught you, abide in him." This verse does not mean that Christians automatically understand astrophysics. It also does not imply that we should fire the pastor and cancel all Sunday school classes, for after all, John—as a God-appointed teacher (cf. Eph. 4:12)—is instructing the church in this very verse. Rather, it means that Christians who are indwelt by the Jesus-sent Spirit do not need anyone to teach them anything new or beyond what they learned about the basics of Christianity from the apostles "from the beginning" (1 John 2:24). Colin Kruse summarizes Johann Michl's work on the Spirit as guarantor of the right faith:

> He argues . . . that an awareness of the truth is given to the whole church, including those who hold the teaching office and the congregation of the faithful. These stand in an organic union and complement one another. The general faith consciousness of the members and the proclamation of the teachers, through the power of the Holy Spirit, lead to an infallible possession of the truth to which it bears witness without error.[11]

---

some combination of the three viewed in their joint function." Robert W. Yarbrough, *1–3 John*, Baker Exegetical Commentary on the New Testament (Grand Rapids: Baker, 2008), 148.

10. I follow I. Howard Marshall, who claims that 1 John 2:20 is "paralleled by what is said in John 14:17; 15:26; 16:13 about the activity of the Paraclete, the Holy Spirit." *The Epistles of John*, New International Commentary on the New Testament (Grand Rapids: Eerdmans, 1978), 153. Cf. Luther's apt summary: "This true anointing is nothing else than the Holy Spirit, who was poured out in the house on the day of Pentecost (Acts 2:1–4)." "Lectures on the First Epistle of St. John," 255.

11. Johann Michl, "Der Geist als Garant des rechten Glaubens," in *Vom Wort des Lebens, Festschrift für Max Meinertz*, ed. Nikolaus Adler (Münster: Aschendorffsche Verlagsbuchhandlung, 1951), 146–47, in Colin G. Kruse, *The Letters of John*, Pillar New Testament Commentary (Grand Rapids: Eerdmans, 2000), 111.

When we recite the Apostles' Creed in church, we should see it as an *external* defense mechanism against heresies. For example, if for years you have recited, "I believe in Jesus Christ," who on "the third day . . . rose again from the dead," and then some antichrist—for example, the professor emeritus of the German Higher Critics Divinity School—comes on the History Channel and denies that claim, the heresy alarm goes off. That's wrong! The anointing, by contrast, is our *internal* defense mechanism. It is personal God-given knowledge that helps us to discern truth from error. As William Tyndale stated, "Ye are not anointed with oil in your bodies, but with the Spirit of Christ in your souls; which Spirit teacheth you all truth in Christ, and maketh you to judge what is a lie, and what truth, and to know Christ from antichrist."[12]

Christian, "you have been anointed by the Holy One" (1 John 2:20). It is by means of that divine anointing that we are called to "abide in him" (v. 27). A few years ago, I set aside one week to read through the whole New Testament. I did this to get a better understanding of and feel for the basic rhythm and themes of God's Word. In doing this, I found that every book of the New Testament was filled with this idea of abiding, commonly called *perseverance*—or, in Reformed circles, *perseverance of the saints*. For example, in his earthly ministry Jesus spoke of perseverance. He said, "The one who endures to the end will be saved" (Mark 13:13). Moreover, in his heavenly ministry, the exalted Christ issues the same call. In Revelation 3:11, he says to the church then and now, "I am coming soon. Hold fast [to] what you have." The apostle John teaches much the same here. Five times he calls us to "abide" or "remain" (*menō*)—or, put thematically, "to endure."

"Endurance is the hall-mark of the saved" is how John Stott correctly summarizes this section.[13] It is not enough to say that we once believed; it is necessary that we continue to believe. "It is not enough merely to have heard and assented to the message in time past. The message must continue to be present and active" in our lives.[14] "Future and final perseverance is

12. Tyndale, quoted in Bruce B. Barton et al., *1, 2 & 3 John*, Application Bible Commentary (Wheaton, IL: Tyndale, 1998), 51.

13. John R. W. Stott, *The Epistles of John: An Introduction and Commentary*, Tyndale New Testament Commentaries (Downers Grove, IL: InterVarsity Press, 1976), 105.

14. Marshall, *The Epistles of John*, 161.

the ultimate test of genuine participation in the life of Christ."[15] If one does not abide in him, it is a sure sign that one has not been anointed. For those anointed by the Spirit abide in Christ and the truth.

As important as it is to emphasize and celebrate how people get into the kingdom, we ought to be just as emphatic and celebratory when people remain under Christ's lordship for life! Who rejoices in the runner who starts the marathon but does not finish the marathon? We must "run with endurance the race that is set before us" (Heb. 12:1). With a "great cloud of witnesses" cheering us on, we are to start *and finish* well. We are to swerve from those on one side who hold out the poison of false religion and those on the other side who offer an easy alternative route through the worldly neighborhoods of Idolatry and Immorality (cf. 1 Cor. 10:1–13; 1 John 2:15–17). Instead, we are to keep to the middle way as we hold fast to the confession (cf. Heb. 4:14) of Jesus as Christ and Son of God.

We all know someone who has left the church. We all know someone who has shipwrecked his faith. Do you fear doing the same? Most of us don't. In the closing line of his poem "A Hymn to God the Father," John Donne wrote:

> I have a sin of fear, that when I have spun
> My last thread, I shall perish on the shore.[16]

It is difficult to know whether Donne's "sin" is that he fears that he will fail Christ or that Christ will fail him. If the latter, it is indeed a sinful anxiety, for Christ will never fail us ("I give them eternal life, and they will never perish, and no one will snatch them out of my hand," John 10:28; cf. 6:36–40). But if the former, then Donne's "sin of fear" might at times be a virtue, for as Hebrews 4:1 states: "Therefore, while the promise of entering his rest still stands, let us *fear* lest any of you should seem to have failed to reach it." Do you have a healthy fear of being stranded on the shore of this fallen and passing-away world? I hope we all do. But I also hope—a hope that is more in line with the apostle John's thinking here—that we are of good cheer because we know that perseverance is possible because God is with us. We remain in the race because

15. James Montgomery Boice, *The Epistles of John: An Expositional Commentary* (Grand Rapids: Baker, 1979), 69.

16. John Donne, "A Hymn to God the Father," in *The Complete English Poems*, Penguin Classics (London: Penguin, 1996), 349.

the Spirit abides in us. God is the author and perfecter of our salvation. The Holy One who saved us is also the One who is saving us and will save us. Trust in the Lord with all your heart, and lean not on your own strength, running shoes, or energy packets—to paraphrase a well-known proverb (Prov. 3:5). God's sovereign and inseparable love in Christ (Rom. 8:38–39) will guard us until the end (2 Tim. 1:12; cf. 1 Peter 1:3–5). Because of God's unchanging character, unwavering promises, and enduring power, we can be assured that God will bring his saving work in us to completion (Phil. 1:6). The Lord who has effectually called us into saving faith will preserve his persevering saints.

Those anointed abide in *the* Anointed. Know it. Believe it. Live it. Rest assured in it.

An Alternative Outline

For years I have met with my interns on Monday afternoons, and we have discussed the Bible passage that I will preach on. I ask them to come prepared with comments and questions. I try to come prepared with a homiletical outline. Because of the timing of our Missions Sunday, we had two weeks to tackle this text. Both weeks I came with different outlines. I scratched the first and just preached the second: the three *D*s (*deceive*, *deny*, and *depart*) and the two *A*s (*anoint* and *abide*). Nevertheless, there was one point from the first sermon outline that was not emphasized in the second. It was what would have been my second point. The first point was "Don't be deceived," the third point was "Abide in him," and *the second point* was "Believe in the promise of eternal life." I will end this chapter with that important point.

First John 2:18 begins: "Children, it is the last hour, and as you have heard that antichrist is coming, so now many antichrists have come." Verse 25 reads, "And this is the promise that he made to us—eternal life." We live, as John lived, in "the last hour." Again, that phrase does not literally mean the final sixty minutes of world history, or John would not have penned the phrase in the first place. Who writes a letter about the last hour, knowing that it would not get to its recipients in an hour? The phrase means the time between Jesus' giving of the Spirit at Pentecost and his return at the end of the world (Acts 2:17; cf. 1 Peter 1:20). Between those points in time, we live in a fallen and frightening world. It is crawling with the lusts of the flesh and eyes and heart. It is filled with those who oppose or try to take the place of King Jesus. One way to survive in such a world is to have an otherworldly vision. The word *last* in 1 John 2:18 is *eschatē*, from which we get words such as *eschatological*. We live in the "last hour" or "last days."[17] And because "the time has been shortened" (1 Cor. 7:29 NASB), to borrow a phrase from Paul, we should not dream of our earthly continuance—as though we will live here forever! Rather, we should abide in the Lord until we go to be with the Lord, or he comes down to be with us in final judgment and salvation. The time is at hand! We live every hour in the last hour. What would you do if you knew that Jesus was returning today? Would you think differently? Would you live differently? Live that way now!

Related to that eschatological vision is "the promise that he made to us—eternal life" (1 John 2:25). In my church, I know five people who have cancer, one who had heart surgery, two who are confined to wheelchairs, and many who have loved ones who are dying or have recently died—including husbands, wives, and children in the womb. The shadow of death hangs over us all, but some of us are blind to it. Death has been dressed up and buried from our sight. In the ancient world, everyone knew the reality of death and feared it. For example, writing to his friend Lucilius near the time that John penned his first epistle, the Roman Stoic philosopher Seneca wrote, "Most men ebb and flow in wretchedness between the fear of death and the hardships of life."[18] Another first-century philosopher, Lucretius, lamented how seeking after "greatness, status, importance, possessions, friendship, [and] pleasure" is evaporated by the grave.[19]

Like all the other New Testament authors, the Gospel writers were also aware of the fears that occupied the general populace. For example, in Mark's Gospel, think of the hurting people who came to Jesus for help:

> a man with an unclean spirit (Mark 1:21–28); a woman with a fever (1:29–31); a leper in his uncleanness (1:40–45); a paralytic (2:1–10); a man with a withered hand (3:1–6); a man with a legion of demons who lives among the tombs (5:1–10); a synagogue official, Jairus, whose twelve-year-old daughter is dying (5:21–23) and then dead (5:35–43); a woman who had been bleeding for as long as the girl had been alive (5:24–34); a Greek woman whose daughter was troubled with a demon (7:24–30); a deaf man with stumbling speech (7:31–37); a blind man who lived in Bethsaida (8:22–26); a father and son,

17. See Acts 2:17; Heb. 1:2; 1 Peter 1:20.

18. Seneca (*Epistle* 4.6), quoted in Peter G. Bolt, *The Cross from a Distance: Atonement in Mark's Gospel*, New Studies in Biblical Theology (Downers Grove, IL: InterVarsity Press, 2004), 41.

19. Lucretius, *De rerum natura*, as summarized by Bolt, *The Cross from a Distance*, 41–42.

> severely afflicted by a spirit that had troubled the boy since childhood and had often tried to kill him (9:14–29); another blind man, by the name of Bartimaeus (10:46–52).[20]

Those thirteen people do not symbolize a few "unlucky" souls but everyone who lives under the everyday curse of death. Perhaps the most informative passage on how death was a constant preoccupation of the New Testament era is the rich man's question in Mark 10:17. This is no poor or powerless man, and yet his question is the question of all: "What must I do to inherit eternal life?" Not even this rich man could ransom his own soul from Sheol.

In Mark's Gospel as well as Matthew's, Luke's, and John's, the message is one of ultimate hope: that the fear of death can be cast aside only by "faith in the one who can raise the dead" because he has conquered death.[21] One window into the gospel—good news!—is the story of the raising of Lazarus. When Jesus arrived too late to save Lazarus,

> Martha said to Jesus, "Lord, if you had been here, my brother would not have died. But even now I know that whatever you ask from God, God will give you." Jesus said to her, "Your brother will rise again." Martha said to him, "I know that he will rise again in the resurrection on the last day." Jesus said to her, "I am the resurrection and the life. Whoever believes in me, though he die, yet shall he live, and everyone who lives and believes in me shall never die." (John 11:21–26)

How long is "never"? Jesus offers "eternal life" in him. "Do you believe this?" (John 11:26) is the question he posed to Martha. I pose it now to you. Do you believe—and live like you believe—in the promise of eternal life in Jesus? Can you answer, as she did (and as John in 1 John 2:18–27 wants us to): "Yes, Lord; I believe that you are *the Christ, the Son of God*, who is coming into the world" (John 11:27).[22] That confession in that person pulls out the sting and rolls away the stone of death. In a world where anti-Christian teachers who have departed from the church seek to deceive us by denying the truth, our only (and eternal!) hope is to abide in the Anointed One by means of our anointing.

20. Bolt, *The Cross from a Distance*, 38.
21. Ibid., 42.
22. This is how the NASB translates the second half of John 11:27: "*even* He who comes into the world."

8

The Appearance Is Everything

1 John 2:28–3:10

And now, little children, abide in him, so that when he appears we may have confidence and not shrink from him in shame at his coming. If you know that he is righteous, you may be sure that everyone who practices righteousness has been born of him. (1 John 2:28–29)

Happy Mardi Gras!" was the greeting I received early last year as I walked into a local coffee shop. Wearing colored beads around their necks and bright smiles on their faces, the two ladies behind the counter greeted each customer with the same greeting I received, as well as with the same suggestive joke, one that reflects the usual atmosphere of Bourbon Street, New Orleans.

Mardi Gras is French for *Fat Tuesday*. Fat Tuesday, with its gluttonous feasting, is a distortion of the season of Lent and the fasting that accompanies it. According to the Western church calendar, Lent begins on what is traditionally called *Ash Wednesday*. Excluding Sundays, the season lasts for forty days, and has been customarily viewed as a time of repentance before the celebration of the resurrection. Those who take to heart this church tradition call the day before Ash Wednesday not *Fat Tuesday* but

Shrove Tuesday. Shrove or *to shrive* means "to cleanse or purify." On that day the faithful are encouraged to prepare their bodies and souls for Lent, and ultimately for Holy Week, by confessing and repenting of their sins.

I do not know how the shriving of sin devolved into the consumption of sin, purifying became partying, and fasting became feasting, but I do know how predictable it is in this fallen world that when the center is removed, "things fall apart."[1] Fat Tuesday is but one of many examples of the law of moral entropy: how that which is pure changes to impure, virtuous to vice, and sacred to sinful. Over time, the world has a way of turning that which is good and right into that which is evil and wrong. My thoughts are divided on whether the season of Lent is good and right. I see its beauty, but I also see (and have experienced) its bondage. Yet about whether the gospel of Jesus Christ is good and right I have no division of mind. God's gospel is the greatest good of the world! And so when it is distorted—when the gospel itself becomes the means or the motivation to sin—then all that is "good" about the "good news" has been sifted out and scattered on the floor.

One of the reasons that the apostle John penned 1 John was to clear up such a mess and showcase afresh the goodness of the good news. Of course, in this letter, the problem is not merely moral entropy but false teachers. Deceivers are out to deceive, and they have deceived. Their deception, like all other skillful lies, was appealing. Put simply, their claim was that a follower of Jesus could still be a child of God and live like a son of Satan. That is, a Christian could know that all his sins are forgiven and yet knowingly continue in sin. That sounds pretty good! That philosophy still sells. John, however, wants us to spew it out of our mouths, and cut it out of our hearts and heads. As a loving and protective parent, he warns Christians, prone to wander from his fatherly fingers, not to be led astray: "Little children, let no one deceive you. Whoever practices righteousness is righteous, as he [Jesus] is righteous" (1 John 3:7). The gospel is life-transforming! Don't let anyone deceive you about its effects. No one "born of God" lives godlessly. There is a black-and-white difference between the "child of the devil" and the "child of God"—the first shoves in sin like barbecue pork on Fat Tuesday, and the latter shrives from sin by daily practicing Christ-abiding righteousness.

1. From William Butler Yeats, "The Second Coming," in *The Collected Works of W. B. Yeats Volume I: The Poems*, ed. Richard J. Finneran, rev. 2nd ed. (New York: Simon and Schuster, 2010), 187.

The Great Theme

A number of pastoral concerns arise from this text, which I will cover by answering three questions in the next three sections. First, in a passage that does not have a clear linear progression and reiterates its point with at least seven verses that sound similar, how do I express clearly John's "big idea," as Haddon Robinson calls it, or "the great theme," as Martyn Lloyd-Jones would say? Here is my shot at it: *In light of the appearance of the Righteous One and our future perfect righteousness, practice righteousness by abiding in him.*

The word *appear* is important to our text. It is used five times, and four of those usages describe the two appearances of Christ. The first appearance was the incarnation, when the preexistent sinless Son of God "appeared [in order] to take away sins" (1 John 3:5). That perspective—that "[t]he self-disclosure of God in his Son, for the purpose of dealing with human sin, stretches from the preexistence of Christ"[2]—is supported by the verb "appeared" or "was manifested," which implies preexistence. It is also supported by the title "Son of God," used for the first time in 1 John 3:8 (then in 4:15; 5:5, 10, 12, 13, 20), along with the phrase "in him there is no sin" (3:5). "Christ is the Righteous One [2:29], the Pure One [3:3], and the Sinless One [3:5]."[3]

In Jesus' incarnation, he also appeared in order "to destroy the works of the devil" (1 John 3:8). How interesting to think of the incarnation as *destructive.* Jesus conquered sin and hell. *Christus Victor!* On the cross, the offspring of Eve crushed the serpent's head (Gen. 3:15). The devil—who sinned before the creation of the world ("from the beginning," 1 John 3:8) and is the source of sin in the world (see John 8:44)—has been defeated in the death of the Messiah. The second appearance is the second coming, referenced by the phrase "when he appears" (1 John 2:28; 3:2). That coming will be *constructive.* We will become like Jesus.

Between those two appearances, we abide and emulate: we remain in Christ and resemble Christ. The Righteous One produces righteous ones—those who practice righteousness.[4] Those whom God births he does not

2. Stephen S. Smalley, *1, 2, 3 John*, Word Biblical Commentary (Nashville: Thomas Nelson, 1984), 156.

3. Daniel L. Akin, *1, 2, 3 John*, New American Commentary (Nashville: Broadman & Holman, 1993), 142.

4. We abide in Jesus as the true Vine, and by abiding in him we bear fruit. Apart from him we can do nothing (see John 15:5).

abandon. "No one born of God makes a practice of sinning" (1 John 3:9). Why? Two reasons—"*for* God's seed abides in him, and he cannot keep on sinning *because* he has been born of God" (3:9). Those who are baptized into Christ the Spirit keeps clean. As Paul writes his warning/encouragement in 1 Corinthians 6:9–11:

> Do you not know that the *unrighteous* will not inherit the kingdom of God? Do not be deceived: neither the sexually immoral, nor idolaters, nor adulterers, nor men who practice homosexuality, nor thieves, nor the greedy, nor drunkards, nor revilers, nor swindlers will inherit the kingdom of God. And such *were* some of you. But you were washed, you were sanctified, you were justified in the name of the Lord Jesus Christ and by the Spirit of our God.

Christians can be called by the awkward but appropriate title *And Such Were Some of You*. The Spirit of God has made an old man born again, raised dry bones to life, and changed a dead tree into a ripe orchard of righteousness.[5] Regeneration *and sanctification* are both God's work in our lives. And for that mighty and miraculous work, let us praise God!

With that clarification made—namely, that our righteous behavior is not the cause or condition of salvation or sanctification and that our source and motivation come from the person and work of God—let us next focus on the phrase "practices righteousness," as summarized in 1 John 2:29. John writes, "If you know that he is righteous, you may be sure that everyone who practices righteousness has been born of him."

John Newton once said, "If I ever reach heaven I expect to find three wonders there: First, to meet some I had not thought to see there. Second, to miss some I had expected to see there. And third, the greatest wonder of all, to find myself there."[6] I admire Newton's humility, and I readily recognize that we all live with various uncertainties. Yet the

5. Note John Calvin's summary of the Spirit's work identified in 1 John: "In short, the apostle ascribes to the Spirit a sovereign presence in the elect; by his power he represses sin and does not allow it to rule and reign. . . . The hearts of the godly are so effectually governed by the Spirit of God that through an inflexible disposition they follow his guidance. . . . The power of the Spirit is so effectual that it necessarily keeps us in continual obedience to righteousness." "1 John," in John Calvin and Matthew Henry, *1, 2, 3 John*, Crossway Classic Commentaries (Wheaton, IL: Crossway, 1998), 59.

6. John Newton, *The Amazing Works of John Newton* (Alachua, FL: Bridge-Logos, 2009), 338.

apostle John wrote this letter so that we might know certain things about ourselves and others within the Christian community, as well as of those who have left it. To him, orthodoxy (right belief in Jesus) and orthopraxy (obedience and love) are accurate indicators of an eternal fellowship with God. Thus, within reason and without a perfectly precise estimation, we can know who is a Christian and who is not. Righteousness is not merely buried in our hearts; it also occupies our feet, hands, eyes, and tongues.[7] In 1 John 2:28–3:10, John reiterates that point in at least seven different verses!

First, he makes the point negatively. In 1 John 3:6, he writes, "No one who abides in him keeps on sinning; no one who keeps on sinning has either seen him or known him." In verse 8, he adds: "Whoever makes a practice of sinning is of the devil," and in verse 9, "No one born of God makes a practice of sinning, for God's seed abides in him, and he cannot keep on sinning because he has been born of God." Finally, 3:10 summarizes the negative data well: "By this it is evident who are the children of God, and who are the children of the devil: whoever does not practice righteousness is not of God."

Second, John makes the same point positively. At the start he writes, "If you know that he [Christ] is righteous, you may be sure that everyone who practices righteousness has been born of him" (1 John 2:29); near the end he adds, "Whoever practices righteousness is righteous, as he [Christ] is righteous" (3:7); and in between he states, "And everyone who thus hopes in him [Christ] purifies himself as he [Christ] is pure" (3:3). In that final verse, John does not express a wish: "*May* everyone who hopes in Christ purify himself." He does not present a possibility: "Everyone who hopes in Christ *might* purify himself." He does not command: "Everyone who hopes in Christ *ought to* purify himself."[8] Rather, he states a fact: "Everyone who hopes in Christ purifies himself." That is the fact of the matter. Hope (in "the appearance") and holiness (our "appearance" now) are linked in the person who "purifies" or "continually purifies" himself. Christians are positionally and practically righteous.

7. See Calvin, "1 John," 57.

8. See Simon J. Kistemaker, "Exposition of the Epistles of John," in *James, Epistles of John, Peter, and Jude* (Grand Rapids: Baker, 2002), 296.

We are saved by grace alone through faith alone in Christ alone, but grace and faith are never alone because Christ has not let us alone. Those he saves he sanctifies. "By virtue of Christ's death and resurrection" and "by his Word and Spirit dwelling within," every believer is "quickened and strengthened . . . to the practice of holiness" (WCF 13:1). As we confess in the Nicene Creed, we believe in "one *holy*, catholic, and apostolic church." All the churches' members are holy, "not merely holy by profession, holy in name, and holy in the judgment of charity." Rather, they are, as J. C. Ryle said, "holy in act, and deed, and reality, and life, and truth. They are all more or less conformed to the image of Jesus Christ."[9]

In Richard Baxter's classic work *The Reformed Pastor*, he stresses how the pastor needs to have his finger on the spiritual pulse of every member of the local church. He does this through home visitations. Two typical questions that he would ask each member of his parish upon his half-hour visit were as follows. First, "Can you truly say, that all the known sins of your past life are the grief of your heart, and that you have felt that everlasting misery is due to you for them; and that, under a sense of this heavy burden, you have felt yourself a lost man, and have gladly entertained the news of a Saviour, and cast your soul upon Christ alone, for pardon by his blood?" In other words, have you recognized yourself to be a damnable sinner and therefore do you come freely and joyfully to Jesus for the forgiveness of your sins? Second, "Can you truly say, that your heart is so far turned from sin, that you hate the sins which you once have loved, and love that holy life which you had no mind to before; and that you do not now live in the willful practice of any known sin? Is there no sin which you are not heartily willing to forsake whatever it cost you; and no duty which you are not willing to perform?"[10] Said simply: Do you practice righteousness? *In light of the appearance of the Righteous One and our future perfect righteousness,* do you *practice righteousness by abiding in Christ?*

We should ask and answer these same questions ourselves. Past sins should grieve our hearts. Do we feel that heavy burden of conscience? Do we acknowledge what lost, damnable sinners we would be without our Savior? And present holiness should thrill our souls! Have we turned from the

9. J. C. Ryle, "The Church," in *Knots United* (Moscow, ID: Charles Nolan, 2000), 228.
10. Richard Baxter, *The Reformed Pastor* (London: Religious Tract Society, 1862), 299.

sins that we once loved? Do we rejoice in our sanctification—the freedom of turning from willful sin to holy habits? Do we practice righteousness?

How Holy?

My second pastoral concern involves our experience as Christians. I think we all understand that if someone professes to be a child of heaven but lives like the offspring of hell, his Christianity is a charade. What we struggle with, however, is grasping how holy we need to be to receive the assurance of our salvation. Put more bluntly, we wonder, "Are we Christians if we habitually sin?" My initial answer was "no." The language seems clear and strong. The habitual sinner is not a believer. Period. Upon further reflection, however, my answer is now "yes." I say this because every Christian habitually sins (cf. 1 John 1:8); that is, we continue to sin in one of two ways. Either we struggle with a particular sin (e.g., an addiction to alcohol, pornography, food, work, shopping, gambling, video games, or [fill in the blank]) or we struggle with a variety of sins that we weekly succumb to (an immoral thought one day, greed the next, anxiety after that, followed by unrighteous anger, then an obscene joke, then hating our parents, then gossip, then gluttony, then deceit, then vanity, then idolatry—or whatever your sin list looks like). We are saints, yet sinners. Those who think they have obtained angelic purity now are deluded. While we are freed from the dominion of sin, we are not freed from the corruption of sin. Though we have confidence (*parrēsian*) of our salvation on the day of his coming (*parousia*, 2:28) because we have "a personal, obedient, abiding relationship" with Jesus,[11] we are not Christ but only Christ*like*. We might have halos on our heads, but they are often dull and broken. We might not walk in sin, but we do fall into it.

And so we pray (weekly? daily? hourly?) the prayer that our Lord taught his disciples to pray, "Forgive us our debts" (Matt. 6:12). And we sometimes sing along with the psalmists:

> O Lord, rebuke me not in your anger,
>   nor discipline me in your wrath!

11. Akin, *1, 2, 3 John*, 129.

> There is no health in my bones
> because of my sin.
> For my iniquities have gone over my head;
> like a heavy burden, they are too heavy for me. (Ps. 38:1, 3b–4)

And:

> Deliver me from all my transgressions. (Ps. 39:8)

And:

> Have mercy on me, O God,
> according to your steadfast love;
> according to your abundant mercy
> blot out my transgressions.
> Wash me thoroughly from my iniquity,
> and cleanse me from my sin! (Ps. 51:1–2)

As Christians, we persistently plea with the publican, "God, be merciful to me, a sinner!" (Luke 18:13). We pray this way because we know that we are still sinners ("If we say we have no sin, we deceive ourselves, and the truth is not in us," 1 John 1:8). Also, we pray this way because we understand that confession provides cleansing ("If we confess our sins, he is faithful and just to forgive us our sins and to cleanse us from all unrighteousness," 1:9). And if we are as self-aware as the apostle Paul, the more we grow in grace, the more we see the spots of sin and our ongoing need for spot removal. How else does Paul go from calling himself "an apostle . . . through Jesus Christ" in the first epistle he penned (Galatians) to "the foremost" of sinners in likely the second to last (1 Timothy)? How else can Paul persistently preach forgiveness—"There is therefore now no condemnation for those who are in Christ Jesus" (Rom. 8:1)—after speaking bluntly about our ongoing struggle with sin (Rom. 7)?

Like Paul, "John is not setting before us a terrifying perfectionism; but he is demanding a life which is ever on the watch against sin, a life in which sin is not the normal accepted way but the abnormal moment of defeat."[12]

12. William Barclay, *The Letters of John and Jude*, Daily Bible Study Series (Philadelphia: Westminster, 1976), 81.

To make this point, look carefully at 1 John 3:1–2 and notice that John sees our fallen nature realistically:

> See what kind of [or "how great a," NASB] love the Father has given to us, that we should be called children of God; and so we are. The reason why the world does not know us is that it did not know him. Beloved, we are God's children now, and what we will be has not yet appeared; but we know that when he appears [then!] we shall be like him, because we shall see him as he is.

Who are we? Children of God. Amazing! In C. S. Lewis's *Screwtape Letters*, the senior demon Screwtape says to his understudy Wormwood that guiding people to hell is sometimes difficult because the "Enemy [God] has a curious fantasy of making all these disgusting little human vermin into sons."[13] It is no small matter to be called *children of God*.

And what does it mean to be called *children of God*? It means that God has bestowed his adoptive and elective love upon us—"see what kind of love the Father has given to us!" The verb *idete*—"see" or "behold" or "take a look at this"—is an imperative. We are commanded to look at how astonishing God's love is for us. Our sonship is a gift, one that cannot be earned, achieved, or rescinded. Beyond God's love, being called *children of God* also means experiencing the world's hatred and the hope of heavenly holiness. "The evil humanistic system" (i.e., "the world")[14] won't like us (see John 15:18–16:4) any more than it liked Jesus (1:10–11). I know that it is paradoxical that someone who embodies the Beatitudes (someone who is humble, meek, merciful, and a peacemaker) is persecuted, but it is also realistic.

Nondiluted disciples—those who are salt to the world—get merciless persecution now and, thankfully, moral perfection later: "When he appears [not before!] we shall be like him" (1 John 3:2). When Jesus returns to judge and save, we will be saved from all our sins. We are now *justified* by faith in Christ (thus perfectly righteous before God), but soon we will be *just* (perfectly righteous like God). Why?—"because we shall see him as he is" (v. 2). Does that mean that once we see Jesus, we will somehow be transformed from this mortal and immoral body into an immortal and moral one? Yes! We will have glorified resurrected bodies, a clean character, and satisfied

13. C. S. Lewis, *The Screwtape Letters & Screwtape Proposes a Toast* (New York: Macmillan, 1962), 17.
14. Akin, *1, 2, 3 John*, 134.

souls. Yet what it all looks like and feels like remains a mystery ("what we will be has not yet appeared," v. 2). Whatever our future heavenly existence resembles, we can trust that it will be quite the sight.

I have seen some beautiful sights. I have seen the Badlands at sundown, the stars that cover the African sky, the mountains of Santiago de Cuba, the ocean waves striking the shores of eastern Australia, and the wild horses that roam over the green hills of Ireland. I have seen the beauty of my wife walk down the aisle on our wedding day and the beauty of her body on our wedding night. All those beauties put together, however, will not match the beatific vision! "As for me, I shall behold your face in righteousness; when I awake, I shall be satisfied with your likeness" (Ps. 17:15). What will make heaven heavenly is not merely seeing old friends, walking the street of gold, dipping in the crystal river, and eating from the tree of life (Rev. 22:1–2), but seeing Jesus—we "will see his face" (v. 4).[15] It will be seeing Jesus *and* being in his presence without sin—being holy before our holy Savior. Is that your desire? Do you "desire . . . to depart and be with Christ" (Phil. 1:23) and like Christ (1 John 3:2)?

The reason that John writes 1 John 2:28–3:10 is not to scare Christians, or even to assure Christians. Rather, he writes to show the incongruity of the attitude of indifference to sin. Do you think it is acceptable for Christians to sin? Don't! Think again. It's not. For us, sin is the exception, not the rule. As Christians, we look like Christ. We are not sinless saviors of ourselves, but we are sin-hating, sin-fighting images of our immaculate Immanuel. While we still have sinful patterns or habits—some of which will plague us for life and others of which we already have or will have conquered or controlled—our new habits of holiness are our prevailing lifestyle. Real and radical change has happened inwardly and outwardly. We have made a decisive break. Our way of life is not characterized by a life of sin, but a life of loving obedience. In other words, we "practice righteousness." *In light of the appearance of the Righteous One and our future perfect righteousness,* we really do *practice righteousness by abiding in Christ.*

15. N. T. Wright answers the question "What will *we* be like?" by saying, "Perhaps we should say: like we are, only much more so. More gloriously physical, not less. Embodied but not subject to sickness or death. Able to celebrate the joys of God's world but no longer lured or seduced into abusing them, into lusting after them, into worshipping them as though they were divine. All that is, I believe, true. But far more important is to say: we will be like Jesus." *Early Christian Letters for Everyone*, New Testament for Everyone (Louisville, KY: Westminster John Knox, 2011), 149–50.

Why So High?

My third pastoral concern follows the second. If we are loved by God and saved by Christ's cross, why is the call to holiness so high? Is it because the depth and breadth of the love of God in Christ are so deep and wide (see Rom. 8:39)? Yes. Is it because holiness matters to a holy God? Yes. Is it because God is our Father? Absolutely!

Parents, does it matter to you if your child behaves properly? Of course it does. That child is a reflection of you. Likewise, as children of God, we are a reflection of God. Thus, we strive against lawlessness as we seek to love (cf. 1 John 3:9–10). Because "we shall be like [Christ]" when he returns (3:2), we attempt to act like God's true offspring now.

And do not think that God is up in heaven laughing at our efforts. He is our Father and we are his children. What earthly father laughs when his five-year-old son falls off his bike or his two-year-old daughter draws outside the lines? What earthly father sneers at his child's attempt to bake a birthday cake for him? The child is trying. I love it when my children try to please me. Do you honestly think that God is "unmoved by our heart-felt attempts at obedience"?[16] Furthermore, do you think that God is unmoved by our rebellious failures? God is like the father in the parable of the prodigal son. When his child wanders from his protection and provision and settles for sharing the slop of sin, the father is surely sad and angry. But when that child comes to his senses and returns home, the father is so overjoyed, it is as though he forgets to formally forgive. He won't even let his son recite his rehearsed lines of repentance, "Father, I have sinned against heaven and before you" (Luke 15:18, 21). He is lost in love. He immediately kills the fattened calf, opens the wine cellar, and puts on his party hat. He extends mercy as quickly as he celebrates grace! He is as happy as a shepherd who has found the lost sheep. If you are a child of God who is now running with the wolves or supping with the swine, get up and walk home. God owns the cattle on a billion hills, and his cellar never runs dry. He forgives "seventy times seven" (Matt. 18:22) our incalculable debt (vv. 24–27).[17] Repent. Return. Rejoice.

16. Kevin DeYoung, *The Hole in Our Holiness: Filling the Gap between Gospel Passion and the Pursuit of Godliness* (Wheaton, IL: Crossway, 2012), 70.

17. The "ten thousand talents" (Matt. 18:24) represents the largest imaginable amount (10,000 was the highest Greek numeral). Robert H. Gundry labels the amount "zillions." *Matthew: A Commentary on His Literary and Theological Art* (Grand Rapids: Eerdmans, 1982), 373–74.

But also, make a fresh effort to pursue holiness! Try to please your Father. Go after the big sins that so easily weigh you down. And root out the small sins—the little bits of worldliness, compromise, inconsistency, and indiscretion.[18] What Robert Murray M'Cheyne said of the pastor—"the greatest need of my people is my own holiness"[19]—I say of the church in the world. What the world needs to see is a holy church that reflects Jesus. It is not just for the evangelism of others, but also for the exaltation of God. What the Father delights in is a Christlike church.

In summary:

- What is the great theme? In light of the appearance of the Righteous One and our future perfect righteousness, practice righteousness by abiding in him.
- How holy do we need to be to receive the assurance of our salvation? We are not sinless saviors of ourselves, but we are sin-hating, sin-fighting images of our immaculate Immanuel.
- Why is the call to holiness so high? It is because God is our Father.

Like Oil to a Flame

In the early fifth century, Augustine preached ten sermons on 1 John. In the prologue to his later book on the sermons, he wrote:

> The person who possesses the thing which he hears about in this epistle must rejoice when he hears it. His reading will be like oil to a flame. For others, the epistle should be like flame set to firewood; if it was not already burning, the touch of the word may kindle it.[20]

Perhaps you are like that first person. You hear about the necessity of holiness and you rejoice that God has so changed your life that that is a reality. It is obvious to all. It is obvious to you. This text has been like oil to flame. You were on fire for Jesus, and now that flame has touched the sky! Or

18. See DeYoung, *The Hole in Our Holiness*, 145.

19. M'Cheyne, quoted in ibid., 144.

20. Augustine, "Ten Homilies on 1 John, Prologue," in *James, 1–2 Peter, 1–3 John, Jude*, ed. Gerald Bray, Ancient Christian Commentary on Scripture, New Testament 11 (Downers Grove, IL: InterVarsity Press, 2000), 166.

perhaps you are like that second person and God is using what has been said like smoldering kindling under dry wood. Give it some time. Let the Word start to spark in your heart. Next thing you know, the whole temple will be on fire! Let this be the Lent of your life—the time to rekindle your relationship with God. Now is the day to put Mardi Gras behind you and strive (and *shrive*!) to live anew by the power of God for the One who died to destroy the works of the devil and who will come again to reign in power and glory forever.

9

What We Know

1 John 3:11–24

We know that we have passed out of death into life, because we love the brothers. Whoever does not love abides in death.
(1 John 3:14)

In *A Short History of Nearly Everything*, Bill Bryson writes about his newly acquired knowledge of science. As a layman and novice, he devoted three years of his life to reading books and journals, as well as consulting experts. His goal was "to see if it isn't possible to understand and appreciate—marvel at, enjoy even—the wonder and accomplishments of science at a level that isn't too technical or demanding, but isn't entirely superficial either." In his introduction, he relays how his ignorance was part of his impetus. As he was looking out the window at a moonlit ocean on a flight across the Pacific, it dawned on him how little he knew.

> It occurred to me with a certain uncomfortable forcefulness that I didn't know the first thing about the only planet I was ever going to live on. I had no idea, for example, why the oceans were salty but the Great Lakes weren't. Didn't have the faintest idea. I didn't know if the oceans were growing more salty with time or less, and whether ocean salinity levels was something I

should be concerned about or not. (I am very pleased to tell you that until the late 1970s scientists didn't know the answers to these questions either. They just didn't talk about it very audibly.)

And ocean salinity of course represented only the merest sliver of my ignorance.[1]

There is much that we do not and cannot know. Yet there is much that we can and should know about our planet, its Creator, and his relationship with us. In 1 John, the concept of *knowledge* is crucial. John's purpose for writing his letter is clear: "I write these things to you who believe in the name of the Son of God that you may *know* that you have eternal life" (1 John 5:13). That statement is followed in verses 14–21 with the repetition of "know" seven times (vv. 13, 20), including *oidamen* ("we know") five times (5:15 [2×], 18, 19, and 20).

In 1 John 3:11–24, the theme of knowledge is likewise prominent. Here various forms of "we know" occur four times:[2]

"We know" (*oidamen*, 3:14)
"We know" (*egnōkamen*, 3:16)
"We shall know" (*gnōsometha*, 3:19)
"We know" (*ginōskomen*, 3:24)

Structurally, "we know" follows the phrase "by this" in all but one occurrence (1 John 3:14). That verse is the key verse, not merely because it differs structurally, but because it summarizes well this text's theme: "*We know* that we have passed out of death into life, because we love the brothers. Whoever does not love abides in death." At issue in 3:11–24 is Christian assurance. It answers the question, "How can we know that we are Christians?" Two answers are provided. The first is that *we demonstrate Christlike love for Christians.*

Christlike Love for Christians

While 1 John 3:11 starts the second half of the epistle,[3] it does not introduce a new theme. John has applied the "love test" before (see 2:7–11), and

1. Bill Bryson, *A Short History of Nearly Everything* (New York: Broadway, 2003), 6.

2. Note also the repetition of "know" in 1 John 4:2, 6, 13.

3. Gary M. Burge argues convincingly for a break at 1 John 3:11: "This is a convenient division for a number of reasons: (1) It gives near balance to the letter's two halves (1:5–3:10 and 3:11–5:12). (2) If the

he is simply continuing his thought from the final phrase of 3:10. We might even say that 3:11–24 is an exposition of 3:10c—"love his brother." What is new is John's illustration and application of love.

John illustrates Christian love with a contrast between Cainlike hatred and Christlike love. John begins with his reminder to love: "For this is the message that you have heard from the beginning, that we should love one another" (1 John 3:11). This "message" came to John's readers from the apostolic evangelists. It is what they heard when the gospel was first preached to them (the meaning of "heard from the beginning"). That message, however, has its origin in Jesus. As Colin Kruse notes, "This is the first of six references in the Letters of John to Jesus' command that his disciples should love one another (the others are found in 1 John 3:23; 4:7, 11, 12; 2 John 5)."[4] Also, this is the first echo in our text of Jesus' Upper Room Discourse. John will take Jesus' words, notably from John 13:34; 15:12, 17–18, and voice Christ's call to love.

The exhortative reminder to love is followed by Cain's negative example: "We should not be like Cain, who was of the evil one and murdered his brother. And why did he murder him? Because his own deeds were evil and his brother's righteous" (1 John 3:12). The story of Cain's murder of Abel (Gen. 4:1–16), a widespread illustration in Judaism and early Christian literature,[5] is the only Old Testament allusion in the letter. The story is so classic that John finds no need to supply the narrative. He assumes that his readers know the tragic tale. For the contemporary reader, perhaps unaware of it, the story can be summarized as follows:

> Cain and Abel were the first two sons of Adam and Eve. Both brothers offered a sacrifice to God. God accepted only Abel's, likely due to Cain's wrongdoing (evil or false motives? see Gen. 4:6–7) and Abel's sincere faith (see Heb. 11:4).

Gospel of John was any model for the structure of the letter, its emphasis on the light and truth of God in the first half is followed by an emphasis on love in the community, a subject found in the second half. (3) First John 3:11 contains the phrase 'This is the message we have heard from the beginning,' a near copy of 1:5, 'This is the message we have heard from him.'" *Letters of John*, NIV Application Commentary (Grand Rapids: Zondervan, 1996), 159; cf. 41–44.

4. Colin G. Kruse, *The Letters of John*, Pillar New Testament Commentary (Grand Rapids: Eerdmans, 2000), 133.

5. See Raymond E. Brown, *The Epistles of John*, Anchor Bible (Garden City, NY: Doubleday, 1982), 442–43. For example, Abel's murder is alluded to elsewhere in the New Testament (Matt. 23:35; Luke 11:51; Heb. 11:4; 12:24; Jude 11), and "Philo wrote four works on Cain! (Loeb vol. 2)." Ibid., 443.

> God's rejection depressed and then angered Cain. Cain envied his brother. He took out his envious anger on Abel by brutally murdering him.

John moves beyond the authors of Genesis (wrongdoing) and Hebrews (lack of faith) and places Cain's motive at the devil's doorstep (1 John 3:12). This is a logical theological connection to Genesis 3:1–4. It also fits Jesus' view of the murder connection ("the devil" has been "a murderer from the beginning," John 8:44). John confidently follows his Lord's lead by equating those who reject other Christians to this satanic source (cf. 1 John 3:10). The apostate antichrists are in view. Did they depart the Christian community because they were envious of John? Envy or no envy, they hated John, and their poisonous gossip and false gospel were spilling into the church's ears. They wanted apostolic Christianity dead.

From Cain's bloody murder of his blood brother John transitions to an eye-opening encouragement to his spiritual siblings ("brothers," 1 John 3:13–14) about an awful reality. Persecution! The reality comes in 1 John 3:13, followed by the affirmation of assurance (v. 14) and warning (v. 15).

> Do not be surprised, brothers, that the world hates you. We know that we have passed out of death into life, because we love the brothers. Whoever does not love abides in death. Everyone who hates his brother is a murderer, and you know that no murderer has eternal life abiding in him. (1 John 3:13–15)

John echoes Jesus' transition in John 15:17, "These things I command you, so that you will love one another," to verse 18, "If the world hates you, know that it has hated me before it hated you." Again the apostate antichrists are in view. (They are lurking throughout this letter.) They embody "the world" (1 John 3:13) (*kosmos* occurs twenty-one times in 1 John, and it generally refers to the evil forces opposing God's rule). Specifically, they are the devil-empowered (3:1; 4:5; 5:19) "false prophets" who have left the church and "have gone out into the world" (4:1) and now "are from the world . . . and the world listens to them" (4:5).

As Jesus' disciples, we must recognize that part of our connectedness to Christ is suffering persecution from the world. We should not be surprised that our sacrificial love fosters Cainlike contempt. This is an important truth to meditate on, for we often fail to see, as Peter reminds us, "the fiery trial" of suffering for Christ as a blessing to be rejoiced in. It is a joyful benediction because it confirms our connection and conformity to Christ:

> Beloved, do not be surprised at the fiery trial when it comes upon you to test you, as though something strange were happening to you. But rejoice insofar as *you share Christ's sufferings*, that you may also rejoice and be glad when his glory is revealed. (1 Peter 4:12–13)

More than rejoicing in persecution, such sufferings produce assurance. If the world hates us when we are practicing righteousness, we are doing something right (see Luke 6:22). The more suffering, the more sanctification; the more animosity, the more assurance. Conversely, if the world warmly embraces us, it is likely because we have warmly embraced the world (see Luke 6:26). Christians are unworldly. We are especially otherworldly in our brotherly love, the theme that John returns to in 1 John 3:14–15:

> We know that we have passed out of death into life, because we love the brothers. Whoever does not love abides in death. Everyone who hates his brother is a murderer, and you know that no murderer has eternal life abiding in him.

Here John is not speaking of love as the cause of our entrance into eternal life, but rather as the evidence of our regeneration, and as our evidence of escaping condemnation![6] The verb *passed* is in the perfect tense, indicating a continuing and abiding life-altering action in the present. The verbs *love* and *hates* are in the present tense, indicating our ongoing affections and actions.

Structurally, in 1 John 3:14, John lays out the warning with a synonymous parallelism (e.g., *does not love* = *hates*) followed, in verse 15, by a thematic explanation and summary:

Whoever	does not love	abides in death.
Everyone who	hates his brother	is a murderer, and you know that no murderer has eternal life abiding in him.

6. Citing Wendy E. Sproston, "Witness to What Was *ap' arches*: 1 John's Contribution to Our Knowledge of Tradition in the Fourth Gospel," *Journal for the Study of the New Testament* 48 (1992): 50, Kruse points out how the expression "we have passed out of death into life" in 1 John 3:14 closely parallels John 5:24, "where the idea of passing from death to life is synonymous with escaping condemnation and obtaining eternal life." *The Letters of John*, 135.

The end stress emphasis falls on the stark contrast between abiding in death and abiding in "eternal life." To John, eternal life is "not an unending extension of life as we know it; rather it is 'having' the Son, Jesus Christ, for eternal life is tied up in him."[7]

Speaking of *life*, and transitioning to 1 John 3:16–17, commentators Philip Comfort and Wendell Hawley explain the significance of John's use of three different Greek words for *life* in verses 15–17:

> The three words are *zōē, psuchē, bios*. The word *zōē* is used in the New Testament to designate divine, eternal life—the life of God. The life resided in Christ, and he made it available to all who believe in him (cf. 3:15). In 3:16, *psuchē* (soul, personality, life) designates the natural life that all human beings are born with; as a human, Jesus had a *psuchē* or "soul." He gave up his soul (*psuchē*) in death so that we might have the *zōē*, the eternal life of God. In 3:16–17, John states that believers should likewise sacrifice their *psuchē* (life, soul) by giving their *bios* (life, livelihood) to those in need. . . . John shows these three aspects of life to be inextricably intertwined: believers demonstrate that they have eternal life (*zōē*) by imitating Christ in surrendering their earthly life (*psuchē*), specifically in giving of their livelihood (*bios*) to sustain the lives (*psuchē*) of other believers. This is the truest and best manifestation of love.[8]

Before we explore our acts of love toward the brothers, we must understand the definition of love in the example of Christ's death, expressed by the phrase "By this we know love, that he[9] laid down his life for us" (1 John 3:16). The theology reflects Isaiah 53:10. Jesus' love is not merely self-sacrificial, but also atoning: "his soul makes an offering for guilt" (Isa. 53:10). Gary Burge concurs and calls 1 John 3:16 "John's version of Mark 10:45, that 'the Son of Man did not come to be served, but to serve, and to give his life as a ransom for many.'" He goes on to explain that Jesus'

7. Kruse, *The Letters of John*, 136. John identifies "eternal life" with Jesus: "Eternal life is promised to those who believe in him (2:25); it is found in Christ, the Son (5:11), who is the true God and eternal life (5:20); this life was with the Father from the beginning and appeared in the person of Jesus Christ to eyewitnesses (1:2); those who believe in Christ may know that they have eternal life (5:13) because they have the Son, and those who have the Son have eternal life (5:12)."

8. Philip W. Comfort and Wendell C. Hawley, *1–3 John*, Cornerstone Biblical Commentary (Carol Stream, IL: Tyndale, 2007), 354–55.

9. The pronoun *ekeinos* (as in "*that* he," ESV) certainly refers to Christ (cf. 1 John 2:6; 3:3, 5, 7; 4:17).

"death is not merely an ethical model; it is a genuine offering, a genuine giving of his life."[10] The language of 1 John 3:16 is also reflective of the Fourth Gospel, where Jesus as "the good shepherd *lays down his life* for the sheep" (John 10:11; cf. v. 15), and later where he commands brotherly love on the basis of his love ("you love one another as I have loved you," 15:12), namely: "Greater love has no one than this, that someone *lay down his life* for his friends" (v. 13). The apostle John makes the transition this way: "By this we know love, that he *laid down his life* for us, and we ought to *lay down our lives* for the brothers" (1 John 3:16).

Such laying down, however, is explained not in martyrdom, as we might have expected and which certainly fits the letter's context (see 1 John 3:13), as well as the historical context (e.g., Rev. 2:2–3; cf. 2:9–10, 13, 19; 3:9–10). Rather, it is explained in material provision.

> But if anyone has the world's goods and sees his brother in need, yet closes his heart against him,[11] how does God's love abide in him? Little children, let us not love in word or talk but in deed and in truth. (1 John 3:17–18)

What is not needed is religious rhetoric, but a looking out for "the interests of others" (Phil. 2:4) in a hands-*on* and hands-*out* way. Heavenly love has an earthiness about it. Christ's incarnational love in Christians makes apathy toward brothers in need intolerable. Brotherly love is as tangible as a roof over the head, as edible as bread on the table, and as foundational as shoes on the feet.

John's shift from Christ's glorious cross to the church soup kitchen is surprising. But what a wonderful surprise! The call to love is within everyone's reach. He is not calling for martyrs. He is not even asking for Zacchaeus-like generosity (Luke 19:1–9). We are not called to give half to the poor, but simply to provide when the opportunity arises (when we see a "brother in need") and out of our abundance (possessing "the world's goods").

10. Burge, *Letters of John*, 162.

11. Deuteronomy 15:7–9 is perhaps the background to this illustration. Note the italicized words below: "If among you, one of *your brothers* should become poor, in any of your towns within your land that the Lord your God is giving you, you shall not harden your heart or shut your hand against your poor *brother*, but you shall open your hand to him and lend him sufficient for his need, whatever it may be. Take care lest there be an unworthy *thought in your heart* and you say, 'The seventh year, the year of release is near,' and your eye look grudgingly on your poor *brother*, and you give him nothing, and he cry to the Lord against you, and you be guilty of sin."

If we ask ourselves to describe our churches in one statement, we might reply "Christ-centered," or "God-exalting," or perhaps "authentically loving." But would any of us describe our churches as "generous"? Would our checkbooks reflect our God-talk and love-language? Our motto might say something of "Christ" and "love," but do we exalt God through Christlike love in the form of financial giving?

In his outstanding book *Neither Poverty nor Riches*, Craig Blomberg provides five applications to his study of material possessions in the Bible. The third is that "if stewardship is a sign of a redeemed life, then Christians will, by their new natures, want to give."[12] That application fits well with John's theology. With the shameful statistics that American Christian tithing (*if* practiced) is all that is needed to "theoretically . . . eradicate world poverty,"[13] how utterly disgraceful it is when American Christians cannot provide for their own poor brother's needs within their own local church. Christlike self-sacrifice is called for. Are we willing to give up on spending money on cut flowers, video games, pets, skin care, chewing gum, diet-related products, sports, and soft drinks so that we might "give something to the poor" (John 13:29)?[14] Are we able to resist the "desires of the eyes" (1 John 2:16) and eager to "remember the poor" (Gal. 2:10)? Are we loving the world and the things of the world (1 John 2:15) rather than the people of God's kingdom? Let us put on compassion, and let us give out generously to "the widow, the fatherless, the sojourner, or the poor" (Zech. 7:10). Let us free up money—for example, stop regularly eating out, buy some clothing at thrift shops, resist lavish entertainment—to give freely to those in need.

God-Given, Spirit-Abiding Heart Confidence

First John 3:11–24 addresses the issue of Christian assurance. In doing so, it answers the question, "How can we know that we are Christians?" The first answer (in vv. 11–18) is that we demonstrate Christlike love for Christians. The second answer (in vv. 19–24) is that *we possess God-given, Spirit-abiding heart confidence.* The last two phrases of that answer are especially important.

12. Craig L. Blomberg, *Neither Poverty nor Riches: A Biblical Theology of Material Possessions*, New Studies in Biblical Theology (Grand Rapids: Eerdmans, 1999), 247.

13. Ibid., 252.

14. These are a few of the items listed in Ronsvalle & Ronsvalle's study of the spending habits of Westerners. Ibid., 19.

But before we explore what I mean by *Spirit-abiding* and *heart confidence*, note first the connection between the two halves of our text. Verse 19 starts with "By this." That phrase takes us backward to verses 11–18, linking our assurance to our acts of love, a theme that John reiterates in verse 23b. (So whatever *heart confidence* entails, it is not merely an internal reality—for its external effects are obvious.) We must read verses 19–24 with this clear connection in mind: the evidence of our assurance is absolutely linked to our obedience of the love command (cf. vv. 23–24).

With that connection in place, we turn now to the second half of our text:

> By this we shall know that we are of the truth and reassure our heart before him; for whenever our heart condemns us, God is greater than our heart, and he knows everything. Beloved, if our heart does not condemn us, we have confidence before God; and whatever we ask we receive from him, because we keep his commandments and do what pleases him. And this is his commandment, that we believe in the name of his Son Jesus Christ and love one another, just as he has commanded us. Whoever keeps his commandments abides in God, and God in him. And by this we know that he abides in us, by the Spirit whom he has given us. (1 John 3:19–24)

These verses can be summarized as follows. Because God abides in us through his Spirit ("the Spirit whom he has given us," 1 John 3:24; cf. 4:13), *he* produces three very visible fruits in his "beloved" (3:21) children:

1. We "believe in the name of his Son Jesus Christ" (3:23);
2. We "love one another" (3:23); and
3. We "keep his commandments" (3:22, 24), which likely centers on the two commandments above.

Therefore, it follows that if we believe in Christ and love the brothers, then God reassures our hearts (1 John 3:19–21), answers prayer (3:22), and, as we will see in the next chapter, casts out fear of God's judgment (4:17–18).

Echoes of Jesus' Upper Room Discourse are clearly heard. Just as Jesus spoke of the love command (John 13), followed by the promise of the indwelling Spirit (John 14) and the call to abide in him so that the disciples' prayers would be heard (John 15–16), so those same themes resurface here. We will explore these themes by moving from the *internal* ("Spirit," "our heart") to the *external* (keeping "his commandments," 1 John 3:22, 24, and answered prayer, v. 22).

Verses 19–20 of 1 John 3 center on the *internal* elements of our assurance:

> By this we shall know that we are of the truth and reassure our heart before him; for whenever our heart condemns us, God is greater than our heart, and he knows everything.

Robert Yarbrough highlights the transition beautifully: "In the wake of a stern command against the hypocrisy of a do-nothing love (3:18), John extends an olive branch of assurance."[15] Demonstrating Christlike love to Christians ("by this") gives us the assurance ("we shall know") that we have *koinōnia* with Christ (John 18:37) and his church (1 John 1:1–4; 4:6). It also "sets our hearts at ease"[16] before God's judgment throne ("before him," 3:19).

But our hearts do not always align with our heads. We might know that we are forgiven, but not feel forgiven. The reason for this heart dis-ease likely relates to our inability to comply flawlessly and continually with the love commandment. "Who loves sufficiently to be free of pangs of conviction in this matter?"[17] First John 3:20 provides two reasons to put our whole weight on this olive branch of assurance: "God is greater than our heart" and "he knows everything." When our hearts accuse us ("you failed the love test . . . again!"), God's benevolent omnipotence and omniscience provide CPR. When our hearts are weighed down with guilt, here John reassures us that "the great God, the great King above all gods" (Ps. 95:3 NIV), eases the burden. When we agonize over our lack of love, "the place to turn is not farther inward but outward and upward toward God."[18] If our hearts are troubled, we should call to mind the greatness of God, a greatness that descends to offer forgiveness each and every time we confess our sins (1 John 1:9).

Moreover, recall the God who "knows everything" (1 John 3:20). While the Bible applies God's omniscience as a warning to refrain from sin (e.g., Eccles. 12:14; Rom. 2:16; 1 Cor. 4:5), here it is a comfort for the sinner. God is not blind to our unloving actions. He knows every detail of every sin. He

15. Robert W. Yarbrough, *1–3 John*, Baker Exegetical Commentary on the New Testament (Grand Rapids: Baker, 2008), 209.

16. Ibid. (Yarbrough's translation).

17. Ibid.

18. Ibid., 211.

knows that even the littlest lack of love carries the weight of eternal condemnation. But (here is the gospel according to John!) God still forgives. Accept his forgiveness through Christ. Rejoice in the renewed relationship. Pray. And return to practicing righteousness (1 John 2:29; 3:7, 10)!

First John 3:21–24 follows, addressing the mostly *external* elements of our assurance:

> Beloved, if our heart does not condemn us, we have confidence before God; and whatever we ask we receive from him, because we keep his commandments and do what pleases him. And this is his commandment, that we believe in the name of his Son Jesus Christ and love one another, just as he has commanded us. Whoever keeps his commandments abides in God, and God in him. And by this we know that he abides in us, by the Spirit whom he has given us.

The logic of the argument is straightforward. If God sets our hearts at ease before him, we have the confidence to approach him in prayer (1 John 3:21–22). What a marvelous truth! "By the blood of Jesus," we have unrestricted access to "enter the holy places" (Heb. 10:19). Let us then press past "internal impediments (deficiency in faith, ethics, or relationship . . .) and external challenges (e.g., the deceivers of [1 John] 2:26; cf. 3:7) . . . [and even] an accusing heart,"[19] and "with confidence draw near to the throne of grace, that we may receive mercy and find grace to help in time of need" (Heb. 4:16). For we should expect our prayers, if made according to his will,[20] to be answered (cf. 1 John 5:14; John 14:13–14). Obedience assures us that the line of communication is open—"because we keep his commandments and do what pleases him" (1 John 3:22). This teaching is similar to James's admonition and Elijah's example, "The effectual fervent prayer of a righteous man availeth much" (James 5:16 KJV), or, as J. B. Phillips phrased it, "Tremendous power is made available through a good man's earnest prayer." Perhaps we might word it this way: the obedience of faith opens God's ears!

God delights in answering his children's prayers when *we trust in his Son*—"we believe in the name of his Son Jesus Christ" (1 John 3:23). To "believe in the

19. Ibid., 212.

20. As the context makes clear, God answers prayers that are pleasing to him (1 John 3:20; cf. John 8:29) and offered "according to his will" (1 John 5:14–15; cf. Matt. 6:10) by the Christian who obeys his will (1 John 3:22).

name" is to confess Jesus' "incarnation (1 John 4:2; 2 John 7), his baptism and atoning death on the cross for sin (1 John 5:6; cf. Rev. 1:5), his self-disclosure and divinity (1 John 5:20), his role as heavenly witness and 'ruler of the kings of the earth' (Rev. 1:5)."[21] God also delights in answering our prayers when we *love like his Son*—who loved "his own" (i.e., "the brothers") until the end (John 13:1), as well as his enemies (Matt. 5:44; Luke 6:27, 35). In John's letters, as in Paul's, faith and love work hand in hand (1 John 3:11; 4:7, 11–12; 2 John 5; cf. Gal. 5:6; Eph. 1:15; 2 Tim. 1:13). Together they open heaven's hand of blessing.

In 1 John 3:24, John ties together his flow of thought with a Trinitarian conclusion. Moving from our confession and commitment to Jesus Christ ("his Son," v. 23), John concludes with the Father ("God"), Son ("his commandments," "he abides in us," "he has given"; cf. John 14:16–20), and Holy Spirit ("the Spirit").

This is the first of six references to the Spirit in the letter (cf. 1 John 4:2, 6, 13; 5:6, 8), and his connection with our assurance is important. As stated in the summary of this section, we know that we are Christians because the Spirit abides in us. We have a God-given, *Spirit-abiding* heart confidence. Here John returns from the external elements of assurance to the internal indwelling of the Holy Spirit. He lives in us! And because he lives (and remains [*meno*]) in us, we remain in the Father and the Son.

> What it means to live [*meno*] in God is not easy to define. The concept is found in ten places in the letter (2:5, 6, 27, 28; 3:6, 24; 4:13, 15, 16; 5:20), including places, as here, where it is part of a broader concept: the mutual indwelling of believers in God and God in believers (3:24; 4:13, 15, 16). In two of the four places where this mutual indwelling is mentioned, the author says that believers can be assured of it because of the Spirit whom God has given to them (3:24; 4:13). This suggests that when the author speaks about believers living in God and God living in believers, as he does here, it involves something more than keeping God's commands. It is the new and very real spiritual existence that believers can enjoy, and this is effected through the agency of the Spirit.[22]

21. Yarbrough, *1–3 John*, 215. Regarding the verb *pisteuō* in John's Gospel, he adds: "Believing is the key to divine sonship (1:12; 12:36), eternal life (3:15, 16; cf. 5:24; 6:40, 47; 11:25; 20:31b), knowing God (6:69; 10:38b; 17:8), receiving the Spirit (7:38–39), worshiping Christ (9:38), and seeing God's glory (11:40)." Ibid., 214n9.

22. Comfort and Hawley, *1–3 John*, 143.

Enjoy the God-given Spirit! Understand that our assurance "does not spring simply from vigorous works of obedience or orthodoxy, but from the interior life."[23] And ask for such knowledge if you do not possess it.

Essential Knowledge

In *A Short History of Nearly Everything*, Bill Bryson discovered how we can know the earth's weight, the age of rocks, the difference between a quark and a quasar, and something about salt. First John 3:11–24 is about acquiring not scientific knowledge but saving knowledge. "We know" something! We know that we are Christians because we demonstrate Christlike love for Christians (vv. 11–18) and possess that God-given, Spirit-abiding heart confidence (vv. 19–24). Such knowledge is invaluable. Incomparable! It is greater than knowing the age of the earth and the intricacies of all its atoms.

23. Burge, *Letters of John*, 171.

10

Who's Got Your Ear?

1 John 4:1–6

We are from God. Whoever knows God listens to us; whoever is not from God does not listen to us. By this we know the Spirit of truth and the spirit of error. (1 John 4:6)

"Doug, you really should come over this afternoon. I would love to see you there." The summer between eighth and ninth grade, I was invited to a pool party. I was invited to a pool party by an older girl. I was invited to a pool party by an older girl who was pretty. I was invited to a pool party by an older girl who was pretty and who had even prettier friends and whose parents didn't care if boys, ugly and otherwise, came to the pool party.

But my parents did.

"No, you cannot go," my mother told me. "We don't want you at pool parties with older girls." She paused. "In bathing suits!" No older girls in bathing suits. That was the new rule.

"But Mom," I carefully reasoned with her, "Tommy said he is going. Billy said he is going."

"I don't care if Tom, Dick, and Billy are going. You're not going. If Tommy jumped in a lake, would you? If Billy jumped in a lake, would you?" No, I thought. "But if they jumped in a pool . . . ," I mumbled beneath my breath.

Moments later, my mom called the other boys' moms. It turns out that both their mothers were as Catholic as mine. Tom, Billy, and Doug, as well as, I'm sure, Tom, Dick, and Harry, were all staying home . . . where they belonged. But who could stay home? She'd asked me! Her alluring voice was still ringing in my ears. I had to go. I came up with a plan as grand in its design and effect as the Tower of Babel. The party began at 2:00 in the afternoon. At 2:05 I approached my mother with that I'm-so-bored/what's-there-to-do look on my face, and then with that I'm-so-bored/what's-there-to-do tone in my voice, I asked, "Mom, can I ride my bike over to Tommy's?" I had no intention of going near Tommy's.

"Sure. That's fine," she said. "I don't see why not."

Off I went, arriving soon at the forbidden destination. Upon arrival, I was spotted by Billy's mom. (I'd neglected to tell my brain that Billy's house backed up to hers!) I was spotted from the kitchen window. She said, "Isn't that Douglas?" In astonishment, she repeated her interrogative. "Billy!" she yelled. My friend was sitting Indian-style on the family-room floor, playing Atari contentedly. "Isn't that Douglas?" she asked a third time. (The cock crowed.) Billy paused the game. This question was of great interest to him. He stood up and walked eagerly to the window. "Yeah." "Yeah!" he said with a rush of excitement. "Yeah, it sure is."

"You go tell Douglas to come over here and his mother won't get a call about this."

My mother did get a call about this. And before all those pretty girls could stare at my pale hundred-pound frame, my mother pulled into the driveway with our two-toned station wagon. My bike, my suit, and my self were all placed in the back of it. I am still not sure whether, in my mother's mind, there are enough acts of contrition in the whole world to absolve me of that sin.

I begin with that amusing anecdote to make a very serious point. Whom we listen to matters. I should have listened to my mother's voice instead of the girl's. Because I failed to listen to the right voice, I suffered for it: two weeks without television and outdoor play. The apostle John, with far greater consequences in mind (the loss of eternal life!), calls the church to listen as well. He wants his readers to listen to the Trinitarian Truth Teachers (*we* and *us*) and not the Worldly Antichrist Liars (*they* and *them*):

> They are from the world; therefore they speak from the world, and the world listens to them. We are from God. Whoever knows God listens to us; whoever

> is not from God does not listen to us. By this we[1] know the Spirit of truth and the spirit of error. (1 John 4:5–6)

Test the Spirits

Before we examine 1 John 4:5–6, however, we must walk through verses 1–4. Transitioning from the themes of brotherly love and the abiding Spirit in 3:11–24, John begins by calling the "beloved" believers "not [to] believe every spirit" (4:1). John will return to the theme of love in 4:7–21. Here he pauses to make sure that the obligation to love is grounded in the apostolic faith. Thus, the twin commands of 4:1 center on doctrinal orthodoxy. Negatively, the readers are "not" to "believe every spirit," and positively they are to "test the spirits." The reason for this testing is that not every spirit is "from God." While John might have many *spirits* in mind (angels, demons, and the spirit inside humans), human teachers are most in mind.[2] No matter how many spirits there are in the world—human or otherwise—John places them all under two main headings: "the Spirit of truth and the spirit of error" (v. 6).

The "Spirit of truth" (1 John 4:6) is "from God" (v. 1), while the "spirit of error" (v. 6) is from "the antichrist" (v. 3). Those of the antichrist "have gone out into the [fallen] world" (v. 1). To have "gone out" speaks of their secession from the church. "The world" is code for unbelieving people whose values are ungodly (2:15–17) and who live under the devil's sovereign sway (5:19). No matter how self-assured, popular, and successful these secessionists have been in winning converts, to have *error* and *antichrist* attached to your cause will not be helpful on judgment day. Those who claim to speak for God now will have their masks removed then. John wants God's people to see what God sees. He wants to expose the impostors now!

The Test

Having issued the warning to "test the spirits" (1 John 4:1), John next provides the test. If both sets of teachers "claim to be indwelt by God, to

1. The final *we* in 1 John 4:6 I take to be an "inclusive *we*," including the readers. See chapter 2, table 1.

2. *Spirits* refers to "a multiplicity of human beings who may be inspired in their spirits by the Spirit of God or the spirit of falsehood." I. Howard Marshall, *The Epistles of John*, New International Commentary on the New Testament (Grand Rapids: Eerdmans, 1978), 204.

have received the Spirit, and to speak in his name,"[3] how will the reader discern between the spirit of truth and the spirit of error? If false teachers look and sound genuine (cf. Matt. 7:15) and often introduce their "destructive heresies" shrewdly and "secretly" (2 Peter 2:1), how does one tell the sheep from the wolves in sheep's clothing? John's test is straightforward. We just listen carefully for their Christology (1 John 4:2–3a). "By this you know the Spirit of God:"

every spirit that	confesses that Jesus Christ	has come in the flesh is from God, and
every spirit that	does *not* confess [that] Jesus	[has come in the flesh] is *not* from God.

Notice the parallelisms (synonymous: "every spirit that"; and antithetical: "confesses"/"does not confess" and "from God"/"not from God"). With that, notice the move from positive to negative (the negative is italicized above). The reader wants to make the positive confession! One reason to pick the positive is the additional sentence that John attached to the person who "does not confess [that] Jesus [has come in the flesh]," namely: "This is the spirit of the antichrist, which you heard was coming and now is in the world already" (1 John 4:3b). The coming antichrist who will arrive near the very conclusion of the age (2:18; 2 John 7) has an *already/not yet* presence that is a spiritual influence over every false teacher in every era. This culminating spiritual force and figure is always at work in those who seek to negate, divide, or destroy Jesus.

We are also to pick the positive confession because it is "from God"—or, put differently, from "the Spirit of God" (1 John 4:2; cf. 1 Cor. 12:3). Following its usage elsewhere in the New Testament (see Matt. 3:16; 1 Cor. 2:11; 3:16),

3. Colin G. Kruse, *The Letters of John*, Pillar New Testament Commentary (Grand Rapids: Eerdmans, 2000), 144. So Rudolf Schnackenburg: "The heretical teachers are now called 'false prophets,' probably because a prophet is one who speaks in the Spirit of God, and these seducers falsely claim to be filled with the Spirit (v. 1a–b)." *The Johannine Epistles: Introduction and Commentary*, trans. R. Fuller and I. Fuller (New York: Crossroad, 1992), 199. Cf. John Calvin, "1 John," in John Calvin and Matthew Henry, *1, 2, 3 John*, Crossway Classic Commentaries (Wheaton, IL: Crossway, 1998), 72.

the latter term—*to pneuma tou theou*—speaks of the Holy Spirit.[4] Notably, in the Gospel of John, "the 'Spirit of truth' is the Holy Spirit [see John 14:17, 26; 15:26; 16:13–15], who proceeds from God and teaches the truth about Christ (cf. 1 John 2:20, 27)."[5]

What, then, is the content of the God-approved confession? There are two theological components, both centering on the person and work of Jesus. First, the true confession acknowledges Jesus as the "Christ" (1 John 4:2; cf. 2:22; 5:1), a title similar but not completely identical to "Son of God" (4:15; 5:5). Jesus is the anointed Messiah.[6] Second, it recognizes that Jesus is the Eternal Incarnate One. I phrase John's claim—"has come in the flesh"—that way because the verb *to come* is in the perfect form, "indicating that it is Christ's status as one come in the flesh, rather than simply the historic act of his coming[,] that he [John] had in mind."[7] Put differently, this participle "points to a settled status: Christ did not merely make an appearance in a fleshly guise but fully assumed the bodily existence common to humanity."[8] Jesus is fully divine and fully human—now and forever.

With the Spirit of God beneath his wings, John presents his Christology—Christology that soars like an eagle![9] His spirit joins the Spirit in glorifying the Son (see John 15:26; 16:13–15) as fully divine (John 1:1) and fully human (1 John 1:1–3; cf. John 1:14). This creed is the death of Docetism (the belief that Jesus only appeared to have a body), Gnosticism (the belief that physical matter is evil), and a hundred other heresies. And it is *life* for those who confess that Jesus is Lord!

4. Robert W. Yarbrough, *1–3 John*, Baker Exegetical Commentary on the New Testament (Grand Rapids: Baker, 2008), 223. Speaking of the Spirit's role in all of Scripture, he notes: "As inheritors of the biblical tradition, John's readers would have been no strangers to God under this rubric. God is heavenly Lord and incarnate Son, yet also ubiquitous Spirit."

5. Philip W. Comfort and Wendell C. Hawley, *1–3 John*, Cornerstone Biblical Commentary (Carol Stream, IL: Tyndale, 2007), 359.

6. Without Jesus' fulfillment of the Old Testament, there is no gospel. To summarize 1 Corinthians 15:1–5, Paul declares the gospel to be that "Jesus died for our sins, rose again from the dead to grant us eternal life, and will come again in power to make everything right . . . *just like the Hebrew Bible said*." Douglas Sean O'Donnell, *Matthew: All Authority in Heaven and on Earth*, Preaching the Word (Wheaton, IL: Crossway, 2014), 814.

7. Kruse, *The Letters of John*, 146–47.

8. Yarbrough, *1–3 John*, 223. "From his incarnation onward, Christ was, and ever is, possessed of true Manhood." Vine 1970:76, quoted in Comfort and Hawley, *1–3 John*, 360.

9. The popular patristic and medieval view that the "eagle" in Revelation 4:7 symbolized St. John the Evangelist (e.g., *The Book of Kells*) prompted my eagle imagery.

It is life because John's Christology is inseparable from his soteriology. Rudolf Schnackenburg says:

> The *sarx* ["flesh"] in which the Logos is veiled has a soteriological import in [the Gospel of] John. It enables the One who became human to take upon himself an atoning sacrificial death in order to give life to the world (6:51). But the very sending of the Son of God to redeem sinners is a concern running all through 1 John (2:2; 3:5, 8; 4:10, 14). . . . The heretical teachers did not need Jesus Christ as the Redeemer from sins and the Mediator of life. They believed they were able to reach the Father and attain salvation by another way. But the author proclaims nothing other than this all through the epistle: the divine life can only be attained through the incarnate Son of God (1:1–3), only by faith in this divine Bearer of life (5:12f., 20).[10]

The incarnation is the foundation for our salvation.[11] Jesus' eternal divinity and preexistence ("has come") and true incarnational humanity ("in the flesh") constitute the "heart of the apostolic gospel."[12]

At the end of the chapter, I will conclude with three applications. I would be remiss, however, not to add at least one application here. A pressing question of the day is: "Who is Jesus?" A mere browsing on the Internet or at the local bookstore will show how many Jesuses there are to choose from. We have the Jesus of our popular "Jesus" authors—of Marcus Borg, Anne Rice, Dan Brown, and Bishop John Shelby Spong, who reject the biblical portrait of Christ. We have the Jesus of the world religions—of Muhammad, Gandhi, and the Dalai Lama. We have the Jesus of the cults and occult—of Deepak Chopra, Joseph Smith, Mary Baker Eddy, and Edgar Cayce. We even have the Jesus of pop culture—from the sports star saying, "I'd like to thank the Big Guy upstairs" to the *Playboy* model sporting across her chest, "Jesus is my homeboy."[13] In this supermarket of spirituality, which Jesus should we choose?

10. Schnackenburg, *The Johannine Epistles*, 201.

11. The earliest extant quote from 1 John comes from Polycarp's *To the Philippians* 7.1. He quoted 1 John 4:2–3. Perhaps this highlights that the church then (the generation after John), as well as throughout the ages, understood the centrality of this doctrinal truth.

12. Stephen S. Smalley, *1, 2, 3 John*, Word Biblical Commentary (Nashville: Thomas Nelson, 1984), 175.

13. These examples are given in chapter 1 of Mark Driscoll and Gerry Breshears, *Vintage Jesus: Timeless Answers to Timely Questions* (Wheaton, IL: Crossway, 2007).

Do not follow the en vogue voices, but rather the old apostolic eye, ear, hand, and *pen* testimony. The clear choice is the canonical Jesus. The New Testament is the only authorized portrait of the true Jesus. Let us stay away from the social-activist Jesus, the merely-a-prophet Jesus, the great-teacher Jesus, the religious-genius Jesus, the pacifist Jesus, the rebel Jesus, the Republican Jesus, the Marxist Jesus, and the vegetarian Jesus.[14] Rather, let us cling to the Jesus whom Peter preached at Pentecost: "Therefore let all Israel be assured of this: God has made *this Jesus*, whom you crucified, both Lord and Christ" (Acts 2:36 NIV).

Victory

As that application turns our attention to the true Christ, so in 1 John 4:4–6 John next turns our attention to our sure victory in Christ over the menace of opposing spirits, false prophets, and evil antichrists. Those dark and destructive powers are real, but they pale in comparison to the light and life we have in Christ. In him, we have already won the victory!

> Little children, you are from God and have overcome them, for he who is in you is greater than he who is in the world. They are from the world; therefore they speak from the world, and the world listens to them. We are from God. Whoever knows God listens to us; whoever is not from God does not listen to us. By this we know the Spirit of truth and the spirit of error. (1 John 4:4–6)

John begins his victory declaration with a fatherly affirmation, "Little children, you are from God" (1 John 4:4a). This is the sixth time (2:1, 12, 28; 3:7, 18; 5:21) John calls the church *teknia*. As church members under his pastoral care, they are John's spiritual children. But more significantly, they are adopted and Spirit-begotten "children of God" (3:10). They are "from God," namely, "born of God" (3:9; 4:7; 5:1, 4, 18) and indwelt by the Spirit of God (4:12–13, 15). That God-possession leads to John's optimism about overcoming: "Little children, you are from God and *have overcome them*, for he who is in you is greater than he who is in the world." The

14. See Scot McKnight, *The King Jesus Gospel: The Original Good News Revisited* (Grand Rapids: Zondervan, 2011), 122.

"them" here refers to the apostate antichrists, and "he who is in the world" is either the spirit of the antichrist or the "ruler of this world" (the devil, John 12:31; 14:30; 16:11). This "overcoming" represents both rejection of error and perseverance in the truth. The logic of the victory looks like this: Because "you are from God" and the triune God[15] "in you is greater than" the evil forces in the world, therefore, you "have overcome" all anti-Christian opponents (both "them" and "he who is in the world"). This overcoming is through God's power! The battle belongs to the Lord. We "have" (present tense) the victory now because Jesus has already "overcome the world" (John 16:33). "As surely as Christ came in the flesh (4:2), died (2:2), rose (implied in every reference to Christ's present existence), and intercedes (2:1), believers can be assured that they will not fall prey to God's opponents."[16]

Believers (*you* below) can also be assured, again due solely to God's strength, that their ears will be open to the right teachers (*we* and *us*) and be closed to the wrong (*they* and *them*). Note the numerous antithetic parallelisms in 1 John 4:

Verse 4a: "You are from God"
Verse 5a: "They are from the world"

There is a world of difference (pun intended) between these two groups, as first demonstrated in the source of commission and revelation:

Verse 5b: "They speak from the world"
Verse 6a: "We are [*speaking* is implied] from God."

Again, the *they* are the apostates and the *we* are the apostles. The *we* is *exclusive* in that it represented the first eyewitnesses in the first century, yet *inclusive* in that it now encompasses any teacher of truth who witnesses

15. Bruce Barton summarizes well the three interpretive options for the phrase "he who is in you": "(1) God (3:20), (2) God in Christ (2:14; 3:24), or (3) the Holy Spirit who indwells every believer (3:24; 4:13–16). Most likely, John was referring to the triune God—the Father, Son and Holy Spirit—not to one member of the Trinity. True believers have all three working within them against the 'one who is in the world,' the devil." Bruce B. Barton et al., *1, 2 & 3 John*, Application Bible Commentary (Wheaton, IL: Tyndale, 1998), 88. Cf. Smalley, *1, 2, 3 John*, 227.

16. Yarbrough, *1–3 John*, 228.

faithfully to the apostolic tradition.[17] Thus, it is the apostolic "children of God" versus the children of "the world," which is the "equivalent of calling them children of the Evil One ([1 John] 3:12–13; 5:19) or children of the devil (John 8:39–45)."[18]

This world of difference is further demonstrated in whose voice people heed. While "the world listens to those who speak its own language,"[19] the Spirit guides God's people to receive and respond to the gospel (see John 14:26; 16:13):

Verse 5c:	"The world listens to them."
Verse 6a:	"Whoever knows God listens to us."

Finally, the divide is as obvious as the difference between heaven and hell: "Whoever knows God listens to us; whoever is not from God does not listen to us. By this we know the Spirit of truth and the spirit of error" (1 John 4:6)—or, viewed poetically:

Whoever	knows God	listens to us;
whoever	is not from God	does not listen to us.
By this we know	the Spirit of truth and	
[by this we know]	the spirit of error.	

To listen to the apostolic *we* is to listen to "the Spirit of truth," while to listen to the false prophets is to listen to "the spirit of error." This final phrase in the final verse offers an excellent summary of 1 John 4:1–6 as a whole. Christians are called to "test the spirits to see whether they are from God" (v. 1). That test involves Christological content. Christians confess that "Jesus Christ has come in the flesh" (v. 2). That test also involves listening. Christians listen to God's voice through his apostolic teaching.

17. On the exclusive nature of the *we*, James Montgomery Boice correctly summarizes that "this 'we' is the same as the 'we' that begins the letter, which verses insist most strongly upon the apostolic teaching and testimony." *The Epistles of John: An Expositional Commentary* (Grand Rapids: Baker, 1979), 111. Yarbrough concurs, yet adds the inclusive element: "Like another 'we' passage of 1 John (1:1–5), . . . 4:6 refers first of all to John and others of the apostolic circle. By extension, then, it applies to readers who receive John's message and thereby join the circle." Yarbrough, *1–3 John*, 229.

18. John Painter, *1, 2, and 3 John*, Sacra Pagina (Collegeville, MN: Liturgical Press, 2002), 262.

19. D. Edmond Hiebert, quoted in Daniel L. Akin, *1, 2, 3 John*, New American Commentary (Nashville: Broadman & Holman, 1993), 174.

Truths for Today

In John's day, Christians gathered to worship in homes throughout the Roman Empire. Some churches had scrolls from the Old Testament and copies of what became the New Testament. While churches might have recited Jewish creeds (such as the Shema) and new Christian creeds (such as the Old Roman Creed, which became the basis for the Apostles' Creed), these early churches certainly did not have the Christological creeds of the fourth century (e.g., the Chalcedonian Creed and the Nicene-Constantinopolitan Creed) to provide doctrinal guidance. They relied on trusted teachers, their oral communication, and endorsed emissaries.

While our situation is certainly different from the early church's, still the local church throughout the world is plagued with the phenomenon of "false prophets" preying on Christians—whether it is through the airwaves, via cyberspace, or in person. Every generation must "test the spirits." Anchored to the apostolic testimony, we must practice discernment with kindness and yet courage. Without being judgmental, we must judge the cultists, the spiritual faddists, the misguided, and the misinformed. Those who twist Scripture, even if they tout "the Spirit," are to be turned out of the church. John's call to the church *then* remains the call to the church *today.*

A Corporate Endeavor

There are many ways to apply 1 John 4:1–6. I will move us from the context of Johannine church life near the end of the first century to our contemporary context in three ways. The first application is that *discernment is a corporate endeavor.*

Because our modern English translations do not differentiate between the singular and plural *you*, we often read phrases such as "you are from God" and "he who is in you is greater than he who is in the world" (1 John 4:4) in an individualistic sense. Yet the context of verse 4 is clear that John is addressing "little *children*," and the Greek *you* is plural, as in *ye* or *you all.* In fact, through 4:1–6 the pronouns and verbs are plural. As individual Christians, we have a personal relationship with Christ and the spiritual indwelling and assurance that goes with it. The call here, however, is to corporate discernment. John addresses not only church leaders, but the whole church body—the "beloved . . . little children"—to distinguish between the Worldly Antichrist Liars and the Trinitarian Truth Teachers. The call here is for "a congregation of 'Bereans' who examine the Scriptures every day to see if what is said is true (see Acts 17:11)."[20]

Custodians of Christology

The second application is that *the church serves as the custodian of apostolic Christology.* On the topic of theological discernment, Gary Burge uses the helpful analogy of radar:

> The Johannine call here is to build a Christian maturity that can use theological radar to spot intruders, who want to upend the church's beliefs. This is high-tech radar that can tell the difference between pleasure aircraft and lethal bombers, between minor issues and colossal errors that deserve a fierce struggle.[21]

The colossal error addressed in 1 John 4:1–6 is the denial of the humanity and divinity of Jesus. At issue was what came to be called *Athanasian Christology*, from Athanasius's summary of the New Testament's teaching on the person and work of Christ. Jesus is fully human, fully divine, and yet one person. As formulated later in the Athanasian Creed:

> It is necessary to everlasting salvation; that he also believe faithfully the Incarnation of our Lord Jesus Christ. For the right Faith is, that we believe and confess; that our Lord Jesus Christ, the Son of God, is God and Man; God, of the Essence of the Father; begotten before the worlds; and Man, of the Essence of his Mother, born in the world. Perfect God; and perfect Man . . . . Who although he is God and Man; yet he is not two, but one Christ.

Today this gospel truth is maligned. The notion of God's becoming a man is deemed nonsensical. And the idea of this God-man's dying a bloody death to atone for human sin and propitiate God's wrath sounds archaic and barbaric. We have "a 'captive audience,'—captive in the sense that they are

20. David Jackman, *The Message of John's Letters*, The Bible Speaks Today (Downers Grove, IL: InterVarsity Press, 1988), 113.

21. Gary M. Burge, *Letters of John*, NIV Application Commentary (Grand Rapids: Zondervan, 1996), 179.

blind to God's truth by the god of this world (2 Cor. 4:4)."[22] Nevertheless, our task is to take this "foolish" message of the "wisdom of God" (1 Cor. 1:20, 24) to the world so that God might set the captives free.

Beyond Christological heresies, we can expand this second application to include other colossal errors. While we must apply the care and skill of a surgeon to any Christological or soteriological cancers that threaten the body of Christ, we must commit ourselves to cutting out any teachers and teachings that cut at the vitals of the faith. At the time of the Reformation, Calvin wrote:

> The heretics in olden times departed from the faith, in one case by denying the divine nature of Christ, and in another case by denying his human nature. People who confess Christ to be God and man are still departing from the faith if they do not adhere to the confession that the apostle requires, because they rob Christ of his own merit. Where free will, merits of works, fictitious modes of worship, satisfactions, and the advocacy of saints are set up, how very little remains for Christ![23]

Some of those same concerns remain today. (The Reformation is *not* over!) Furthermore, as Jacques Ellul wrote of the "tendencies of thought and behavior that are inflicting our age with dreadful spiritual diseases," there are *The New Demons* as well.[24] These "new demons" have produced "a decaying intellectual environment that has no use for truth, no interest in a transcendent God, and indeed no way to conceptualize any notion of revelation."[25] The question "Who is Jesus?" remains. But because there is no interest in the quest for truth, added to it are questions such as: "Who cares who Jesus was?" and "Why does it matter who he was?" and "Aren't there many ways to God?" and "In the end, who can know the truth, anyway?" We are not to go on theological witch-hunts, but we are to go to war, fighting against this stealth army of postmodernism, and whatever other false philosophy rears its diabolical head.

The Spirit and the Word

The third application is that *the Spirit and the Word work together.* The problem addressed in our text is the refusal of some to "listen to the word of

22. Barton, *1, 2 & 3 John*, 89.
23. Calvin, "1 John," 75.
24. This summary of Ellul's book *The New Demons* is from Burge, *Letters of John*, 182–83.
25. Burge's remarks on David Wells's *No Place for Truth*. See ibid., 183.

God in the apostolic teaching."[26] That same problem plagues our churches. Beneath the problem is the misunderstanding that the Holy Spirit works independently from scriptural revelation. In his excellent summary of "The Role of the Holy Spirit in 1 John," Colin Kruse speaks on how the role of the Spirit in John's first letter "builds upon the teaching about the Spirit in the Fourth Gospel,"[27] for example, where the Spirit is identified as "the Spirit of truth" (John 14:17) who bears witness about Jesus' death (19:34–35). Kruse concludes his "survey of the Spirit texts of 1 John," saying:

> [John] has portrayed the role of the Spirit primarily as testimony to the tradition, not as a source of new revelation. In all probability he did this because the secessionists were claiming the Spirit as the source of their new and heretical doctrines concerning Christ. The author, therefore, felt that it was necessary to hold together the word and the Spirit, or, put in other words, he felt that it was necessary to stress the Spirit's role as witness to the truth of the gospel concerning Jesus as it was proclaimed from the beginning.[28]

Many movements today want to move us *beyond* the Word *to* the Spirit. That is a strange estrangement, as well as one that is moving in the wrong direction. We are not missing some Spirit-filled experience when we *only* read and teach the Bible. There is not a time for the Spirit (singing and praying) and then a time for the Word (preaching). To be led by the Spirit in corporate worship or private devotion is to be led back to the inspired apostolic testimony. When the apostles received the Holy Spirit, they were Christ's witnesses to the world via the Word preached (Acts 1:8) and later written (e.g., 1–3 John). As we together (*discernment is a corporate endeavor*) resist the antichrist spirits of our age and guard the truth (*as the custodian of apostolic Christology*) "once for all delivered to the saints" (Jude 3), let us not divide this God-ordained union of *the Spirit and the Word.*

26. Jackman, *The Message of John's Letters*, 115.
27. Kruse, "A Note on the Role of the Spirit," in *The Letters of John*, 153.
28. Ibid., 155.

11

The Two Loves

1 John 4:7–21

In this is love, not that we have loved God but that he loved us and sent his Son to be the propitiation for our sins. Beloved, if God so loved us, we also ought to love one another. No one has ever seen God; if we love one another, God abides in us and his love is perfected in us. (1 John 4:10–12)

In his *Autobiography*, Mark Twain wrote, "Repetition is a mighty power in the domain of humor. If frequently used, nearly any precisely worded and unchanged formula will eventually compel laughter if it be gravely and earnestly repeated, at intervals, five or six times." Twain knew from experience the truth of his claim. On his first lecture tour of the United States, he began "with a scheme so daring a nature," as he put it, that he wondered how he "ever had the courage to carry it through." He began his talk in a level, colorless, monotonous voice by telling a short story of no interest, and certainly no humor.

His first telling was met with dead silence, as he anticipated. Fifteen hundred people stared at him with looks of sorrow, insult, resentment, and pity. Twain tried to look embarrassed. He took a long pause. He stood fumbling his hands, trying to appeal to his audience for sympathy. Then he began again. He told the same story in the same way. Once more he was met with looks of confusion and indignation. Twain paused and started up again. He told the same story in the same way for the third time. But this time, the reaction was quite different. "All of a sudden," he recalls, "the front row recognized [the joke of it] and broke into a laugh. It spread back, and back, and back, to the furthest verge of the place; then swept forward again, and then back again, and at the end of a minute the laughter was as universal and as thunderously noisy as a tempest." Forty years after the fact, the great American humorist wrote of that laughter, saying, "It was a heavenly sound to me," and one of his colleagues called the whole event "a triumph of art."[1]

The art of repetition, as Twain proved, can be used to engender riotous laughter. But the art of repetition can also be applied to produce other results. In 1 John 4:7–21, repetition provokes sober reflection on the theme of love. The word *love*—including *loves*, *loved*, and *beloved*—is repeated twenty-nine times, averaging nearly two occurrences per verse. To put that into perspective, *love* is addressed here more than in the four Gospels. With 1 Corinthians 13 a close second, this portion of 1 John is the most highly concentrated section on the theme of love in the whole of Scripture. Of all the biblical writers, John loves to talk about love. That is why some ancient Christian writers called him "the doctor of love" and "the theologian of love." In this study, let us sit at his feet and learn from this apostle of *agapē*.

While John certainly says a lot about love, he repeats many of the same words to express the same ideas. This makes it easy to recognize his point, and to find a verse or two or three or four (!) to summarize his thought. Perhaps the best summary verse of this section is 1 John 4:11: "Beloved, if God so loved us, we also ought to love one another."[2] John has written the sermon outline for us. Point 1 is that God has loved us. Point 2 is that we ought to love one another. The two loves! It is that simple. At least it is that simple to say. To put it into practice, however, is another matter altogether.

1. Recounted in Mark Twain, *Autobiography of Mark Twain*, ed. Charles Neider (New York: HarperPerennial, 1990), 143–47.

2. Cf. "We love because he first loved us" (1 John 4:19).

God Has Loved Us

John acknowledges this difficulty. That is why he speaks of the need for prayer (1 John 3:22), the Holy Spirit (3:24; 4:13; cf. 4:2, 6), and abiding in Jesus (4:15) and the Father (i.e., "God," 3:24; 4:15–16). That is also why he bases the command to "love one another" (4:7, 11–12), namely, our Christian brothers (4:20–21), on the sure foundation of the triune God and his love for us in Christ through the Spirit.

Many verses in Scripture start with "God is . . ." and then add an attribute (e.g., "mighty," Job 36:5, and "merciful," Ps. 116:5), but only a few speak of God's essence. John gives us the three most memorable. In his Gospel he records Jesus' words to the Samaritan woman, "God is spirit" (John 4:24). In 1 John we read near the beginning that "God is light" (1:5) and now toward the end that "God is love" (4:8, 16). We might say, "Grandma Smith is a very loving person," but what is said here is different. John is not saying that love is a quality that God possesses; rather, he is saying that love is the essence of God's divine being.[3] The eternal love between the Father, Son, and Spirit that existed before creation (John 17:24) spills over into his creation, as God perpetually gives of himself for the benefit of his creation. That is what makes the statement "God is love" so remarkable.

What also makes it remarkable is its uniqueness among the world's religions. In his *New York Times* best seller *The Reason for God: Belief in an Age of Skepticism*, Timothy Keller shares about his exploration into Buddhism, Hinduism, Islam, and Confucianism, and how his theory that at the core of all world religions was the belief in a loving God was debunked. He came to understand that only Christianity speaks of a living God who "is love" and who also personally loves his creation. For example, "Buddhism doesn't believe in a personal God at all, and love is the action of a person," not a divine being. And Islam speaks of God's mercy, but never about God's loving mercy extended to the world in Jesus, our Bridegroom who so loved us that he laid down his life for us. To a Muslim, such language of love would be considered disrespectful of the divine. Quite simply, Keller discovered that to all the major world faiths (save Christianity!), love is not "the dominant, ruling attribute of God." He also shares how, through

3. David Jackman, *The Message of John's Letters*, The Bible Speaks Today (Downers Grove, IL: InterVarsity Press, 1988), 118.

that season of searching, this central Christian concept brought him back to the "God of Love."[4]

But what does it mean when the Christian confesses, "God is love"? Years ago, when my daughter Evelyn was learning to read, I asked her to read aloud from 1 John 4:8. I wanted "God is love" to be the first Bible words she ever read. So I pointed and she pronounced. When she finished, I said, "Good job!" At first, that simple reading exercise pleased me both spiritually and academically. Yet it did not take long for a strange sinking feeling to settle in my soul. My sensitive theologian conscience convicted me that I needed to clarify the concept of God as love. In sum, I said, "Evelyn, listen. God is holy; we are not. But because God is love, in love he sent Jesus to die for our sins. Okay?" She nodded.

Perhaps I was overprotective. Perhaps such overprotection has its benefits. I think that just as it is good to be protective with my daughter's purity of body, so, too, it is good to be protective with her purity of mind. I want my children to know who God is. I want the picture to be as clear as possible. I want them to know that "God is all-loving and, equally, all-holy (1:5)," and that these "two characteristics do not stand in opposition to one another but belong together and determine his actions."[5]

That same burden of conscience compels me to clarify this same concept for you, for as you know, there is a great difference between how people today define God's love and how the apostle John defines it. The contemporary concept of a loving God—or a God whose very essence is love—is that he cannot and will not judge anyone for anything. "God is love" means that God is tolerant of all theological perspectives and lifestyles. This is the god of the flower children fully blossomed!

For example, on August 28, 2013, America celebrated the fiftieth anniversary of the March on Washington, which included Martin Luther King Jr.'s famous "I Have a Dream" speech. On that day, a number of the speakers (and plenty of the pundits) made the connection between civil rights and gay rights. According to the Bible, that is a faulty logical leap—racism and homosexual behavior are both sins. Today, from the lips of America's

4. See Timothy Keller, *The Reason for God: Belief in an Age of Skepticism* (New York: Dutton, 2008), 81–82. Cf. I. Howard Marshall's claim that the statement "God is love" is "simply the clearest expression of a doctrine of the nature of God." *The Epistles of John*, New International Commentary on the New Testament (Grand Rapids: Eerdmans, 1978), 213.

5. Marshall, *The Epistles of John*, 213.

president and even from the mouths of the Boy Scouts of America, we are repeatedly told that the loving thing to do is to embrace sexual lawlessness. On this issue, Christians are scolded for advocating that love and moral constraint are necessarily bound together. Such accusations are ridiculous. Blind! They reflect a dark world walking and talking in darkness. Christian love has its limits, and those limits are set by the law of God, which is the law of perfect freedom. Live by it and love by it, and you will take on wings. On a grander scale than civil liberties, you'll be "free at last"!

John's definition of love, based on Christ's command to love, is "not a simplistic call to indiscriminate tolerance and affirmation of all human expression and action."[6] Rather, love is a characteristic that finds its ultimate explanation in Christ's incarnation and crucifixion. "By this we know love, that he laid down his life for us" (1 John 3:16). We will not understand what is meant by "God is love" in 4:8 until we grasp some important words in the surrounding context, namely, "that Jesus Christ has come in the flesh" (4:2) to be "the propitiation for our sins" (4:10).

In approaching 1 John 4:7–10, it is important that we begin by walking through the context of 4:1–6, where John starts with a call to discernment: "Beloved, do not believe every spirit, but test the spirits to see whether they are from God, for many false prophets have gone out into the world" (v. 1). This "test" is simple enough: "By this you know the Spirit of God: every spirit that confesses that Jesus Christ has come in the flesh is from God, and every spirit that does not confess Jesus is not from God. This is the spirit of the antichrist, which you heard was coming and now is in the world already" (vv. 2–3). "Spiritual activity is not necessarily Godly activity."[7] It is anti-Christian spirituality to think that Jesus the Christ was not born of Mary, and that he did not walk and talk and heal throughout Galilee, suffer under Pontius Pilate, die on a cursed tree, rise bodily from the grave, and ascend victoriously into heaven.

John starts with spiritual discernment. Next, he offers a word of apostolic (*we* and *us*) encouragement against the false teachers (*they* and *them*). In 1 John 4:4–6, he writes:

6. Robert W. Yarbrough, *1–3 John*, Baker Exegetical Commentary on the New Testament (Grand Rapids: Baker, 2008), 87.

7. Daniel L. Akin, *1, 2, 3 John*, New American Commentary (Nashville: Broadman & Holman, 1993), 171.

> Little children, you are from God and have overcome them, for he who is in you is greater than he who is in the world. They are from the world; therefore they speak from the world, and the world listens to them. We are from God. Whoever knows God listens to us; whoever is not from God does not listen to us. By this we [i.e., all Christians] know the Spirit of truth and the spirit of error.

Then, arriving at our text, he gives Christ's command and the reason behind it:

> Beloved, let us love one another, for love is from God, and whoever loves has been born of God and knows God. Anyone who does not love does not know God, because God is love. (1 John 4:7–8)

God is the source of love ("love is from God"). Thus, his children (those "born of God," those who "know God"), by the very definition of their new nature, "love." Conversely, those who do not love have not been born of God (do "not know God") because God's essence and actions are completely loving. "God is love."

First John 4:9–10 informs us in what manner God is love:

> In this the love of God was made manifest among us,
> that God sent his only Son into the world,
> so that we might live through him.
> In this is love,
> not that we have loved God but that he loved us
> and sent his Son to be the propitiation for our sins.

"Amazing love! How can it be that Thou, my God, shouldst die for me?"[8] Our relationship with God is not based on our initial love for God and his affirmative response to us. We did not first love God; he first loved us. He is the "great initiator."[9] Love is not best demonstrated by *God's people's* heeding the Shema ("Hear, O Israel: The LORD our God, the LORD is one. You shall love the LORD your God with all your heart and with all your soul and with

8. Charles Wesley, "And Can It Be That I Should Gain" (1738).

9. Bruce B. Barton et al., *1, 2 & 3 John*, Application Bible Commentary (Wheaton, IL: Tyndale, 1998), 95.

all your might," Deut. 6:4–5); rather, it is through *God's* sending his Son to be "forsaken" by him so that we might be forgiven through him. God's unique Son offered a unique sacrifice for our sins. Through his propitiatory *death* he removed the guilt of our sins, appeased God's wrath, and gave us eternal *life*—we "live through him" (1 John 4:9).

> If the propitiatory death of Jesus is eliminated from the love of God, it might be unfair to say that the love of God is robbed of all meaning, but it is certainly robbed of its apostolic meaning. It has no longer that meaning which goes deeper than sin, sorrow, and death, and which recreates life in the adoring joy, wonder and purity of the first Epistle of John.[10]

So, then, when we confess those great words "God is love," we ought never to do so without the thought of God's essence being explained and illustrated in the life and death of Christ. God is love and God has loved. He has loved us in Christ's incarnation and propitiation. That is the only foundation of our genuine Christian love toward others.

We Should Love Others

God, who is love, has loved. That is the first point. The second follows. The *beloved* are to love. If God has loved us, then we are to love others. "Beloved, if God so loved us, we also ought to love one another" (1 John 4:11). But how are we to do this? What are the characteristics of Christian love? Is Christian love emotional? Yes, but that is not what is taught here. Is it mystical? Perhaps, but that emphasis is not expounded either. Is it social activism? Yes, in part, but not in terms of the secularist ethics so popular today. According to 1 John 4:7–21, Christian love has three characteristics. First, Christian love is orthodox. Second, Christian love is active. Third, Christian love is assuring.

Christian Love Is Orthodox

We start with the orthodoxy of Christian love. While there is no mention of *love* in 1 John 4:1–6 (note, however, *beloved*, 4:1), John intentionally places that text on spiritual discernment between two love-dominated verses (3:11–24, where *love*-words are mentioned seven times; 4:7–21, twenty-nine

10. James Denny, *The Death of Christ*, quoted in Marshall, *The Epistles of John*, 215.

times). Thus, the contextual point is that just as John bound orthodoxy and love thematically together, so should we. Right love naturally flows out of right theology.

Notice how John connects these two themes. In the middle of his talk on love (1 John 3:11–4:21), he addresses orthodoxy. We have already covered 1 John 4:1–6 and seen how confessing Jesus Christ has come in the flesh, testing the spirits, and resisting the error of the antichrist go hand in hand with the commandment to love. The orthodoxy of incarnational confession is wed with the orthopraxy of incarnational compassion. Three other verses support this God-ordained marriage. In 3:23 we read, "And this is his commandment, that we believe in the name of his Son Jesus Christ," followed later in 4:14–15 by: "And we have seen and testify that the Father has sent his Son to be the Savior of the world. Whoever confesses that Jesus is the Son of God, God abides in him, and he in God."

As taught in 1 John 3:23 and 4:14–15, Christian love is orthodox in that it acknowledges two truths. First, Jesus is "the Son of God" who "stands in a unique relationship with God," and therefore "mediates salvation (v. 14), the indwelling of God with us (v. 15) and the love of God (v. 16)."[11] Second, Jesus is "the Savior of the world" whose limited atonement has an unlimited sphere: those throughout the world—regardless of age, sex, or nationality (cf. John 4:39–42)—who confess their need for Christ's atoning sacrifice are cleansed from their sins. Christian love acknowledges that Jesus is "the Divine Son, the incarnate Deity, the sinless Human, the Messianic Savior."[12] It is orthodox!

Today, medical error is simply not tolerated. Sadly, theological error is. We do not sue doctors of theology if what they teach is false. We rarely take away a pastor's position if his sermons are unorthodox. We no longer burn heretics. While I am not for torturing Gnostics and Marcionites, I am of the opinion that there is nothing so deadly in the entire world as theological error. Moreover, I believe that there is nothing so *unloving* as theological error. In fact, it is better to have a millstone tied around your neck while swimming in the Mediterranean Sea than to teach a child that Jesus has not come in the flesh to die for our sins. Theological error is far more deadly

11. Marianne Meye Thompson, *1–3 John*, IVP New Testament Commentary Series (Downers Grove, IL: InterVarsity Press, 1992), 125.

12. Akin, *1, 2, 3 John*, 167.

than medical error, for theological error can cause the loss of both body *and soul* (Matt. 10:28).

We must not be confused by the media elites, pop philosophers, and antichrist celebrities who sound so broad-minded, humble, and loving when they talk about Jesus. They claim to have high regard for him but deny his deity, atonement, and resurrection; they tout him as a great moral teacher, but reject his ethic of love—on issues such as adultery and fornication. They call the Golden Rule their rule while they crush those who oppose their pluralism. Such tolerance without truth so easily tantalizes. But the Word of God thunders against such triviality, saying that there is nothing loving about theological error. Nothing! The wrong view of Jesus is a deadly plague that will kill the church. Right belief and right conduct have been joined together by God,[13] and what God has joined together let no one put asunder.

Christian Love Is Active

First, and foundationally, Christian love is orthodox. We cannot have a right love toward others unless we also have a right perspective on Jesus. The second characteristic follows, namely, that Christian love is active. John expressed earlier the necessary transition from "Christian love is orthodox" to "Christian love is active." Christian love is not just in the head; it also extends through the hands. As John summarized in 1 John 3:18, "Little children, let us not love in word or talk but in deed and in truth," or, as Raymond Brown paraphrases it, "Let us love, not by word of mouth but by real deeds."[14] In 1 John 3:12–16, the examples of Cain and Christ were put before us. On one hand, we have Cain, whose hatred resulted in murder. On the other hand, we have Christ, whose love resulted in self-sacrifice. Needless to say, Christians are to be like Christ, not Cain. Thus, like Christ—who knowingly and deliberately "laid down his life for us"—so, too, "we ought to lay down our lives for the brothers" (v. 16).

One expression of Christlike love is self-sacrifice, even the most extreme—the once-in-a-lifetime sacrifice of one's life. The other expression of Christlike love is compassion—practical every-day-of-our-life concern, consideration, and care for others. This is what was taught in 1 John 3:17, "But if

13. "You cannot believe without loving nor love without believing." R. C. H. Lenski, *The Interpretation of the Epistles of St. Peter, St. John and St. Jude* (Minneapolis: Augsburg, 1966), 479.

14. Raymond E. Brown, *The Epistles of John*, Anchor Bible (Garden City, NY: Doubleday, 1982), 451.

anyone has the world's goods and sees his brother in need, yet closes his heart against him, how does God's love abide in him?" John's rhetorical question is similar to James's in James 2:15–16: "If a brother or sister is poorly clothed and lacking in daily food, and one of you says to them, 'Go in peace, be warmed and filled,' without giving them the things needed for the body, what good is that?" Whether the sense of "be warmed and filled" is "I wish you well as you take care of yourself" or "May God feed and clothe you, because I certainly won't,"[15] the seemingly sweet words are filled with the bitter poison of hypocrisy. Just as faith without works is dead, so God-talk about God's love without looking out for the physical and financial needs of our brothers and sisters in Christ is poppycock.[16] "If anyone says, 'I love God,' and hates his brother, he is a liar; for he who does not love his brother whom he has seen cannot love God whom he has not seen" (1 John 4:20). As God's love is manifested to us in Christ (4:9; cf. John 1:18; 6:46), our love for God is manifested in our love for others. In this way our love for the *invisible* God is made *visible*. The one who truly "love[s] God" will love "his brother" (1 John 4:20)—sacrificially and compassionately. That is God's "love . . . perfected in us" (4:12). God's love for us is completed, is made whole, or "reaches its extended goal" when we actively extend it to others, or, as Thompson put it, "when it flows from God, through us, to our fellow believers."[17]

> The shape of perfect love is triangular: love comes as a gift from God that enables us to love each other and so return to God the gift that is given to us. . . . Where any one leg of the triangle is missing, love remains incomplete and immature. But where the triangle is whole, love is complete.[18]

Christian love is not mystical visions or warm words, "but practical down-to-earth actions."[19] It is, as David Jackman points out, "the modern equivalent of washing one another's feet."[20] It is, as I will add, as hands-on as Christ's

15. Daniel M. Doriani, *James*, Reformed Expository Commentary (Phillipsburg, NJ: P&R Publishing, 2007), 84–85.

16. Cf. Galatians 6:10: "So then, as we have opportunity, let us do good to everyone, and especially to those who are of the household of faith."

17. Thompson, *1–3 John*, 123.

18. Ibid., 126–27.

19. Jackman, *The Message of John's Letters*, 123.

20. Ibid.

incarnation and as hands-out as Christ's crucifixion. It is "love so amazing, so divine," that it "demands my soul, my life, my all"[21]—our all for all.

Christian Love Is Assuring

Christian love is orthodox. Christian love is active. Finally, Christian love is assuring. Francis Schaeffer called this active and observable oneness of love between true Christians "the final apologetic."[22] That is, he believed that the love shown between Christians was the best way for the world to recognize the reality of Christianity. I agree. Yet such love is more than an apologetic for unbelievers; it is also an assurance for believers.

First John 3–4 contains three sections that center on that theme of assurance. The first section, found in 1 John 3:10–15, focuses on *the evidence of our eternal identity.* First John 3:10 begins: "By this it is evident who are the children of God, and who are the children of the devil: whoever does not practice righteousness is not of God, nor is the one who does not love his brother." John continues by saying that this is nothing new. This is what you have heard the first time we taught you the gospel: "For this is the message that you have heard from the beginning, that we should love one another" (v. 11). Then, as a good pastor, John illustrates with an Old Testament allusion: "We should not be like Cain, who was of the evil one and murdered his brother. And why did he murder him? Because his own deeds were evil and his brother's righteous" (v. 12). Cain is the perfect example of "the world" because it was his evil attitude that led to his bloody "butchering" (*esphaksen*) of his own blood brother. Similarly, John states, "Do not be surprised, brothers, that the world hates you" (v. 13). We should be ashamed if the world hates us for being difficult, obnoxious, fanatical, overzealous, or foolish. But we should not be ashamed (or surprised!) if the world hates us for "righteousness' sake" (Matt. 5:10) and on account of Christ (v. 11). Like Christ himself, Christians are "a fragrance of death" to "those who are perishing" (2 Cor. 2:15–16). No wonder we are persecuted. The children of Cain hate the children of Christ. Yet ironically, such hatred is a sign of our assurance. Along with our love for others, it assures us that we are forever alive in Christ: "We know that we have passed out of death into life, because

21. Isaac Watts, "When I Survey the Wondrous Cross" (1707).

22. See Francis A. Schaeffer, *The Mark of the Christian*, IVP Classics (Downers Grove, IL: InterVarsity Press, 2006), 29.

we love the brothers. Whoever does not love abides in death. Everyone who hates his brother is a murderer, and you know that no murderer has eternal life abiding in him" (1 John 4:14–15).

In 1 John 3:10–15, we were reminded of *the evidence of our eternal identity.* We can be certain that we are eternally saved because, unlike the Cainlike world, we love others as Christ has loved us. Then in the second and third sections focusing on the theme of assurance, we learn about our *fearless confidence before God.* In 3:19–24, we read:

> By this we shall know that we are of the truth and reassure our heart before him; for whenever our heart condemns us, God is greater than our heart, and he knows everything. Beloved, if our heart does not condemn us, we have confidence before God; and whatever we ask we receive from him, because we keep his commandments and do what pleases him. And this is his commandment, that we believe in the name of his Son Jesus Christ and love one another, just as he has commanded us. Whoever keeps his commandments abides in God, and God in him. And by this we know that he abides in us, by the Spirit whom he has given us.

Then in 4:12–18, we read:

> No one has ever seen God; if we love one another, God abides in us and his love is perfected in us.
>
> By this we know that we abide in him and he in us, because he has given us of his Spirit. And we have seen and testify that the Father has sent his Son to be the Savior of the world. Whoever confesses that Jesus is the Son of God, God abides in him, and he in God. So we have come to know and to believe the love that God has for us. God is love, and whoever abides in love abides in God, and God abides in him. By this is love perfected with us, so that we may have confidence for the day of judgment, because as he is so also are we in this world. There is no fear in love, but perfect love casts out fear. For fear has to do with punishment, and whoever fears has not been perfected in love.

Those thirteen verses can be summarized as follows. Because the invisible God ("no one has ever seen God," 1 John 4:12; cf. v. 20) now abides in us through his Spirit ("he has given us of his Spirit," 4:13; cf. 3:24), his love produces two very visible fruits in his "beloved" (3:21; 4:1, 7, 11) "children" (3:10; cf. 3:18; 4:4):

1. We "believe the love that God has for us" (1 John 4:16) in "his Son Jesus Christ" (3:23; cf. 4:14–15), "the Savior of the world" (4:14), and therefore,
2. We abide in God's "love" (4:12, 16) by loving "one another" (3:23).

It follows that if we believe in God's love and love the brothers, then God reassures our hearts (1 John 3:19–21), answers prayer (3:22), and casts out fear of God's judgment (4:17–18).

I say "fear of God's judgment" because the famous phrase "there is no fear in love" (1 John 4:18) does not mean that true love conquers all earthly phobias. The "perfect love [that] casts out fear" (v. 18) is not casting out the fear of the unknown, public speaking, heights, clowns, or blimps. The context is clear that perfect love casts out fear of eternal punishment. If we love our neighbor, then we ought not to fear what will happen on "the day of judgment" (4:17), that is, the ultimate and eternal "day" when Christ will return ("at his coming," 2:28) to judge the world (John 5:22, 27). Think of it this way: If you love your wife, you have no fear of the state's punishment for murder. You will not murder her if you do not hate but love her. Similarly, if you love other Christians, the fear of divine judgment is averted. There is no fear when we love. Only those who are hateful need to fear. "Perfect love"—God's love for us expressed in our love for others—"casts out" the fear of judgment (1 John 4:18). Put simply and in summary, Christian love is assuring. If we love our brothers, we know who we are and how we stand before God.

"Loving God: Head, Heart and Hands"

I am uncertain whether the Irish Bible Institute's slogan "Loving God: Head, Heart and Hands" and the design of its theological training "to develop the whole person: head (mind), heart (attitudes) and hands (skills)"[23] are borrowed from 1 John. What I do know is that these serve as a fitting summary of our study of 4:7–21, for here John seeks to develop our heads (Christian love is orthodox), our hands (Christian love is active), and our hearts (Christian love is assuring). He teaches us that if we think in love and walk in love, our hearts can be reassured of God's steadfast love (cf. 3:19–21).

23. http://ibi.ie/.

12

The Nature and Knowledge of Faith

1 John 5:1–12

Everyone who believes that Jesus is the Christ has been born of God, and everyone who loves the Father loves whoever has been born of him. By this we know that we love the children of God, when we love God and obey his commandments.
(1 John 5:1–2)

Ancient tradition says that when the apostle John was near death, his voice grew so weak that he could no longer preach to the congregation in Ephesus. Yet each Sunday, as he arrived at the church, he would offer the identical exhortation: "Little children, love one another." When the congregation grew tired of this same sentence, someone finally asked John why he so frequently repeated it. He replied, "I say what I say because it is the Lord's command, and if this is all you do, it is enough."[1]

1. From Jerome (*Gal.* 6.10), cited in Alfred Plummer, *The Epistles of St. John*, Cambridge Greek Testament for Schools and Colleges (Cambridge: Cambridge University Press, 1894), xxxv. Cf. Jerome, *Commentary on Galatians*, trans. Andrew Cain, Ancient Christian Writers 121 (New York: Newman, 2010), 260.

In the previous chapter, we learned that Christian love is orthodox, active, and assuring. Love, of course, is not all there is to Christianity, but it certainly is the defining ethic. In this chapter, without detaching completely from the theme of love, we turn our attention to a theme no less foundational—faith.[2] In 1 John 5:13, John says, "I write these things to you who *believe* in the name of the Son of God that you may *know* that you have eternal life." That verse serves as a good summary of the two points addressed in 5:1–12: the nature of faith (vv. 1–5) and the knowledge of faith (vv. 6–12).

The Nature of Faith

What, then, is the nature of true Christian faith? First John 5:1–5—where John writes about the object, author, and effects of faith—provides an excellent summary. We will begin with the object of our faith.

The Object of Faith

Christian faith begins with the object of our faith, namely, the apostolic Jesus. Christian faith believes that Jesus is the promised Messiah ("the Christ," 1 John 5:1; cf. v. 6). Christian faith believes that Jesus is the divine Christ ("the Son of God," v. 5; cf. vv. 9–12),[3] "he who came" (v. 6; cf. John 6:14; 11:27) to die ("the blood," 1 John 5:6, 8) for us. Christian faith believes the apostolic testimony about Jesus: his coming in the flesh, teachings, miracles, exorcisms, sufferings, crucifixion, resurrection, bodily appearances, ascension, eternal mediation, glorification, and ongoing offer of forgiveness and call to faith in light of the coming judgment.[4] Christian faith believes in the Jesus of 1 John: "the one with whom believers enjoy fellowship (1:3), the Righteous One, who makes intercession with the Father (2:1), the one whom the antichrist denies (2:22), the one in whose name (alone) people

2. "Now in 5:1–5 John will begin to shift emphasis in a pistic (faith) direction—of the ten occurrences in 1 John of the Greek noun or verb for 'faith' or 'believe,' seven of them are in 1 John 5." Robert W. Yarbrough, *1–3 John*, Baker Exegetical Commentary on the New Testament (Grand Rapids: Baker, 2008), 268. Also, Yarbrough says: "The road to love, he will now affirm, is paved with faith." Ibid., 269.

3. While Daniel L. Akin argues that 1 John 5:1–5 is structured chiastically (see *1, 2, 3 John*, New American Commentary [Nashville: Broadman & Holman, 1993], 188) and thus "the Christ" (v. 1) and "the Son of God" are viewed as "virtual synonyms" (ibid., 194), nevertheless, the title "Son of God" has a divine edge. Jesus is more than the Jewish Messiah; he is also the Son of Israel's God. How else can he be tried for blasphemy—"he claimed to be the Son of God" (John 19:7 NIV)?

4. See Acts 10:34–43; cf. 2:14–36; 3:17–26; 4:8–12; 5:29–32; 7:2–53; 13:16–41; 17:22–31.

are commanded to trust (3:23), and the one who has come from God in the flesh (4:2)."[5]

Years ago, I met Pastor Jon Dennis for coffee at the Harper Center's cafeteria of the University of Chicago Booth School of Business. As we were waiting in line inside this sleek silver-and-white edifice of higher education, Jon asked what I wanted to be when I grew up. Playing along, I responded, "When I grow up, I want to graduate from this business school and make lots of money." The cafeteria cashier, overhearing our curious conversation, gave a shy but sure smile. That same smile resurfaced as Jon paid for our drinks with his church credit card. Our identity was revealed. We were not aspiring businessmen but poor pastors. This woman's name was Porscha. She spelled it (if her nametag is trustworthy) with an *a* at the end rather than with the *e* of the luxury sports car. Making the most of the opportunity, Jon asked, "Porscha, do you go to church?" She replied, "No, but I am a believer." Pointing to her heart, she added with depth of sincerity, "What I believe is in here."

Porscha's name may be novel, but sadly, her perspective on faith is not. Most people have "faith." Someone might say, "I have faith, but not as much as I would like." Another might claim, "I have a strong faith," and go on to describe some deep internal emotion and abstract spirituality that is based on a religious experience that provided some meaning or authenticity to life.[6] Such definitions of faith are different from the apostle John's. To him, it is not the experience of having faith in faith. In 1 John 5:1, when he writes of faith, he does not say, "Everyone who believes in whatever or whoever has been born of God"; rather, he writes, "Everyone who believes *that Jesus is the Christ* has been born of God." Moreover, verse 5 does not read, "Who is it that overcomes the world except the one who believes in belief"; rather, "the one who believes *that Jesus is the Son of God.*" According to John, the nature of Christian faith begins with the object (or in this case, *person*) of our faith, namely, the apostolic Jesus.

The Author of Faith

The second aspect of authentic Christian faith involves the author of our faith. Who is the source of our faith? The common experiential answer

5. Yarbrough, *1–3 John*, 269.

6. See David Jackman, *The Message of John's Letters*, The Bible Speaks Today (Downers Grove, IL: InterVarsity Press, 1988), 135.

would be "us." Our faith is self-birthed. The scriptural answer, however, is that our faith is God-birthed, as made clear in 1 John 5:1: "Everyone who believes that Jesus is the Christ has been born of God, and everyone who loves the Father loves whoever has been born of him." Just as the birth of a child comes before his first grin, word, and step, so spiritual birth comes before belief. I say that with confidence based on the linguistic evidence. The verb "believes" or, more literally, "the one believing" is in the present tense, which indicates a present, continuing activity. The word "born" or "has been born" is in the perfect tense. The perfect tense indicates a past event with continuing consequences. This means that our present, continued belief is a result of a past event. What event? The event of being born "*of* God"—"given spiritual rebirth."[7] David Jackman explains: "It is God who takes the initiative in the new birth, or the work of salvation, faith being both its gift and the first active sign of the new life."[8]

Let me illustrate God's authorship. When my sister Julie was in college, she invited me to visit because her roommate, Anne, had some questions about Christianity. I was a recent convert, zealous for evangelism, and thus I welcomed the opportunity. Anne was reading the Baltimore Catechism. She was thinking of joining the Catholic Church. She began the conversation with a question about the apparently odd phrase "born again" used under the answer to question 315, which quotes John 3:5. "What does that mean?" she asked. I gladly explained by opening to John 3 and retelling the story of Nicodemus, where Jesus instructed that old, knowledgeable religious leader that no one can enter the kingdom of God unless he is born from above, or, as 1 John 5:1 puts it, "born of God."

After another twenty minutes of explanation, illustration, and exhortation, I gave the evangelical altar call. Sadly, Anne wasn't interested. I had answered her question. She had lost her curiosity about Christianity. I left, frustrated. Yet God's grace was not frustrated that day. While I was speaking to Anne, I forgot that my sister was in the room. She was lying on the top bunk bed and seemed distracted. (Or, as older brothers so often do—I simply ignored her.) Anne was my target, not Julie. Yet God had a different

7. Ibid., 275. Cf.: "In Johannine theology, spiritual rebirth seems to precede and ultimately create faith: those who believe do so not so much as the result of human volition as of prior divine intention (cf. John 1:12–13)." Ibid., 270.

8. Jackman, *The Message of John's Letters*, 36.

plan. He used my words on his Word to open Julie's heart. Soon after my dorm-room sermon, she gave her life to Christ, God's having birthed a new life in her through his Word.

Years later, as I reflected on my sister's conversion, I penned a poem celebrating her supernatural re-creation. I called it "And Julie, Also," based on the phrase in Genesis 1:16, "He made the stars also" (KJV). The first stanza goes:

If in divine decree, the stars were spun in but an "also,"
    and moons and suns did
        f
            a
                l
                    l
    with gravity to their determined dwellings,
Fairer still September's daughter, whose nativity—
    not from maiden's womb, but of God
        conceived, delivered, caressed—
            was November's second birth.

The poem has its flaws, but the awe it expresses in God's amazing grace is the awe that we all should express. Julie's conversion wasn't a glitch in grace. It was as much an afterthought as the creation of the sextillion-plus stars. The way that she came to Christ is the way that everyone comes to Christ: "God, being rich in mercy, because of the great love with which he loved us, even when we were dead in our trespasses, made us alive together with Christ . . . . For by grace you have been saved through faith. And *this is not your own doing; it is the gift of God*" (Eph. 2:4–5, 8).

The Effects of Faith

The nature of authentic Christian faith is threefold. We have looked at the object (Jesus) and the author (God). We come now to the final aspect—the Spirit-empowered effects of faith.

You may know of the popular Campus Crusade drawing of the train, with *fact* as the engine pulling along *faith* and *feelings*. That picture seeks to illustrate that just as a train will run without the caboose, we should not depend on our feelings or emotions to determine the truth of God's promises. Our faith—with or without feelings attached—should attach through faith to the facts. Today, many Christians have *obedience* as the caboose (i.e., that one can still be a Christian and have obedience attached or not attached to faith). John disagrees. He teaches that the living bond with God creates a life of lawfulness and love. This is why he writes in 1 John 5:1–2 of the necessity of Christian love and obedience:

> Everyone who loves the Father loves whoever has been born of him. By this we know that we love the children of God, when we love God and obey his commandments.

Christianity today is a thousand miles wide and an inch deep because we have pictured the effects of faith as an unnecessary caboose. Love and obedience don't drive the train. They are dependent on the engine of the source and object of faith. Still, they are not optional extras. So if we say that we "love God," but we never lift a finger to help others, especially those in need within the church ("whoever has been born of him," 1 John 5:1), our faith is a farce. If we say that we "love God," but our sexual ethics are no different from the world's, our creed is not credible. If we say that we "love God," but we are greedy, not generous, our trust is untrue. I can go on, but you get the point. Lawlessness is unloving.[9] The gospel has vertical and horizontal dimensions. And showing our faith through love and obedience is the natural, yet supernatural, effect of authentic Christian faith.

We might agree that love and obedience are essential effects of authentic Christian faith. But theological acknowledgment of a truth is different from living out that truth. How do we live a life of love and obedience? In 1 John 5:3, John provides some motivation: "For this is the love of God, that we keep his commandments. And his commandments are not burdensome." Unfortunately, we do not often take this verse as an encouragement. Instead, we object. We advocate a divorce from love and keeping Christ's commandments. For example, a number of years ago a group of theologians gathered together to promote a "new morality," one freed from traditional

9. "If God means little to you, people will become worthless to you too, and love even for them will die out." Adolf Schlatter, quoted in Yarbrough, *1–3 John*, 273. "Love is not *only* obedience to the commandments, of course, but John's point is that it is no less." Ibid., 274.

rules and regulations. When someone asked that there be some guidelines, they agreed on one guiding principle: "Anything that flowed from love was permissible. Anything was allowed so long as it did not hurt anyone." This did not sit well with one of the more conservative theologians. He reacted by refraining from participating in the discussion. His silence stood out. Finally, someone asked him, "Don't you agree that the only limiting factor in any ethical decision is love?" He replied by quoting Jesus, "If you love me, you will keep *my commandments*" (John 14:15).[10]

Sadly, what was then called the *new morality* is now simply called *morality.* But John reminds us, just as Jesus did, that *morality* has its definition in the commandments of Jesus Christ. Moreover, authentic discipleship defines itself not on the basis of a confident affirmation, "I know Jesus," but on a humble submission to the revealed will of God. We cannot say that we love God and others if we break God's rules.[11] "Love divorced from obedience to the commands of God is not love."[12]

A second objection to 1 John 5:3 is that we might believe that Christ's commandments *are* burdensome. This objection should also be overruled. Scripture teaches that we cannot perfectly keep the law, and thus that we cannot use our obedience as the means of obtaining right standing before God. I agree with the answer to question 82 of the Westminster Shorter Catechism:

> *Question*: Is any man able perfectly to keep the commandments of God?
>
> *Answer*: No mere man since the fall is able in this life perfectly to keep the commandments of God, but doth daily break them in thought, word, and deed.

That aspect of the commandments, however, is not what John is addressing. The idea here is not that Christians keep the commands perfectly, but rather that believers keep them *characteristically.*[13] This is the glory of living under the new covenant. The new birth of the new covenant gives us a new desire

10. James Montgomery Boice, *The Epistles of John: An Expositional Commentary* (Grand Rapids: Baker, 1979), 48.

11. Cf. John 14:15, 21, 23–24, 31; 15:10.

12. Boice, *The Epistles of John*, 126.

13. Jackman, *The Message of John's Letters*, 141.

to obey the new commandment. As James Montgomery Boice said, "The life of God within makes obedience to the commands possible, and the love the Christian has for God and for other Christians makes this obedience desirable."[14] Slavery to sin is hollow (makes us feel empty inside), yet heavy (weighs down our consciences). We have all been enslaved to sin. How fun-filled and free is that feeling? But the yoke of keeping Christ's commands is gentle on the back, restful on the soul, and absolutely emancipating.

John turns to that theology in 1 John 5:4–5. God's commandments are not burdensome, "for [or because] everyone who has been born of God overcomes the world" (v. 4). Verses 4–5 use three forms of a Greek word that many of us are familiar with, the noun of which is transliterated *nikē*. The Nike shoe company is named after the Greek goddess of victory, Athena Nike. My translation will give you a sense of Greek *victory*-wordplay: "Because everyone who has been born of God gets the victory [*nika*] over the world; and this is the victory [*nikē*], the one having victory [*nikēsasa*] over the world, our faith. Who is the one having victory [*nikōn*] over the world except the one believing that Jesus is the Son of God?" The logic looks like this:

> Major premise: (Because) we have been born of God.
>
> Minor premise: We have faith in Jesus as the Son of God.
>
> Conclusion: That God-given faith in God's Son makes us victorious over God's enemies—the loveless world, its dictator the devil, and its deceivers the antichrists.

This is John's version of Philippians 4:13, "I can do all things through him who strengthens me."[15] Through faith we have the victory! "Christians don't

14. Boice, *The Epistles of John*, 127. Yarbrough also summarizes the biblical data and theology well: "In the OT itself Moses insists, 'Now what I am commanding you today is not too difficult for you or beyond your reach' (Deut. 30:11 NIV). Jesus taught that heavy-laden people should come to him, 'For my yoke is easy and my burden light' (Matt. 11:30 NIV). Moses and Jesus agree that from one viewpoint, the closer one grows to God, the more delightful his moral and ethical guidelines become (cf. Ps. 119)." *1–3 John*, 274.

15. It is John's rendition of the exhortation to follow the heroes of Hebrews 11, and Jesus' call to the churches in John's Revelation: "'The one who overcomes' is repeatedly extolled in John's letters to the seven Asia Minor churches (Rev. 2:7, 11, 17, 26; 3:5, 12, 21; cf. 12:11; 15:2; 21:7)." Yarbrough, *1-3 John*, 275–76.

fight *for* victory; we fight *from* victory. Christ has already won the victory for us on Calvary."[16] "The devil, the flesh, and everything that is evil" has been crushed by Christ.[17] All who war against God's Word and ways have been disarmed. God has given us "victory through our Lord Jesus Christ" (1 Cor. 15:57). Yes, "we win an overwhelming victory through him who has proved his love for us" (Rom. 8:37 Phillips).

Authentic faith has Jesus as the object, God as the source, and love and obedience as the effects. In Christ and through love and obedience to God, we have the *nikē*.

The Knowledge of Faith

Christian faith has Christ as its object, God as its author, and Spirit-empowered love and obedience as its effects. From the theme of the nature of faith (1 John 5:1–5), we turn our attention to the knowledge of faith (vv. 6–12).

In October 2013, I traveled to Nagoya, Japan, to teach at Christ Bible Seminary and preach at All Nations Fellowship. Before I preached, Nozomu shared his testimony. In it, he recalled the time a pastor asked him, "Are you saved?" That question brought back memories. Having been raised as a Roman Catholic, I remember how strange that question was when it was first posed. I was not sure whether it was the question itself or, more likely, the questioner that I thought was presumptuous. Today if I am asked that question, I sometimes answer, "Yes, I was saved two thousand years ago when Jesus died on the cross," or, with more theological sophistication, "Yes, I was saved, I am saved, and I will be saved." Such answers always confuse the questioner.

But I do not want to confuse you; and I want, without presumption, to ask that same straightforward inquiry: "Are you saved?" Or, with a Johannine touch: "Do you know that you have eternal life?" John takes that question quite seriously. In fact, he wrote this epistle because he wanted Christians

16. David L. Allen, *1–3 John: Fellowship in God's Family*, Preaching the Word (Wheaton, IL: Crossway, 2013), 220–21. Or, more broadly, as Rudolf Schnackenburg said, "the victory that Christ won once for all in salvation history." *The Johannine Epistles: Introduction and Commentary*, trans. R. Fuller and I. Fuller (New York: Crossroad, 1992), 276.

17. That is how Martin Luther defined "the world." See "Lectures on the First Epistle of St. John," in *The Catholic Epistles*, vol. 30 of *Luther's Works*, trans. and ed. Jaroslav Pelikan and W. A. Hansen (St. Louis: Concordia, 1972), 313.

to know the answer to it. One way in which we can know that we have received the gift of salvation is to accept through faith the testimony of God concerning Jesus. *Martyria* (*testimony*) and *martyreō* (*testify*) are the key words here, repeated ten times in 1 John 5:6–12 in reference to God's testimony. Verses 6–8 tell of his testimony:

> This is he who came by water and blood—Jesus Christ; not by the water only but by the water and the blood. And the Spirit is the one who testifies, because the Spirit is the truth. For there are three that testify: the Spirit and the water and the blood; and these three agree.[18]

These verses are challenging to comprehend. What is clear is that the Holy Spirit has testified concerning Jesus, and that his testimony is trustworthy. What is confusing is what "the water and the blood" signify. Interpretive solutions abound. Some take a sacramental view, understanding the water and blood as foreshadowing the sacraments: the water of baptism and the blood (i.e., red wine) of the Eucharist.[19] Martin Luther understood the two elements as baptism alone, but a baptism "which is colored with the blood" (i.e., in view of Christ's death).[20] Others, such as John Calvin, take the water and blood to symbolize Christ's fulfillment of the ancient rites of the law—the water representing ritual cleansing and the blood signifying animal sacrifices.[21] Both these views are unlikely because they do not fit the context. Unlike the end of John's Gospel, the end of his first epistle holds no motif of promise/fulfillment; and unlike other places in the New Testament,

18. The KJV renders 1 John 5:7b–8a this way: "in heaven, the Father, the Word, and the Holy Ghost; and these three are one. And there are three that bear witness in earth." There is overwhelming evidence that this material was not in the original text of 1 John. As Yarbrough summarizes, "They contain great truth, but they are not original. Only a single Greek text (fourteenth-century cursive 629) dating from before ca. 1500 contains them in the original scribal hand." *1–3 John*, 293.

19. See Brooke Foss Westcott, *The Epistles of St. John: The Greek Text with Notes and Essays* (Cambridge and London: Macmillan, 1892), 182.

20. Luther, "Lectures on the First Epistle of St. John," 314.

21. Calvin comments: "I have no doubt this alludes to the ancient rites of the law. Moreover, the comparison is intended not only to teach us that the law of Moses was abolished by the coming of Christ, but so we will seek in him the fulfillment of those things that the ceremonies formerly typified." "1 John," in John Calvin and Matthew Henry, *1, 2, 3 John*, Crossway Classic Commentaries (Wheaton, IL: Crossway, 1998), 92.

1 John makes no direct reference to baptism or the Lord's Supper, and it never explores sacramental theology.

Three interpretations take into view the context of the letter and its theological themes. The first view advocates that the water and blood have to do with Jesus' birth, saying that, like any other human birth, Jesus had real water and blood flowing from his mother upon delivery. This slightly grotesque view certainly fits with John's emphasis on the incarnation, but it fails to make sense of the emphasis he lays on the blood—"not by the water *only* but by the water and the blood." The second view comes from Augustine, who teaches that the blood and water speak of the blood and water that came from Jesus' pierced side (John 19:34). Jesus' death (and a scarred resurrected body!—cf. 20:20, 25–27) proved that he was truly human. It is mere speculation that John had this piercing in mind. Further, it makes little sense how this human affirmation in any way serves as a divine witness to Jesus' divinity. The third view, which is the majority opinion and my opinion, is that the blood and water symbolize two events in Jesus' incarnational ministry that summarize the whole of his ministry. The water is representative of his baptism in the Jordan, where the Spirit descended on him as a dove, and the Father testified, "This is my beloved Son" (Matt. 3:16–17). The blood represents the crucifixion,[22] at which, according to John's Gospel, Jesus obtained all power and authority through his glorification at Golgotha.[23] So like the Gospel of Mark—bookended with Jesus' baptism and crucifixion (Mark 1, 15)—the baptism ("the water") and the cross ("the blood") embody the story of Jesus' life.

With this view in mind, some scholars believe that John is intentionally attacking an early Christian heresy—that of Cerinthus—that taught that Jesus became the divine Son of God at his baptism (not before), and that then the divine Son left the body before the crucifixion. Therefore, here, by stressing that it was the same divine Jesus who was baptized in the flesh and died in the flesh (both "the water" and "the blood"), John is combatting that heresy. To John, Jesus was fully and thoroughly the eternal Son

22. Yarbrough lists a number of New Testament verses that use "blood" as symbolic of the cross (Matt. 26:28; Acts 20:28; Rom. 3:25; Eph. 1:7; Col. 1:20; Heb. 9:12; 13:12), including 1 John 1:7; Rev. 1:5; 5:9; 7:14; 12:11 from John's corpus. *1–3 John*, 282.

23. Gary M. Burge, *Letters of John*, NIV Application Commentary (Grand Rapids: Zondervan, 1996), 202.

of God at his baptism, and he was fully and thoroughly the eternal Son of God at his death.

Now, to place an emphatic exclamation point on that point, John next calls the Holy Spirit to the witness stand! In the middle of 1 John 5:6–7, we read: "And the Spirit is the one who testifies, because the Spirit is the truth. For there are three that testify: the Spirit and the water and the blood; and these three agree." John was possibly an eyewitness to Jesus' baptism and certainly his death, and yet he calls on the Spirit to take the stand. This is a safe move, since the Holy Spirit is God and, as Hebrews 6:18 says, "It is impossible for God to lie." Most legal systems require that witnesses take an oath (e.g., "Do you swear to tell the truth, the whole truth, and nothing but the truth, so help you God?"). There is no need for God the Spirit to swear by himself. We should know and trust that he will tell the truth, the whole truth, and nothing but the truth. The Spirit collaborates with the testimony of "the water and the blood" (1 John 5:8). "These three agree" (v. 8);[24] that is, (1) the baptism and (2) the death of the earthly Jesus agree with (3) the Holy Spirit of heaven. It is a double—Jesus and the Spirit—divine testimony!

In 1 John 5:9–12, the Father ("God," "he," "his," and "him" in the text) adds his affirmation. It is a triple Trinitarian testimony! "If we receive the testimony of men, the testimony of God is greater, for this is the testimony of God that he has borne concerning his Son" (v. 9). The Creator's witness causes the testimonies of his creatures to pale in comparison. Philosophically speaking, it is the argument *a minori ad maius* ("from smaller to bigger"). If we usually believe human testimony—two or more people who testify in a court of law (ecclesial, Matt. 18:16, or otherwise, Deut. 17:6; 19:15)—how much more should we trust a threefold divine testimony. "Whoever believes in the Son of God has the testimony in himself" (1 John 5:10a). There is an internal testimony that coincides with this external testimony. The reason that we are to accept and internalize God's true testimony about his Son is given next: "Whoever does not believe God has made him a liar, because he has not believed in the testimony that God has borne concerning his Son. And this is the testimony, that God gave us eternal life, and this

24. "According to the Greek text, the three witnesses 'are one.' In German one would say: 'And these three belong together' (*und die drey dinge gehören zu sammen*). The water and the blood—and much less the Spirit—are not actually one thing, but they 'are one,' they belong together (*sie gehören zusammen*)." Luther, "Lectures on the First Epistle of St. John," 316.

life is in his Son" (vv. 10b–11). Here John targets the apostate antichrists. Through their deception, denial, and departure, they are in the process of an ever-growing unbelief ("whoever does not believe" is present tense). They do not believe "God's witness concerning the person (came in the flesh) and work (came by water and blood) of the historical Jesus."[25] The result of their rejection deserves the strongest possible rebuke: they have made God a liar! Their so-called enlightened knowledge of God is in fact dark, deadly, and damning. For that reason, John follows with a clear line of demarcation: "Whoever has the Son has life; whoever does not have the Son of God does not have life" (v. 12). It is because the Father and the Spirit have taken the stand as the ultimate witness to Jesus that the stakes are so high. That is why the choice between belief and denial has such dramatically different consequences. Only in Jesus Christ, who is "eternal life" (5:20), are we granted "eternal life" (5:13). Believe in him! Or, put more relationally and ontologically—"have the Son of God." Trust the testimony.

The Choice and the Consequences

Fifteen years ago, I traveled with a small group of American missionaries to Malawi and Zambia. One day the group visited a remote village. A few of us went off exploring. We found a dry riverbed on which we found hundreds of fresh hippo and crocodile tracks. Later, someone told us to watch out for scorpions in the huts. We paid no attention to the animal dangers around us. It took a spitting cobra to get our attention. This snake is small, but it can spit venom up to twenty feet. It was spitting twenty-two feet away from us. Thankfully, a local man saved the day. He took his machete and cut off the creature's head.

Sometimes we approach the clear but controversial claims of the Bible as I did Africa's wild terrain. We think we are invincible or immutable. Or we think the warnings are not real or are exaggerated. The end of our text shares one quality with the spitting cobra: it is worthy of cautious respect. To reject God's witness is "a serious evil, and to oppose it is a futile project."[26] If there was ever a time in world history that God appeared as a witness, spoke

25. Colin G. Kruse, *The Letters of John*, Pillar New Testament Commentary (Grand Rapids: Eerdmans, 2000), 182.

26. Schnackenburg, *The Johannine Epistles*, 239.

clearly, and gave proof of his will, it was in the incarnation.[27] The water. The blood. The Spirit. To dismiss such divine disclosure is deadly dangerous. To be apathetically indifferent, to willfully ignore, or to maliciously attack is the height of folly.[28] Don't be a fool!

Jesus is a theological exclusivist—he believes he is the only way to God (John 5:39–40; 6:40; 14:6). Here and elsewhere (John 3:36), John joins Jesus in his exclusivity. Based on the Trinity's testimony, he believes that Jesus is the only way of salvation. Thus, he states quite emphatically that if you do not accept God's testimony about Jesus, then not only do you make him out to be "a liar" (1 John 5:10), but you also do "not have life" (v. 12)—both now and forevermore. Right thinking about Jesus is a matter of life and death. Our faith in faith, or our faith in our homemade personal Jesus, will not save us from our sin and the wrath to come. Only faith in the water-and-blood Jesus will. We can "grumble that God didn't provide a smorgasbord of salvation options,"[29] we can construct "a god figure toward whom all religions are alleged to be striving by their various means—and who regard all religious beliefs as equally valid,"[30] or we can humble ourselves before the true and living God, and in gratitude accept the one sure way of salvation. We can get a life! We can believe and receive God's gift. We can *know* that we are saved.

27. "One time in the course of world history God appears as witness, speaks clearly, and gives proof and secure direction. That took place at the sending of the Christ." Schlatter, in Yarbrough, *1–3 John*, 286.

28. "Opposite to dynamic trust (5:10a) lie any number of contrasting postures (summarized in 5:10b), as some Johannine examples may illustrate: willful ignorance (John 4:22), apathy (12:37), cowardly or disenchanted withdrawal (6:66), hypocritical lip service (8:31, 48), malicious misappropriation (12:6), secret contempt (7:28; 8:19), open hostility (11:57; 15:21), misplaced skepticism (20:25)." Yarbrough, *1–3 John*, 288. As Calvin puts it: "Though people may in other parts of their lives be like angels, their sanctity is diabolical as long as they reject Christ." "1 John," 96.

29. Bruce B. Barton et al., *1, 2 & 3 John*, Application Bible Commentary (Wheaton, IL: Tyndale, 1998), 114.

30. Yarbrough, *1–3 John*, 291.

13

Festival of Faith

1 John 5:13–21

I write these things to you who believe in the name of the Son of God that you may know that you have eternal life. (1 John 5:13)

It is a strange day in which we live when doubt is deemed a virtue, skepticism hallowed as humility, and absolute truth viewed as absolutely false. Reflective of this trend, a chaplain at a nearby college held what he called "A Festival of Doubt,"[1] during which various campus activities underscored the importance of religious uncertainty.

The spirit of our age is so different from the Spirit of God: in 1 John—from the beginning of chapter 1 through the end of chapter 5—the chaplain in Ephesus holds a "Festival of Faith." It is a celebration that crescendoes and concludes with certainty: "I write these things to you who believe in the name of the Son of God that you may know that you have eternal life" (1 John 5:13). John's call to confidence escalates in verses 14–21, where the word *oidamen* ("we know") is repeated five times (5:15 [2×], 18, 19, and 20) and the phrase "that *you* may know" is used in verse 13 and "that *we* may know" in verse 20. That is seven *knows* in nine verses! But what are we to

1. For this illustration, see Gary M. Burge, *Letters of John*, NIV Application Commentary (Grand Rapids: Zondervan, 1996), 222.

know? Here John teaches that we are to know that (1) God hears our prayers, (2) Jesus protects us from sin and the evil one, and (3) Jesus is the true God and in him we have eternal life.

We Know That God Hears Our Prayers

In 1 John 5:14–17, John begins his final lecture at his "Festival of Faith" by talking about prayer—which is "the most direct expression of faith."[2] He reminds those who have been "born of God" that God hears their prayers. He begins:

> And this is the confidence that we have toward him, that if we ask anything according to his will he hears us. And if we know that he hears us in whatever we ask, we know that we have the requests that we have asked of him. (1 John 5:14–15)

First, note that *God* is the recipient of our prayers. I illuminate the obvious because the simple fact that prayer is to be directed "toward him" (1 John 5:14) has not always been, and still is not, so obvious to many professing Christians. It is a common and encouraged practice in both the Roman Catholic and the Eastern Orthodox churches to pray to and/or through saints and angels. As a former Roman Catholic, I had such prayer as a part of my everyday life. I even set up a Marian shrine in my basement, where I lit three candles—for God, Jesus, and Mary. It wasn't until I read the New Testament, which doesn't offer a hint of praying to anyone but God, that the Holy Spirit changed my prayer life. The last time I prayed, "Holy Mary, Mother of God, pray for us sinners, now and at the hour of our death," was the day before I was converted. Our praises and petitions should be offered to God. It is acceptable for us Protestants to *protest* if someone tells us otherwise. Moreover, as Reformed evangelicals, we should rejoice in this gospel reformation! "It is no small claim to affirm confident access into the very presence of the invisible, eternal, and almighty God."[3] We have immediate and interminable access to the Creator of the heavens and the earth. Imagine that. Celebrate that. Act on that. Pray to him.

2. Adolf Schlatter, quoted in Robert W. Yarbrough, *1–3 John*, Baker Exegetical Commentary on the New Testament (Grand Rapids: Baker, 2008), 298.

3. Yarbrough, *1–3 John*, 299.

Second, note that prayer to God is offered with confidence: "And this is the confidence that we have toward him" (1 John 5:14). If we can stand with confidence before God in view of the final judgment, as taught in 1 John 2:28 and 4:17, then surely we can come with confidence before God in prayer. Yet such confidence does not mean presumption. To view God as a pushover father, indentured servant, or butler who is at the beck and call of our every wicked whim is evil. Neither should we cower in the corner, thinking that our harsh parent gives us only what we deserve. Both extremes must be avoided. Rather, in agreement with the author of Hebrews, 1 John teaches that we can "draw near to the throne of grace" with confidence that "we may receive mercy and find grace to help in time of need" (Heb. 4:16).

This real confidence, however, does not allow us "an unbridled liberty" to ask for whatever comes into our heads.[4] Third, note that we can have confidence that God will hear our prayers "*if* we ask anything according to his will" (1 John 5:14). We can ask absolutely "anything" of God that is "according to his will." Thus, foolish and sinful requests fly like arrows against a brick wall. Prayers for a passing grade on a plagiarized essay, vengeance on a stingy boss, or a new spouse who will better understand our love language are three of three hundred thousand requests that fall dead to the ground. Just as prayer is hindered by disbelief (we are to ask in the name of Jesus; see John 14:13–14), disobedience (1 John 3:22), and wrong motives (James 4:3), so prayers that are contrary to God's will never reach our Father in heaven. But conversely, prayers that accord with his will do reach him.

Prayer That God Will Answer

The person and petitions of Christ provide the perfect example of praying according to God's will. In John's Gospel, we learn that Jesus' will was always one with the Father's (John 4:34; cf. 6:38–40), and that he always spoke what the Father wished him to say (3:34; 8:55; 14:10; 17:8). In Matthew's Gospel, as Jesus taught his disciples to pray—"Our Father in heaven, . . . *your will be done*" (Matt. 6:9–10)—so he also embodied that last petition at Gethsemane when he "fell on his face and prayed, . . . 'My Father, if it be possible, let this cup pass from me; nevertheless, not as I will, but *as you will*' " (26:39).

4. John Calvin, "1 John," in John Calvin and Matthew Henry, *1, 2, 3 John*, Crossway Classic Commentaries (Wheaton, IL: Crossway, 1998), 98.

Jesus teaches and models that proper prayer is not that we change God's mind to accept our will but rather that God changes our minds to accept his.[5] "Prayer is the means that God uses to give his people what he wants."[6]

One certain way to pray in line with God's will is through meditation on God's revealed will—the Bible. When I was in college, God used an answer to a simple question to change my comprehension and practice of prayer. A visiting pastor answered the question "How do you pray?" in this way: "Each morning, I read my Bible. When I come to an area addressed in a passage in which I feel I need prayer, I simply stop reading and pray there and then." How fully in line with God's will! Read the Word. Pray the Word.

I have brought this personal practice to my church's congregational prayer. At New Covenant Church, we pray through the prayers of the Bible. We pray through the Lord's Prayer, Paul's prayers, and the Psalms, as well as any other part of the Scripture that is applicable to the needs of the body or relevant to the sermon series. For example, from our study of 1 John we might pray, "Lord, help us to have assurance of our salvation," and "Lord, help us to love you and others by keeping your commandments," and "Lord, forgive these sins that we now confess to you." Those are prayers that God delights to hear because they are prayers prayed according to his revealed will.

This practice does not mean that our prayers are limited to biblical revelation. You can pray for anything that you need. Paul prayed that his thorn in the flesh would be removed (2 Cor. 12:7–9). God said "no." Solomon asked for wisdom (1 Kings 3:5–12). God said "yes." I once prayed to be an All-American basketball player. God said "no." I prayed for a best friend. God said "yes." I prayed for pain-free molars. God said "wait for heaven." But whether the answer is yes, no, wait, maybe, or not this time, we should "ask in faith" (James 1:6), believing that we will always receive what is best for God's kingdom and its heirs.

Emily and I are watching the television series *The West Wing*, a drama about the President of the United States, his staff, and the everyday decisions and operations of the White House. While we are not God's advisers ("Who has been his counselor?," Rom. 11:34), we do have access to God; and just as the president's advisers have his ear, so we have God's. He listens to everything we

5. James Montgomery Boice, *The Epistles of John: An Expositional Commentary* (Grand Rapids: Baker, 1979), 139.

6. Yarbrough, *1–3 John*, 299.

say to him. And like the president, he may or may not do what we ask or suggest. The analogy breaks down, of course, in at least one major way: the president may not have thought through all the options until they are presented to him, while God knows all that will be asked even before we ask him (Matt. 6:8).

While our prayers do not determine God's decisions, they do develop our relationship. Even unanswered prayer can deepen the bond. As Robert Yarbrough states and illustrates:

> John may understand prayer not primarily as *communicating* in order to acquire petitions or to somehow force God's hand but as *communing* with God. . . . Moses's high esteem in God's sight lay in his "face-to-face" interchange with God, not his ability to direct God's ways with his prayers (Exod. 33:11; cf. Num. 12:8; Deut. 34:10). Jesus's Gethsemane request for the cup to be removed was not granted, but far from diminishing his sense of the Father's closeness, it intensified it (as implied, e.g., by John 17).[7]

To have God's listening ear and to hear "yes" *or "no"* is one of the many ways that God has designed to draw us closer to him. Bernard of Clairvaux said it masterfully: "Brothers, do not despise our prayer; for when it has gone forth from your mouths, it has been heard in heaven. And be sure either that what you have asked for will be granted us or that what has been asked for has not been beneficial."[8] God loves us, and thus he always lovingly answers our prayers.

In 1 John 5:16–17, John gives his own example of a prayer—perhaps one very different from what is expected—that God loves to lovingly answer "yes." He writes:

> If anyone sees his brother committing a sin not leading to death, he shall ask, and God will give him life—to those who commit sins that do not lead to death. There is sin that leads to death; I do not say that one should pray for that. All wrongdoing is sin, but there is sin that does not lead to death.

Setting aside the question of "sin that leads to death" (1 John 5:16), let us notice that this phrase is the kind of prayer that God will answer. It is a

7. See ibid., 302.

8. Bernard, quoted in Martin Luther, "Lectures on the First Epistle of St. John," in *The Catholic Epistles*, vol. 30 of *Luther's Works*, trans. and ed. Jaroslav Pelikan and W. A. Hansen (St. Louis: Concordia, 1972), 323.

prayer for a fellow Christian who has fallen into sin (literally, "sinning a sin," *hamartanonta hamartian*).

A friend of mine has an intriguing object hanging on his family-room wall. It is an oblong claylike mold that has various letters mixed in it. Noticeably in the middle of it are the letters *T*, *H*, *E*, *R*, and *S*. At first glance, as I made out the word *hers*, I thought it had something to do with a woman or girl. But I couldn't figure out what the *T* was doing. It took my host to point out what should have been the most obvious letter—the letter *O*, which was used as the border of the whole piece. *Others* is what the artwork said.

In our prayer lives, we can be so preoccupied with ourselves and our own concerns that we fail to see and do the obvious: pray for others, as John is encouraging us to do here. This should come as no surprise to us as we finish 1 John. This epistle so often speaks of others. Loving others makes John's top three themes. So, too, does the theme of holy living. Therefore, naturally, to pray for the person struggling with sin fits. God commands holiness. God commands that we love our brothers. So if a brother is being unholy, we should pray for him.

John Calvin said: "Surely it is an iron hardness not to feel pity when we see souls, redeemed by Christ's blood, going to ruin."[9] Ah, but iron hardness is sometimes in our hearts. Who of us has not seen some Christian entangled in iniquity and turned a blind eye, given the evil eye, pointed the finger, wagged our heads in disgust, gossiped, or felt superior?[10] We need soft hearts and tamed tongues so that we might petition God for those who are too heavy laden to lift their own heads to heaven. Can you think of someone like this—a stumbling sibling in the household of God? Most of us can. Pray for that person. Pray even now. Pray that God would save the person "by snatching [him or her] out of the fire" (Jude 23). Pray that God would forgive the person's trespasses (Matt. 6:12). Pray that God would grant the person "life" (1 John 5:16)—new life, renewed life, eternal life.

A Prayer That God Won't Answer

Prayer for a struggling spiritual sibling is a petition acceptable in God's sight. It is a prayer that he is pleased to hear. But this wideness of

9. Calvin, quoted in Yarbrough, *1–3 John*, 307.
10. See Yarbrough, *1–3 John*, 307.

God's mercy, we are told, has its limits. John makes it clear that there are two categories of sin: a sin "not unto death" (*mē pros thanaton*) and sin "unto death" (*pros thanaton*). We should pray for the person who committed the former but not the latter.

These two categories can be called *venial* ("forgivable") and *mortal* ("unforgivable" because such sins lead to the loss of eternal life), as long as we change the traditional definition. In traditional Catholic theology—following Tertullian, Aquinas, and other theologians—deliberate sins against the self (such as suicide), others (such as adultery), and God (such as blasphemy) are classified as mortal sins. From the context of 1 John, we know that such sins are not what John has in mind, for those specific sins are not mentioned in his epistle. Moreover, from the context of the whole of Scripture, we know that even one violation of God's law makes us guilty of violating all of it (James 2:10). Further, we know that every "wrongdoing"—even an everyday unintentional fault (what Catholics call a *venial* sin)[11]—is so detestable in God's sight that it deserves death, as Romans 6:23 attests: "The wages of sin is death."

So what is this "sin to which no hope of forgiveness is left"?[12] It could be the "resolute rejection of the true doctrine about Christ, chronic disobedience to God's commandments, persistent lack of love for fellow believers" that John warns about throughout the letter.[13] In other words, it is the sin of deliberately denying the need for the life-transforming gospel offered in Jesus Christ. It is the major "sin" of your everyday unbeliever. Yet John's target seems smaller than that. Just as Jesus' warning about the unforgivable "blasphemy against the [Holy] Spirit" (Matt. 12:31–32) targeted the false teachers of his day, so John targets the secessionists of his ecclesial community.[14] Those sinning the sin of death are the epistle's apostate antichrists.

If you synthesize the characteristics of John's false teacher, the following picture emerges. A man professed to believe all that the apostles taught about Jesus. Then he denied the faith and left the fellowship. But he did not stop there. Next, he became an exponent of error, sharing his

11. See *Catechism of the Catholic Church* (New York: Doubleday, 1994), 1458.

12. Calvin, "1 John," 101.

13. *ESV Study Bible* (Wheaton, IL: Crossway, 2008), 2437.

14. Raymond E. Brown, *The Epistles of John*, Anchor Bible (Garden City, NY: Doubleday, 1982), 617–18.

testimony of disbelief, hoping to lead others astray. That sin is diabolically dark and deadly. Someone who has known the light but now hates and makes an earnest effort to extinguish the light should not be prayed for.[15] Put simply, we should not pray for long-standing, hard-hearted Christological heretics.

With that said, we ought not to be rash in our judgment as to who fits into this category, nor are we to be less merciful than God himself. Would you have prayed for Judas but not Peter? Just as we cannot always know what prayers will be efficacious or not, so we cannot always know who has fallen from the faith or who has fallen in his faith. Do not pray against God's will, but also do not always assume the worst of people. When in doubt, pray. Who would have thought that the centurion who crucified Christ would confess him as the Son of God? Who would have thought that Saul the persecutor would become Paul the poster boy for forgiveness?[16]

Yet with that charitable attitude applied to this tough text, let us not do away with its straightforward teaching. It is true, as is said here and in places such as Hebrews 6:4–6, that one can "fall away" in such a way that it is impossible to restore that person again to repentance. Like Dr. Faustus in Christopher Marlowe's tragedy of that title, some do experience an irreversibility of fate and in essence cry out, as Faustus did in that play, "My heart's so hardened I cannot repent."[17] As it was with Pharaoh (Ex. 9:12), God does harden hard hearts; he does give people over to their own depravity (Rom. 1:24). And in this manner, his present judgment foreshadows the final judgment to come.

We Know That Christ Protects

This grave reality should lead us to "work out [our] own salvation with fear and trembling" (Phil. 2:12). There is great value in that, for a healthy fear of the fragility of our faith can bring us to the place where God wants us, and where John takes us next in 1 John 5:18–19. In these verses, we learn that we must find refuge from our fear in our love-casts-out-fear Savior.

15. Cf. Douglas Sean O'Donnell, *Matthew: All Authority in Heaven and on Earth*, Preaching the Word (Wheaton, IL: Crossway, 2013), 333–34.

16. Perhaps this was because they acted in ignorance (Acts 3:17; 1 Tim. 1:13; cf. Luke 23:43; 1 Cor. 2:8).

17. Marlowe, quoted in David Jackman, *The Message of John's Letters*, The Bible Speaks Today (Downers Grove, IL: InterVarsity Press, 1988), 165.

> We know that everyone who has been born of God does not keep on sinning, but he who was born of God protects him, and the evil one does not touch him.
>
> We know that we are from God, and the whole world lies in the power of the evil one.

Recently I was asked to contribute two chapters to a book about sermon preparation. In my first contribution, "Spirit-filled *Sitzfleisch*: The Prayerful Art of Sermonizing,"[18] I talk about the preacher's need for "sitting flesh"—*sitzen* ("to sit") and *fleisch* ("flesh")—that is, the ability to stay glued to a chair for hours in order to see what God's Word says. I add the adjective "Spirit-filled" before *sitzfleisch* to emphasize that the art of observation of the holy canon requires the illumination of the Holy Spirit. When I sat, stared, and "gave room" for the Spirit in the study, I wrote down three questions and answers regarding 1 John 5:18–19.

First, what does John mean by "everyone who has been born of God does not keep on sinning" (1 John 5:18)? By deduction, we can arrive at the answer. John knows that Christians will sin. He made that clear in 1:8–10, but also in the immediate context. In 5:16, Christians are commanded to pray for other Christians who have sinned. The sense of verse 18 must, then, be something like this: for Christians, sin is no longer the primary pattern of our lives (cf. 3:8–9); as Boice memorably wrote, "the new birth will result in new behavior."[19] Why? The reason is Jesus' protection. This leads us to the second question.

Second, who is "he who was born of God" in 1 John 5:18? I have already answered "Jesus," but let me explain why. At first I thought this reference could be to another Christian, the sense being that Christians do not continue in a pattern of sin because other Christians pray for each other's protection. I love that reading! It is a true statement. But for grammatical, theological, contextual, and canonical reasons, the protector here must be Jesus Christ, "the only begotten of the Father" (John 1:14 KJV), the Savior who *keeps* us, as John 17:2 and Revelation 3:10 state. It is Jesus, "who in his physical birth was 'born of God' in that he was sent from God the Father and was

18. Douglas Sean O'Donnell, "Spirit-filled *Sitzfleisch*: The Prayerful Art of Sermonizing," in *Unashamed Workmen: How Expositors Prepare and Preach*, ed. Rhett Dodson (Ross-shire, Scotland: Christian Focus, 2014).

19. Boice, *The Epistles of John*, 145.

conceived by the Holy Spirit (Luke 1:35) and in his resurrection from the dead was 'born of God' in that he was brought back to life (Col. 1:18)."[20] This name or title is "shorthand for the numerous ministries performed for believers by Jesus: coming to bring eternal life (1:2), cleansing from sin (1:7), interceding in the Father's presence (2:1), dying a propitiatory death (2:2), confirming knowledge (2:20), destroying the devil's works (3:8), [and] teaching believers the meaning of love (3:16)."[21]

Third, whom does Jesus protect us from? We are protected from "the evil one" (1 John 5:18) and his evil world (v. 19). In the Western world, Satan's existence is questioned and the notion that the world lies under the spell of some evil being is laughable. But whom are we to believe? I hold to the testimony of God. I take the water-blood-Spirit witness to be the most reliable witness to reality. As the devil-attentive Martin Luther said: "The world is a realm of wrongdoing, and the devil is lord over it."[22] We live in enemy territory, and we war against invisible enemies (see Eph. 6:12), and whether we are aware of it or not, Jesus has our back. And he has our front, as well as right and left sides! Like Simon Peter, Satan demands that he sift us like wheat, but Jesus persistently and prayerfully protects us (see Luke 22:31). We might fall, as Peter did, but we get up. We repent. We are forgiven. We return to the front line. Jesus assures believers that no one—not even the devil!—is "able to snatch them" out of his "hand" (John 10:29). He is our Good Shepherd. He is our Great Warrior. He is our Full Armor of God. Nothing can separate us from his protective love (Rom. 8:35–39).

We Know That Jesus Is the True God and That in Him We Have Eternal Life

So what do we know as Christians? We know that God hears our prayers. We know that Jesus protects us from sin and from the evil one. And finally, as attested in 1 John 5:20, we know that Jesus is the true God and that in him we have eternal life: "And we know that the Son of God has come and has

20. *ESV Study Bible*, 2437.

21. Yarbrough, *1–3 John*, 316.

22. Luther, "Lectures on the First Epistle of St. John," 326. On Luther's awareness of the devil, see Heiko A. Oberman, *Luther: Man between God and the Devil* (New Haven, CT: Yale University Press, 1989).

given us understanding, so that we may know him who is true; and we are in him who is true, in his Son Jesus Christ. He is the true God and eternal life."

We should grasp three points from this key verse. First, Jesus is the true God. Second, in him we have eternal life. Third, we come to this understanding as a gift from him. Since we explored that third point in the previous chapter, we will focus on the other two.

First, Jesus is the true God. Throughout John's writings, he promotes and defends the full divinity of Jesus,[23] and nowhere is this more plainly stated than at the end of 1 John 5:20. As I. Howard Marshall states: "It is fitting that at the climax of the Epistle, as at the beginning and climax of the Gospel of John (John 1:1; 20:28), full deity should be ascribed to Jesus."[24]

Second, Jesus, who is "the word of life" and "the life . . . made manifest" (1 John 1:1–2), bestows "eternal life" (1:2; 5:20). John pushes us toward the promise that is being fulfilled. It is helpful to highlight this point (notice the final sentence below) within the context of the epistle as a whole, as well as in light of the four Gospels:

> By all indications this is a Jesus conceived very much along the lines of the individual presented in the canonical Gospels. He was a human being (1 John 4:2) but also somehow deserving of the appellation "God" (5:20) despite God's indubitable transcendence (1:5; 4:12). By connection with him, people can receive the Holy Spirit (3:24). Jesus was preexistent, with the Father in the beginning (1:1–2). He lived a life worthy of emulation (2:6). He died as a sacrifice for sins (2:2; 4:10). He must have been raised, for he is the source of eternal life (5:11), and he is going to return (2:28). In the meantime he is at the Father's right hand in a mediatorial role (2:1). At the end of all things, Jesus will bring his followers to eternal life (5:11, 20), which is already inaugurated but has yet to be consummated in the current age.[25]

First John 5:20 reminds us of John's purpose statement in 5:13: "I write these things to you who believe in the name of the Son of God that you may know that you have eternal life." Both verses speak of Jesus' divine identity

23. See Burge, *Letters of John*, 219; cf. John 1:1, 18; 20:28; Rom. 9:5; Titus 2:13; 2 Peter 1:1.

24. I. Howard Marshall, *The Epistles of John*, New International Commentary on the New Testament (Grand Rapids: Eerdmans, 1978), 254n47. Cf. Rudolf Schnackenburg, *The Johannine Epistles: Introduction and Commentary*, trans. R. Fuller and I. Fuller (New York: Crossroad, 1992), 262.

25. Yarbrough, *1–3 John*, 16–17.

("the Son of God," v. 13; "the true God," v. 20), as well as our knowledge and assurance of eternal life in Christ ("that you may know that you have eternal life," v. 13; "that we may know him," namely, "the true God" who possesses and in whom we possess "eternal life," v. 20). John wants us to be assured of our faith! He desires to develop in us a deeper understanding and appreciation of our everlasting relationship with Jesus.

A Concluding Command

John could have stopped there. He could have ended with that eschatological yearning for eternal life. He could have put down his pen, sealed the letter, and sent it on its way. Or he could have added a line, as he did in 2 and 3 John, about having much more to write but hoping to soon see the letter's recipients face-to-face. Instead, he gives a concluding command. He will not let us "luxuriate in the bubble bath of Christian assurance."[26] First John concludes with this unconventional and somewhat abrupt ending: "Little children, keep yourselves from idols" (1 John 5:21). What has this apparently enigmatic imperative to avoid idolatry to do with anything that John has said thus far?

The ending fits the immediate context. If Jesus is the true God (1 John 5:20), then we Christians must keep ourselves from false gods or "idols" (v. 21). It fits the whole context of the epistle as well. "The letter ends as it began, with an admonition to worship the one true God alone. Everything else that John says is contained in this one golden rule."[27] It is a simple comprehensive summary of what John is combatting. The apostate antichrists were promoting an idolatrous image of Jesus—denying his coming in the flesh, his dying for our sins, and his teachings on love and obedience. As Marshall summarizes, "Having emphasized that Jesus is the true God, John warns against being misled into the worship of any other alleged manifestation or representation of God."[28] It is "an exhortation not to accept the false teaching of the secessionists."[29]

26. Jackman, *The Message of John's Letters*, 171.

27. Hilary of Arles, "Introductory Commentary on 1 John," in *James, 1–2 Peter, 1–3 John, Jude*, ed. Gerald Bray, Ancient Christian Commentary on Scripture, New Testament 11 (Downers Grove, IL: InterVarsity Press, 2000), 229.

28. Marshall, *The Epistles of John*, 255.

29. Colin G. Kruse, *The Letters of John*, Pillar New Testament Commentary (Grand Rapids: Eerdmans, 2000), 202; following Brown, *The Epistles of John*, 627–28.

It also fits the historical context. In the Greco-Roman world, Ephesus was a central city of pagan idolatry. It housed the famous Temple of Artemis, one of the seven wonders of the ancient world. When Paul preached Jesus as the true God and "that gods made with hands are not gods" (Acts 19:26), it caused "no little disturbance" with the idol-making silversmiths union (v. 23). The people sided with the silversmiths, rushed into the possibly twenty-five-thousand-seat theater, and chanted for two hours "Great is Artemis of the Ephesians!" (v. 34). Moreover, we know from John's letters to the churches in Asia Minor (Rev. 2–3) that Christians were tempted to compromise with their culture (yield to pagan practices of idolatry) in order to avoid persecution and possible martyrdom. John was writing to a church that lived and breathed in a culture of idolatry.

How the times have *not* changed! This ending fits our context as well. Our neighbors likely do not go to a temple to worship a mythological goddess or bow before a religious object made of wood, stone, or metal. But as the philosopher Friedrich Nietzsche said, "There are more idols in the world than there are realities."[30] If we understand idolatry as "trusting, obeying, revering, and following—that is, in effect, worshipping—anyone or anything other than God himself, and his Son Jesus Christ" (cf. Eph. 5:5; Col. 3:5),[31] there are as many idols in contemporary America as there were in classical antiquity. *Idols* can have an elastic interpretation, one that represents a reality that seeks to stretch around our souls. As Calvin put it, "Dry wood when coals are put under it will not burn as easily as idolatry lays hold on and engrosses our minds when it is given the chance. And who does not see that images are sparks or rather torches, that are sufficient to set the whole world on fire?"[32] The whole world lives in Idolville. So, "little children," if you want to cling to the kingdom of Christ, "keep yourselves from idols" (1 John 5:21).

The Greater Chicago Fire

When I was out of town, a former intern filled the pulpit. His sermon began by calling everyone in our congregation *snobs*. After the initial shock

30. Nietzsche, quoted in David L. Allen, *1–3 John: Fellowship in God's Family*, Preaching the Word (Wheaton, IL: Crossway, 2013), 250.

31. *ESV Study Bible*, 2437.

32. Calvin, "1 John," 105.

subsided, he carefully and cleverly explained himself. In that introduction I was labeled a *book snob* because if you gave me a book to read, I likely would not read it. This is not because I do not read but because I think I have better books to read than what others choose for me. When I returned to town, I quickly disproved this theory and read the very next book that a congregant handed me: Pastor Jim Cymbala's *Fresh Wind, Fresh Fire: What Happens When God's Spirit Invades the Heart of His People*. Here is a breath from that book:

> As a preacher myself, let me be blunt here. Preaching itself can easily become just a subtle form of entertainment. When I stand at the Judgment Seat of Christ, he is not going to ask me if I was a clever orator. He is not going to ask me how many books I wrote. He is only going to ask whether I continued in the line of men and women, starting back in the time of Adam's grandchildren, who lead others to call upon God.[33]

Powerful.

Another powerful part of that book is the story that Cymbala shares about D. L. Moody. "Moody was haunted all his life by an occasion when he felt he got too clever in presenting the gospel."[34] In the fall of 1871, the Chicago evangelist intended to devote six Sunday nights to preaching on the life of Christ. Twenty-two years afterward, he recalls:

> I had spent four Sunday nights on the subject [i.e., the life of Christ] and had followed him from the manger along through his life to his arrest and trial, and on the fifth Sunday night, October 8, I was preaching to the largest congregation I had ever had in Chicago, quite elated with my success. My text was "What shall I do then with Jesus which is called the Christ?" That night I made one of the biggest mistakes in my life. After preaching . . . with all power that God had given me, . . . I closed the sermon and said, "I wish you would take this text home with you and turn it over in your minds during the week, and next Sunday we will decide what we will do with Jesus of Nazareth."

Moody regrets that final sentence because he would never preach that final sermon. That Sunday night, fire bells sounded throughout the city as

33. Jim Cymbala, *Fresh Wind, Fresh Fire: What Happens When God's Spirit Invades the Heart of His People* (Grand Rapids: Zondervan, 1997), 59.

34. Ibid., 125.

the Great Chicago Fire blazed for twenty-seven straight hours, leaving the Windy City destroyed and hundreds dead. Moody learned his lesson, and declared, "I would rather have [my] right hand cut off than give an audience a week to decide what to do with Jesus."[35]

I am no D. L. Moody, and I need my right hand to finish writing this chapter. Like Moody, however, I am from Chicago, and I am just as serious about pressing the point of decision *now*! Reader, you have a decision to make. Will you worship Jesus as the true God, or will you keep playing with lifeless idols? I will warn you again with John's final imperative: keep away from idols! Those who put anything or anyone before God will be forever without God. And I will press you again with the positives. Don't you want to know that God will hear your prayers? Don't you want to experience the powerful protection of Jesus? Don't you want the assurance of eternal life? Don't you want to know the true God and be truly known by him?

35. Moody, quoted in ibid., 125–26.

14

In Truth and Love

2 John

Grace, mercy, and peace will be with us, from God the Father and from Jesus Christ the Father's Son, in truth and love. (2 John 3)

In 1665–66, the bubonic plague swept through London. In less than twenty months, at least 20 percent of the population died (about two hundred thousand deaths). Medical authorities, who were about a decade shy of the first microscopic sighting of bacteria (Anton van Leeuwenhoek in 1675), theorized that the disease might be due to the sickness of livestock, emanations from the earth, or the contaminated air. For those who advocated the bad-air theory, clearing the contamination was the remedy. Fires were lit day and night. Pepper, frankincense, and other strongly scented substances were tossed in. People were even encouraged to smoke tobacco!

Those doctors were dead wrong. The plague was not an airborne disease but a bacterial one (*Yersinia pestis* on rat fleas), and it was the rats, not the air, that carried it. This medical mishap cost many lives, especially of the poor who lived in rat-infested slums. Death records state that by September 1665, at the height of this outbreak, seven thousand persons died per week. It was not until the following September, with the Great Fire of

London and its destruction of much of the city's housing, that the plague was finally eradicated.[1]

Imagine that you were a doctor living during this outbreak, working day and night to find the cure, and you came across the existence of the culprit bacteria on the rodents. You test and retest. Sure enough, the rats must go, and those thousand fires will do. The solution is the rats-in-the-fires combination. You inform the authorities. "I know the cause. I have a cure!" This is good news. Everyone listens with interest and excitement as you explain. Now, also imagine that another doctor comes along. He sounds more sophisticated. He has better credentials. He speaks a more traditional medical language. He ridicules the theory, equating the existence of bacteria to that of the Irish fairies. People are persuaded. They change their minds. They denounce the first doctor and follow the second. But sadly, they follow the second to their demise.

The Cause, the Cure, and the Coming Crisis

When the apostle John first preached the gospel by sharing both the *cause* of our disease (the plague of Adam's sin and ours) and its *cure* (the coming in the flesh of the God-man Jesus Christ), it was good news, and many received it gladly. Soon after, however, eloquent self-appointed authorities came to town (2 John 10), questioned the cause, and scoffed at the cure. They claimed that sin was not so serious a problem. They taught that Jesus had not come "in the flesh" (v. 7). We learned from 1 John 2:18–27 and 4:1–3 that these apostates taught the opposite error of the heretic Arius.[2] Arius denied the full divinity of Jesus. To him, Jesus was a created being—"There was a time when He was not."[3] These earlier heretics—*deceivers* or *antichrist*, as John labels them in verse 7—were denying the full humanity of Jesus. It is not that they wanted to

1. It should be noted that historians now debate the effects of the fire on the stop of the plague.

2. "It is possible to view 2 John as the accompanying letter introducing 1 John to a circle of house churches." John Painter, *1, 2, and 3 John*, Sacra Pagina (Collegeville, MN: Liturgical Press, 2002), 335. As Marianne Meye Thompson notes: "It is possible that 2 John served as a cover letter, sent along with 1 John, to include personal greetings from the Elder to a specific congregation in his care. It is also possible that 1 and 2 John were intended for different audiences: 1 John was circulated in the Elder's immediate vicinity, while 2 John was sent to those at a distance, whom the Elder could contact only by letter (v. 12) or by messenger (v. 4). In any case, it is safe to say that the two letters illumine each other and are so obviously written with the same situation in view that each may be used to interpret the other." *1–3 John*, IVP New Testament Commentary Series (Downers Grove, IL: InterVarsity Press, 1992), 150.

3. Arius, quoted in Alister E. McGrath, *Christian Theology: An Introduction*, 5th ed. (West Sussex, UK: Wiley-Blackwell), 275.

take Christ out of Christmas; rather, they wanted to take the human body out of the cradle. They would be fine with that old line, "Be near me, Lord Jesus; I ask Thee to stay / Close by me forever, and love me, I pray," but not with this one: "Away in a manger, no crib for a bed; the little Lord Jesus laid down His sweet head." They wanted a headless/bodiless Christianity.

How did they arrive at this conclusion? Syncretism: a fusion of pagan beliefs with Christian ones. On one hand, they found the new story of Jesus compelling; on the other hand, they wanted to hold on to their old pagan religion, which was highly influenced by Greek philosophical thought. Put differently, these heretics didn't shake all the Hellenism out of their heads. While they were hundreds of years removed from the time of Socrates (d. 399 B.C.), something of his system of thought still prevailed. If you believed what Plato's teacher taught—that the soul is "pure when it leaves the body and drags nothing bodily with it"[4]—how would you reconcile Christianity's doctrine of the incarnation and bodily resurrection? If you saw the frail and transient human body as intrinsically unspiritual or even evil, wouldn't you view God's taking on human flesh as uncouth and his dying a human death as scandalous (1 Cor. 1:23)? Apostolic Christianity had its appeals. These pro-Jesus, proto-Gnostic evangelists knew that and believed that. They deemed their high calling in the evolution of this fine burgeoning religion to be to remove the reprehensible elements. Their mission was progressive thinking in line with ancient Neoplatonic dualism and their present-day Docetism. Cut out the crude cradle/cross, and Christianity will sing! Update John's primitive doctrines, and the message of Jesus will successfully spread. Remove the word *bodily* from the apostolic announcement "For in him the whole fullness of deity dwells" (Col. 2:9), and Christianity will spiritually conquer the Greco-Roman world.

Perhaps I have misread their motives. What I have not misread is their false and deadly theology. John knew that Jesus had come in the flesh: he had heard, seen, and touched the man (1 John 1:1–4). He also knew that this spreading plague needed to be stopped immediately. The heart of his Gospel was at stake. To him, on one hand, "In the beginning was the Word [*logos*], and the Word was with God, and the Word was God," and on the other hand, "the Word became flesh and dwelt among us" (John 1:1, 14). To him, as it should be to us, "a nonincarnate Christ is not the true Christ," and

4. From *Phaedo* 80e, in Plato, *The Complete Works*, ed. John M. Cooper (Indianapolis: Hackett, 1997), 71.

"anything short of the true Christ will not deliver on the gospel's promises either in this life or the next."[5] Jesus became flesh, and "he gave that flesh in death so that we might have life."[6] To deny the fleshiness of Jesus Christ, as well as the inseparable and now-eternal unity of the two natures in one person, is to take the mercy, grace, peace, and joy out of the gospel. It is antichrist!—against the person and work of Jesus Christ. For, you see, John's emphatic answer to the question "Why did God become man?" is this: to be the "propitiation for our sins" (1 John 2:2). Without a fully human/fully divine Savior, we humans have no assurance of God's full salvation.

Second John is a short letter (only 245 words in Greek), and perhaps it is so short because the problem was so serious. John[7]—"the doctor of love"—needed to get word to the church via next-day mail (a "postcard" on one piece of papyrus) and soon in person (v. 12). The matter was life-and-death urgent![8] The plague-ridden propaganda needed to be set aflame before the church in Ephesus, or perhaps another nearby city (Smyrna, Pergamum, Thyatira, Sardis, Philadelphia, or Laodicea? [Rev. 2–3]), was wiped out. The rats needed to go.

The Truth Abides in Us

Second John 7 informs us of the cause of the plague—false teachers were denying the incarnation: "For many deceivers have gone out into the world, those who do not confess the coming of Jesus Christ in the flesh. Such a one is the deceiver and the antichrist." The rest of the epistle is a reminder of the remedy. In verses 1–4, John reminds the church that "the truth . . . abides in us" (v. 2), and in verses 5–11, he exhorts believers to continue to "abide" in the truth (v. 9).

We begin with the greeting: "The elder to the elect lady and her children, whom I love in truth, and not only I, but also all who know the truth,

5. Robert W. Yarbrough, *1–3 John*, Baker Exegetical Commentary on the New Testament (Grand Rapids: Baker, 2008), 344.

6. Thompson, *1–3 John*, 154.

7. The shared terminology, style, and theological themes of 1 John and 2–3 John, as well as their position in the Christian canon, make it most likely that the apostle John wrote all three epistles that bear his name around the same time (near the end of the first century, likely between A.D. 85 and 95).

8. "Second John 7–8 is the core of the epistle and probably reveals the immediate occasion for writing. Once John arrives there to visit, as he hopes (2 John 12; cf. 3 John 14 [14a NIV]), he can stabilize matters in person." Yarbrough, *1–3 John*, 343.

because of the truth that abides in us and will be with us forever" (2 John 1–2). In verse 1, John calls himself "the elder" and the local church and its members "the elect lady and her children" (v. 1; cf. "dear lady," v. 5). He designates himself as "the elder" both because of his age and because of his position of ecclesial authority. He is not "an elder" (i.e., one of the elders in Ephesus) but "the elder," a unique title that best symbolizes his role as the church's "old man"—her spiritual father and apostle. In a culture that honored the aged, he is not demanding respect, but assuming it.

He addresses the church cryptically with an honorable and endearing title, "the elect lady [*kyria*, the feminine form of *lord*] and her children" (and later "the children of your elect sister," 2 John 13). The *ESV Study Bible* provides an excellent summary of the scholarly consensus:

> "The elect lady" . . . more likely refers to a congregation than to an individual, because much of 2 John is written in the second-person plural. It is also questionable whether John would write to a female Christian that he and she should "love one another" (v. 5); the phrase makes better sense if addressed to a church. There are three additional reasons why "elect lady" may refer to a whole congregation. First, the word "church" in Greek is feminine in gender, and "lady" would go along with that. Second, the church is depicted as "bride" elsewhere in John's writings (Rev. 21:2, 9; 22:17). [For the church symbolized as a woman or bride, see also John 3:29; 2 Cor. 11:2; Gal. 4:25–26; Eph. 5:22–23; Rev. 18–19.] Third, the Greek word *kyria* ("lady") referred to a social subunit in the Greek city-state. John may use this word for a local congregation instead of the more common feminine word *ekklēsia*.[9]

This title "the elect lady and her children" represents the vertical (God graciously chooses us as his own beloved children)[10] and horizontal (he places us in a new human family) aspects of our salvation. We are children of the Father, brothers and sisters of Christ, and united in love by the Spirit of truth.[11] John does not hold back his expression of *agapē*. He directly

9. *ESV Study Bible* (Wheaton, IL: Crossway, 2008), 2439. Scholars who hold to this view include I. Howard Marshall, Raymond E. Brown, and Stephen S. Smalley.

10. For John's use of the verb *to choose*, see John 6:70–71; 13:18; 15:16, 19. According to John, we are not God's children by our own initiative and will, but solely by God's sovereign grace.

11. Commenting on verse 2, Painter notes: "The assurance that the truth 'will be with us forever,' is similar to the promise that the Spirit 'will be with you forever' (John 14:16)." *1, 2, and 3 John*, 338.

expresses his love for them ("whom I love in truth")[12] and shares that the sentiment is universal ("and not only I, but also all who know the truth").[13]

Then at the end of his greeting, he reemphasizes the horizontal: "Grace, mercy, and peace will be with us, from God the Father and from Jesus Christ the Father's Son, in truth and love" (2 John 3). While John's greeting or prescript (vv. 1–3) contains the usual components of "early Hellenistic letters—sender (*superscriptio*), addressee (*adscriptio*), good wishes for the recipient's well-being (*salutatio*)"[14]—his triad is a gospel-centered celebration of God's promise of salvation. John Stott explains our God-wrought salvation in this way:

> Grace and mercy are both expressions of God's love, grace to the guilty and undeserving, mercy to the needy and helpless. Peace is that restoration of harmony with God, others and self which we call "salvation." Put together, peace indicates the character of salvation, mercy our need of it and grace God's free provision of it in Christ.[15]

This God-centered gospel is "the truth" that John speaks of five times in the first four verses (11× in 2 and 3 John). It is this "truth" that is from the Father and the Son that abides now and forever within true believers. That is why, following the greeting of 2 John 1–3, John rejoices in verse 4 that some of the church have continued in the truth: "I rejoiced greatly to find some of your children walking in the truth, just as we were commanded by the Father."[16] By *some* John might mean "a few out of many" or simply "those he knows from that congregation." However many people the *some* represents, this walking is wonderful to John. He adds a thanksgiving (v. 4) to his greeting (vv. 1–3). He is grateful to God that

12. "'I' is emphatic, and 'love' is in the present tense. 'Whom I, myself, love as a constant expression of my heart' is what John is saying." Daniel L. Akin, *1, 2, 3 John*, New American Commentary (Nashville: Broadman & Holman, 1993), 220–21.

13. While I don't favor Jerome's view that "the elect lady and her children" are the church universal (see "Letter cxxiii," in *Nicene and Post-Nicene Fathers*, 2nd ser., 6:234, in ibid., 219), that reading fits the phrase "all who know the truth" (v. 1).

14. Rudolf Schnackenburg, *The Johannine Epistles: Introduction and Commentary*, trans. R. Fuller and I. Fuller (New York: Crossroad, 1992), 277.

15. John R. W. Stott, *The Epistles of John: An Introduction and Commentary*, Tyndale New Testament Commentaries (Downers Grove, IL: InterVarsity Press, 1976), 204.

16. While I agree with the consensus of commentators that verses 1–3 of 2 John constitute the "greeting," I disagree that verse 4 starts the body of the letter. I take verse 4 to function, as typical of the characteristics of a Hellenistic letter, as the "thanksgiving." See Painter, *1, 2, and 3 John*, 346; Thompson, *1–3 John*, 152. Moreover, linguistically and thematically John's "and now" of verse 5 most clearly indicates the beginning of the body of the letter, or at the very least a change of topic or emphasis.

some are *walking*—idiomatic for the idea of *doing* or *obeying* (John 3:21)—in the *truth* (believing in Jesus and loving others as Christ commanded, 1 John 3:23).

Abide in the Truth

John's remedy begins by reminding Christians that they already have the saving truth abiding within them. With that groundwork established, he next exhorts them to abide in the truth. How so? In 2 John 5–11, he provides two very practical ways. First, walk in the commandment of love; second, don't let false teachers walk all over you. Put differently, be loving to all by being inhospitable to some. That seeming contradiction will, I hope, make sense as we explore this second section.

Opened Door: Walk in the Commandment of Love

How would you define love? Cartoonist Kim Casali is famous for her definitions. For four decades, nearly every major newspaper in the country featured her captions under her drawings of a chubby, childlike, modestly undressed couple. For example:

Love is . . . not picking the most expensive dish on the menu.
Love is . . . massaging her toes.
Love is . . . like wine, better as it matures.[17]

Those are healthy definitions, certainly better than some of what passes as definitions and expressions of love today, such as:

Love is . . . tolerance without truth.
Love is . . . never insisting on changing or challenging someone's views.
Love is . . . refusing to label anything "wrong."

Today, love is defined by "the cult of 'tolerance,'" which is "the moralistic invention of the modern secular world."[18] This cult borrows Christian

17. These three examples are taken from Kim Casali, *Love Is . . . in Bloom* (New York: Abrams Image, 2007), 13, 313, 349.

18. N. T. Wright, *Early Christian Letters for Everyone*, New Testament for Everyone (Louisville, KY: Westminster John Knox, 2011), 178.

language—such as *love*—and twists it to mean something very different from Jesus' intent and then accuses Christians of being arrogant, unloving, and, ironically, *unchristian*.[19] In this prevalent school of thought, *love* has even become a common excuse for immorality.

Recently, Emily and I took our two youngest children to the Oriental Museum at the University of Chicago. Before our six-year-old deciphered Egyptian letters (no joke) and our eight-year-old recited some Hittite code of ethics (perhaps a joke), we walked past the First Unitarian Church of Hyde Park. On the side of that magnificent building is featured a rainbow flag (a representative of the homosexual movement) on which is written: "We Stand on the Side of Love." There, love is defined in contrast with Old Testament law and New Testament ethics. Of course, the love-covers-a-multitude-of-truths movement doesn't stop there. "But we love one another" now trumps God's truths on fornication, adultery, and even incest. When Woody Allen faced questions about his sexual relationship with the adopted daughter of his wife, he shrugged his shoulders and said, "The heart wants what it wants." When asked whether he had fallen in love with her, he replied, "Yes, yes. My flair for drama. What can I say?"[20] At least he didn't say that "love" made him do it. Or did he? The irony is thick, and sadly in our sex-crazed society only growing thicker.

Needless to say, John defines love differently—by the Book. To him, authentic love arises from God's revealed truth:

> And now I ask you, dear lady—not as though I were writing you a new commandment, but the one we have had from the beginning—that we love one another. And *this is love*, that we walk according to his commandments; this is the commandment, just as you have heard from the beginning, so that you should walk in it. (2 John 5–6)

While in the Bible love can express itself romantically and sexually (see the Song of Songs), here John connects love to God's commandments.[21] We

19. Ibid.

20. Walter Isaacson, "The Heart Wants What It Wants" (interview with Woody Allen), *Time*, August 31, 1992, 59.

21. Akin's chiasmus (*1, 2, 3 John*, 226) visually highlights the connectedness:

A command (5b)
  B love (5d)
  B' love (6a)
A' commands (6b)

might illustrate by imagining that John writes the caption *love is . . . that we walk according to his commandments* under two pictures. The first picture is of the Christian community holding hands. It symbolizes our acting out of Christ's "new commandment" (cf. John 13:34–35; 15:12, 17), what the Johannine community "heard from the beginning" (i.e., the original oral proclamation of the Christian message). The second picture is of the Christian community holding hands as we lift them up to God. It is a picture of worship, which most often in the New Testament is a picture of adoration through obedience.

In John's letters, God is often called *Father.*[22] One reason for that designation is that God functions in a fatherly way. I am a father of five children. As their father, I love them and want what is best for them. To my knowledge, I have never given my children a commandment that I do not think is in their ultimate best interest. In Matthew 7:9–11, Jesus calls earthly fathers "evil," yet notes that they still "give good gifts to [their] children." He adds, "How much more will your Father who is in heaven give good things to those who ask him!" Let me take that analogy a step further. If imperfect Christian fathers give commandments that they think are for their children's good, how much more does the perfect heavenly Father give his children good commandments. "His commandments are not burdensome" (1 John 5:3). There is a lightness to loving the Lord and loving neighbor (Mark 12:29–31). And obeying the commandments—for example, treating others the way we would like to be treated (Luke 6:31), considering others better than ourselves (Phil. 2:3), honoring our parents (Matt. 19:19), putting on kindness (Col. 3:12), submitting to one another (Eph. 5:21), abstaining from anxiety (Matt. 6:25, 31, 34), fleeing from youthful lusts (2 Tim. 2:22), and keeping ourselves from idols (1 John 5:21)—brings freedom because "if the Son sets

---

It also shows in my mind (not his; see page 227) that *command* and *commands* are virtually synonymous. In a way similar to Jesus in Mark 12:28–31—"There is no other commandment greater than these [two commandments]"—John interweaves *commandments* and *commandment.*

Visually, it looks like this:

according to his	commandments
this is the	commandment

That said, nevertheless, the love commandment covers all the commandments. Thus, my exhortations are based on more than one command.

22. Fifteen times *Father* is used of God: 1 John 1:2, 3; 2:1, 13, 15, 16, 22, 23, 24; 3:1; 4:14; 2 John 3 [2×], 4, 9.

you free, you will be free indeed" (John 8:36). Walking in God's ways will give you wings!

The reason that John gives for keeping the commandments, however, is not related directly to our personal advantage—the lightness of living in the light. Rather, he connects commandment-keeping to the plague of false teachers. Look at 2 John 7. Why love one another? Why obey all that God has to say? The reason returns to the plague problem—the false teachers' worldly behavior and erroneous belief: "For many deceivers have gone out into the world [behavior], those who do not confess the coming of Jesus Christ in the flesh [belief]." Do you see the connection that John is making? It is because of heresy that truth and love in the church must join hands and walk forward together. For if you have just truth without love, or love without the truth, you do not have the church. You might have a political party, country club, or workers union, but you do not have Immanuel's *ecclesia*. The church is not a society where you can come as you are, stay as you are, do as you like, and think as you might. Rather, Christ's church is a place (or a people, to be more precise) where truth and love reside and preside, where love (*agapē*) and truth (*alētheia*) necessarily join hands and walk forward together.

Therefore, when movements arise in the church—often today under the umbrella of ecumenism—that promote unity at the expense of truth and blanket the essential doctrines of the Christian faith with a "love" defined as tolerance rather than obedience, it is then that the true church must show forth the full gospel. We must not allow anyone to base Christian unity on the foundation of a false compromise, for to do so is to band-aid the problem of disunity and to widen the wound caused by false teaching. It would be like the United Nations' legitimizing terrorist regimes, universities' tolerating plagiarism, or the Food and Drug Administration's approving tainted meat and arsenic-laced aspirin. Love must walk hand in hand with truth.

Closed Door: Inhospitality to False Teachers

In 2 John 5–11, John provides two very practical ways to abide in the truth. First, as we have seen, we are to walk in the commandment of love. Second, according to verses 8–11, we abide in the truth by being hostile toward false teaching and inhospitable toward false teachers. We must resist false teaching (vv. 8–9) and false teachers (vv. 10–11).

There are only two imperatives in 2 John, and the first comes at the beginning of verse 8: "Watch yourselves."[23] We are not told to burn heretics but rather not to be burned by them. Discernment is the remedy for dealing with theological errors. In a fallen world that is filled with lies about God and his gospel, we must train our minds, as some of us do our muscles, to get stronger at discerning truth from error. The two reasons for self-watchfulness follow: (1) "so that [we] may not lose what we have worked for" and (2) so that we "may win a full reward." One is negative (so that we may not lose); the other is positive (that we may win). Both involve the motivation of future rewards. As Robert Yarbrough puts it: "In addition to the daily gratification of things like love, truth, joy, peace, mercy, and fellowship," there are "eschatological incentives" for watchfulness.[24]

Second John 9 reminds us that the stakes are high. We have a life-or-death choice to make regarding false teaching. We can accept it or we can reject it. To embrace falsehood is to no longer "abide in . . . Christ," the consequence of which is to sever fellowship with God. John makes this plain when he says, "Everyone who goes on ahead and does not abide in the teaching of Christ, does not have God. Whoever abides in the teaching has both the Father and the Son" (v. 9). Again we have negative and positive remarks. Negatively, to run on ahead with the "spiritual know-it-alls," as Akin calls the false teachers, is to leave God behind.[25] This is not a "true progression but a fatal and flawed digression."[26] Positively, perseverance in Jesus' teaching (or the teachings about him) is proof of authentic Christian faith.

Following the imperative, incentives, and encouragements to resist false teaching (2 John 8–9), John continues his plea to abide in the truth with the imperative and motive to shut the doors on false teachers (vv. 10–11): "If anyone comes to you and does not bring this teaching, do not receive him into your house or give him any greeting, for whoever greets him takes part in his wicked works." Christians in John's community are to "not receive" (v. 10) or welcome any false teacher into their homes because to do so would be to share or take part "in his wicked works" (v. 11).

23. The verb *watch* (*blepete*) is the same word used in the warnings of Jesus (Matt. 24:4; Mark 13:5; Luke 21:8) and Paul (Acts 13:40; 1 Cor. 8:9; Gal. 5:15; Eph. 5:15; Phil. 3:2 [3×]; Col. 2:8) against false teachers.

24. Yarbrough, *1–3 John*, 346.

25. Akin, *1, 2, 3 John*, 232.

26. Ibid.

In the ancient world, there was a high regard for hospitality. It was commonplace to open one's home to welcome travelers. Homes served as hotels. Christian missionaries, like the first disciples of Jesus (Mark 6:10–11) and the early church (3 John 5–8), including John himself (2 John 12), were dependent on such Christian hospitality. So why, then, in this little letter on love, do we find this striking command to be inhospitable?

The inhospitality arises from the insidious nature of heresy.[27] As with the plague, total avoidance of the plagued is the only solution. Here John is not talking about Christians' refusing to house a Muslim exchange student or the church's canceling a debate with an atheist. He is not talking about making sure that our unbelieving brother sits outside for Thanksgiving dinner or our unbelieving friend stands in the narthex to hear the sermon. He is not even saying that we cannot invite a skeptic into our homes for an honest discussion about the claims of Christ. And certainly he is not saying that we should refuse to eat in the homes of sinners. What he is saying is that home-owning Christians should not house traveling heretics and that the local church (perhaps the reference to "house" in 2 John 10 is to a house church) should not provide a base for their anti-gospel evangelism. To let someone who denies the incarnation and crucifixion of Christ use the church building, preach a sermon, or take from missions funding is to have *koinōnia* with that person. Why would the church support those "who are engaged in the systematic dissemination of lies"?[28] It is "spiritual suicide" to give false teachers a platform to propagate their deceptive doctrines.[29] And quite simply, it lacks love.

> It does not show love to the rest of the flock, because it exposes them to heresy's insidious undermining of their faith. It does not even show love towards the "deceiver," since it simply confirms him in his error, which he might now never be brought to admit. Above all, it does not express love for God, because it sides with evil in actively encouraging the spread of that which is most destructive of the truth (v. 11).[30]

27. "Heretical teaching is so insidious and lethal a danger that total avoidance is the only solution." Judith Lieu, *The Second and Third Epistles of John: History and Background* (Edinburgh: T&T Clark, 1986), 97.

28. Stott, *The Epistles of John*, 213.

29. David Jackman, *The Message of John's Letters*, The Bible Speaks Today (Downers Grove, IL: InterVarsity Press, 1988), 185.

30. Ibid.

It not only lacks love, but also (as John concludes) threatens the church's mutual joy:

> Though I have much to write to you, I would rather not use paper and ink. Instead I hope to come to you and talk face to face, so that our joy may be complete.
>
> The children of your elect sister greet you. (2 John 12–13)

How can a church lose its "joy" (2 John 12)? The answer: by not being *aware* of false teaching (v. 9), and also by not being *active* in avoiding it (vv. 10–11). Imagine that two Jehovah's Witnesses knock at my door. They introduce themselves and what movement they are a part of. At that moment, I know that they deny the deity of Christ and his physical resurrection. Nevertheless, I dismiss those differences by embracing them with a holy kiss and a salvation-sharing greeting: "Grace, mercy, and peace will be with us, from God the Father and from Jesus Christ the Father's Son, in truth and love" (v. 3).[31] "Come in, come in," I say. "Please make yourselves at home. Can I get you some coffee or tea?" Then imagine that when our charitable conversation concludes, I invite them to stay the night so that they might preach the next day at my church. Then as they sleep, I phone the treasurer and ask that he cut a check for tomorrow's guest preachers. I also e-mail the missions committee to see whether they might add our guests to those whom we regularly support. "We'll surprise them after the service with our generosity!"

Needless to say, these actions would not bring about church unity. And where there is no Christian unity on the person and work of Christ, there is certainly no shared joy. John hopes to talk to these Christians "face to face" (literally, "mouth to mouth" [*stoma pros stoma*]). This is not a reference to a "holy kiss" (e.g., Rom. 16:16)—when he gets to town, they are to greet him with the traditional expression of brotherly love, but not the false teachers. And it is not an allusion to Elijah's healing of the widow's son (1 Kings 17:17–24)—that is, John needs to breathe the living-giving truth back into them. Rather, as translated, it is simply a Greek idiom for the

31. "Christian greetings generally carried a recognition of the true Christian standing of those being greeted." Colin G. Kruse, *The Letters of John*, Pillar New Testament Commentary (Grand Rapids: Eerdmans, 2000), 214. Moreover, note the greetings that include a kiss (Rom. 16:16; 1 Cor. 16:20; 2 Cor. 13:12; 1 Thess. 5:26; 1 Peter 5:14).

English expression *face-to-face*. The idea is that if John's joy and their joy is to be "complete" (fulfilled or perfected), they need to see eye-to-eye on Jesus.

"Lord, Have Mercy upon Us"

In the Great Plague of London, if people caught the disease, they were quarantined in their houses. Such a house was then known as a "plague house," was marked with a red cross, and had the words "Lord, have mercy upon us" written on it. Second John—an epistle written in love and exhorting us to love—was also written to warn. "Lord, have mercy upon us" if the church becomes the world, the truth becomes lies, the commandments of God become the deceptions of the devil, and Christ becomes the antichrist.[32] The world is infected with a deadly plague. The cure is known. It is the coming in the flesh of the God-man, Jesus. Believe in him and live forevermore!

32. For these antitheses, see Stott, *The Epistles of John*, 205.

15

Seven Important Lessons from 219 Inspired Words

3 John

Beloved, do not imitate evil but imitate good. (3 John 11)

In 1994 the World Council of Churches held a conference that called for a "Second Reformation." It was a reformation, in their estimation, that would not only give the church a much-needed facelift, but also remove from the body of Christ what had once been deemed vital organs. For example, Delores Williams proclaimed, "I don't think we need a theory of atonement at all. I don't think we need folks hanging on crosses and blood dripping and weird stuff. . . . We just need to listen to the god within." The conference's stated purpose was to reimage God. Such reimaging involved removing the Father's testimony through the Spirit about Jesus and replacing it with worship of the goddess Sophia, the female psyche that "takes a historic, particularistic form, but appears in many ways and in many spiritual traditions."[1] The irony of this unorthodox "reformation" should be obvious to the orthodox. In 1 Corinthians 1:23–24,

1. This retelling is found in Gary M. Burge, *Letters of John*, NIV Application Commentary (Grand Rapids: Zondervan, 1996), 206–7.

Paul wrote: "We preach Christ crucified, a stumbling block to Jews and folly to Gentiles, but to those who are called, . . . Christ the power of God and the wisdom [*sophia*] of God." To believers, the cross is the very show of *sophia*!

Around A.D. 94 (nineteen hundred years before that heretical council meeting in 1994), the apostle John is dealing with similar opposition to apostolic authority and testimony. In a church in Asia Minor, likely in or near Ephesus, a Christian leader named Diotrephes has strayed off course. He is not teaching false doctrine. He is not denying the incarnation or the atonement of Christ. He is simply being egotistical and stubborn. He refuses to heed John's teaching (the letter John wrote: "I have written something to the church," 3 John 9). Then he refuses to welcome John's apostolic delegates ("brothers," vv. 3, 5, 10). More than that, he is acting so wickedly (v. 11) that he seeks to exclude or perhaps even excommunicate (put "out of the church," v. 10) those who wish to be hospitable to the orthodox teachers who come to his church.

Faced with this crisis, John refuses to retire from his apostleship even in his old age. He picks up his pen again and writes 3 John. The letter is *personal*, between two persons—John and Gaius. It is *obscure* because we do not know precisely where his audience is located. (Other than what we have in this letter, we do not know anything about its three major characters.) And it is *short*. It has only 219 words in the Greek text, which makes it the shortest book in the New Testament. While we can understand something of the nature of the church conflict, we also grasp the apostolic assessment, which is to imitate good, not evil. Given its nature, this private, obscure, and short letter seems at first as applicable to us as having read a stranger's e-mail. What does this ancient situation, and this little letter in response to it, have to do with us or say to us?

Thankfully and providentially, we trust that all Scripture is inspired and applicable (cf. 2 Tim. 3:16–17). In my estimation, we can learn at least seven important lessons from these 219 inspired words.

The Christian Retirement Age

The first lesson comes from the first two words, "the elder" (3 John 1). John's greeting shows that *the retirement age for Christian ministry is death.* The term "the elder" connotes two truths. First, John was an important authority figure in the early church. Second, he was aged. We do not know how old John was when he wrote 1, 2, and 3 John, but we can surmise from the dating of the letter (c. A.D. 90–95) that he was at least an octogenarian. And how did this old man spend his time? Gospel work! He wrote, traveled, prayed, tried to resolve church conflicts, and was exiled for the gospel. He did not view ages sixty-five to ninety-five as the time of earthly bliss and rest. He would rather die in the pulpit than on the golf course. When I say that the retirement age for Christian ministry is death, I mean that the most aged can pray and give; some can even write, teach, counsel, and host. We never retire from gospel work.

John Calvin was an industrious man. For decades he preached every day, gave three divinity lectures a week, penned over a million words, and handled hundreds of church conflicts. When poor health forced him to stay at home, he still worked. He gave pastoral counsel to those who visited him, and he dictated letters to his secretaries. When Theodore Beza encouraged him to give it a rest, he answered, "Would you that the Lord should find me idle when He comes?" He died shortly thereafter.[2]

The Gospel Value of Godly Friends

The second lesson takes us beyond the first two words to the whole of the first verse, and in many ways the whole of the letter. The lesson is that *without godly friends, our gospel witness weakens.* If you cut out the conflict, 3 John is a "fatherly and friendly letter" from one gospel worker to another.[3] As John ends the letter on the theme of Christian friendship ("I hope to see you soon.... The friends greet you. Greet the friends," vv. 14–15), so it begins with an expression of personal love from one friend to another: "The elder to the beloved Gaius, whom I love in truth" (v. 1). We know nothing about Gaius other than what we read here.[4] We do know that these two are joined

2. From William Wileman, *John Calvin: His Life, His Teaching, and His Influence*, available at http://www.reformed.org/calvinism/index.html?mainframe=/calvinism/jc_character.html.

3. Rudolf Schnackenburg, *The Johannine Epistles: Introduction and Commentary*, trans. R. Fuller and I. Fuller (New York: Crossroad, 1992), 291.

4. "'Gaius' was a common name in the Roman Empire of the first century, and three men by that name appear in the New Testament: Gaius of Corinth (Rom 16:23), Gaius of Macedonia (Acts 19:29), and Gaius of Derbe (Acts 20:4). Because the name was common, it is unlikely the Gaius of 3 John should be identified with any of these." Daniel L. Akin, *1, 2, 3 John*, New American Commentary (Nashville: Broadman & Holman, 1993), 239.

by the truth and work of the gospel. Gaius is one of John's "beloved" (vv. 2, 5, 11) spiritual "children" who has kept the faith (v. 4) and supported the spread of the gospel (vv. 5–6). "Gaius has effectively embodied the teaching of his colleague or mentor John (1 John 3:17–18)."[5] He possessed the necessary doctrinal, ethical, and relational aspects of genuine Christian faith. He believed in the apostolic message, obeyed the apostolic teachings, and opened his heart and home and wallet to the apostolic ambassadors. He aced the three tests of 1 John! Grounded in the "truth" (mentioned six times), Gaius and John have grown into close friends.

Ecclesiastes 4:9 teaches, "Two are better than one, because they have a good reward for their toil. For if they fall, one will lift up his fellow. But woe to him who is alone when he falls and has not another to lift him up!" Qoheleth's "commendation of community" is a welcome "antidote to the individualism that infects" many local churches.[6] Just as the body of Christ "does not consist of one member but of many" (1 Cor. 12:14), we need one another for service (v. 21), perseverance in holiness (Heb. 10:24–25), and mission (Mark 6:7).

When Paul wrote 2 Timothy under house arrest in Rome, he was tired, cold, and discouraged. He needed a few friends to pick up his spirits and pray with him. At the conclusion of 2 Timothy, Paul lists his friends—old friends such as Prisca and Aquila and new friends such as Linus and Carpus—because he wants them all to stand by him in the hour of his death. Paul also enlists Timothy, his good friend and "soul-son," as Kent Hughes calls him,[7] because he wants Timothy to stand literally by him at the hour of his death. He writes, "Do your best to come to me soon" (4:9), "Get Mark and bring him with you" (v. 11), and "Do your best to come before winter" (v. 21).

Do you need a friend to comfort you and pull you through? Embrace the *ecclesia*! As Paul leaned on his friends in his hour of death, and as John counted on Gaius in his hour of need, we must do the same. Fellowship is more than sharing a cup of coffee after the service; it is sharing life

5. Robert W. Yarbrough, *1–3 John*, Baker Exegetical Commentary on the New Testament (Grand Rapids: Baker, 2008), 371.

6. The first phrase comes from Iain Provan, *Ecclesiastes/Song of Songs*, NIV Application Commentary (Grand Rapids: Zondervan, 2001), 105–6, and the second from Sidney Greidanus, *Preaching Christ from Ecclesiastes: Foundations for Expository Sermons* (Grand Rapids: Eerdmans, 2010), 107.

7. R. Kent Hughes and Bryan Chapell, *1–2 Timothy and Titus*, Preaching the Word (Wheaton, IL: Crossway, 2000), 258.

together—the joys and sorrows, triumphs and defeats—so that together we might fight the good fight, finish the race, keep the faith, and long for the glory of God's gospel to cover the earth.[8]

PHYSICAL AND SPIRITUAL WELL-BEING

The third lesson is that *a healthy body without a healthy soul makes for an unhealthy person*. Observe John's prayer in 3 John 2: "Beloved, I pray that all may go well with you and that you may be in good health, as it goes well with your soul." John knows that Gaius has done well thus far. He needs for him to keep it up. So he prays for Gaius to remain in good health both spiritually and physically.

Praying for our physical well-being is biblical. Before I first preached this chapter, I was sick all week. It is difficult to do gospel ministry when you are in bed. So I prayed repeatedly the first half of 3 John 2, "Lord, may I be in good health . . . at least by Sunday morning!" I had no voice on Wednesday, Thursday, Friday, and Saturday, but *not Sunday*!

Christians are not Gnostics. We value the human body. Nevertheless, we must emphasize that a healthy body without a healthy soul makes for an unhealthy person because in our world the body's value seems higher than the soul's.[9] Six times out of ten when I turn on Christian radio, I hear about health matters. This seems odd to me. Physical well-being should concern Christians, but the amount of concern seems off-balance. Has diet and exercise become Christianity's new idol? For better (in many ways) but also for worse (in idolatrous ways), our culture is obsessed with health. The Walgreens slogan "Be Well" is everyone's attitude.

Ah, but how well are our *souls*?

When I was in college, Dr. Lyle Dorsett would sincerely ask his students, "Brother (or sister), how's your soul?" One day, I was depressed. I ran into

8. Parts of the three paragraphs above were taken, with permission, from Douglas Sean O'Donnell, *Ecclesiastes: Enjoyment East of Eden*, Reformed Expository Commentary (Phillipsburg, NJ: P&R Publishing, 2014).

9. "The word translated 'soul' refers to the whole being of a person. In the Gospel of John, Jesus is said to lay down his *psyche* which certainly means more than to give his 'soul' (compare Jn 10:15, 17–18)." Marianne Meye Thompson, *1–3 John*, IVP New Testament Commentary Series (Downers Grove, IL: InterVarsity Press, 1992), 159. I used the word *soul* because our culture often separates the body from the soul. By *soul* I mean "what's inside us" as well as our bodily frames.

Dr. Dorsett in the hallway and the line came out, "Brother Doug, how's your soul?" It caught me off guard. I paused for ten seconds and then said, "Not good." He stopped walking, brought me into his office, and listened to me. Then he prayed for me, gave me a book from his library, and sent me back into the mission field with a renewed soul.

In 3 John 2, John is doing more than following the typical pattern of Hellenistic epistles in offering a blessing or prayer-wish of health;[10] he is getting to the heart of the issue. Diotrephes is in good physical health (as demonstrated by his strenuous opposition), but his soul is sick. And a Christian leader with a sick soul is sickening. His moral health is "evil" (v. 11). The spiritually well soul walks in the truth (v. 3) and imitates what is good (v. 11). This is the regimen that Diotrephes needs to get on—and perhaps some of us as well.

The Greater Joy of the Gospel

The fourth lesson is that *gospel faithfulness should bring us supreme joy.* This lesson is derived from 3 John 3–4: "For I rejoiced greatly when the brothers came and testified to your truth, as indeed you are walking in the truth. I have no greater joy than to hear that my children are walking in the truth." John sent Christian evangelists ("the brothers" of verse 3) to Gaius's church, and they eventually returned to John to share the good and bad news. The good news was Gaius's faith, warm welcome, and support. This report of Gaius's faithfulness brought John "no greater joy" (v. 4). Raymond Brown notes that *meizoteros* is "a Hellenistic double comparative," which we might render "more greater."[11] However we render it, this is emphatic and emotive language.

What brings you joy? Not just a momentary physical or emotional thrill, but a more lasting, deep-seated, and cheerful pleasure? Is it your spouse's embrace, children's obedience, financial reward for a week's hard work, playing a sport, or eating a delightful meal? Those are all godly joys. Enjoy such joys! But what brings you "no greater joy"? Is it John's joy? Is it when you hear the news of friends' keeping and promoting the good news?

10. Walter Elwell and Robert Yarbrough list two examples of this convention: "Papyrus Oxrhynchus 292 (ca. A.D. 25) records Theon writing to Tyrannos, 'before all else you have my good wishes for unbroken health and prosperity.' A second-century letter states, 'Before all else I pray you are in good health.'" *Readings from the First-Century World* (Grand Rapids: Baker Academic, 1998), 194.

11. Raymond E. Brown, *The Epistles of John*, Anchor Bible (Garden City, NY: Doubleday, 1982), 706.

In chapter 12, I shared part of my sister's conversion story. My sister's name is Julie Roper. There is another Julie Roper who is a member of my church. There is a connection. My sister (Julie) married the other Julie's brother. It's confusing, I know. Both ladies are following the Lord. When I weekly see the church-member Julie giving her life for the church—my home church—it gives me life and joy. Why? It is because part of her story is my story. A regeneration chain reaction occurred over twenty years ago: I became a Christian, then my sister became a Christian, and then Julie became a Christian. I would have no deeper sorrow than to learn that one or both of those Julies had left the Lord. But thankfully, that is not the case. The fact remains that they have remained—abided in Christ. And that reality causes great rejoicing. What are your stories? Whom do you celebrate? Who is your crown *and your joy* (cf. Phil. 4:1; 1 Thess. 2:19)?

Financial Ethics and Generosity

The fifth lesson is that *the financial ethics of the sent are as important as the generosity of the supporters.* In 3 John 5–8, we read:

> Beloved, it is a faithful thing you do in all your efforts for these brothers, strangers as they are, who testified to your love before the church. You will do well to send them on their journey in a manner worthy of God. For they have gone out for the sake of the name, accepting nothing from the Gentiles. Therefore we ought to support people like these, that we may be fellow workers for the truth.

In 3 John 5, John recounts and praises Gaius's generosity, which took the form of hospitality. Gaius has taken in these "strangers" because they are "brothers." In verses 6 and 8, John exhorts Gaius and all other Christians to "support people like these." He is talking about hospitality, but also financial giving. "Send them on their journey in a manner worthy of God" can be paraphrased "send them on their way with a generous gift" (TLB). "Pay for their ticket to travel" and "Give them some money for their mission" are two ways that we might say it today.

Third John 7 states why the "strangers" are worth the church's support: their motivation is right. They are on their mission "for the sake of the name." That is, they came "for the sake of Christ or for his honor."[12] They are not out to earn their own fame but to lift up Christ's name. They are to exalt the only name under heaven whereby we can be saved (Acts 4:12)—the one name that bestows the forgiveness of sins (2:38) upon even the Gentiles (9:15; cf. Eph. 2:12). Furthermore, their actions are commendable. They are not preaching the gospel for gain. Contrary to the popular pagan practices of the day, they were not accepting money after giving their message,[13] at least not from those who were unbelievers or "the Gentiles" (3 John 7). If the "*unbelieving, worldly, polytheistic*"[14] person wanted to open his pocketbook after a great gospel message, these men refused to bank the bounty. They offered the free grace of God in Christ for free.

Those two reasons prove their legitimacy, and thus commend the church's participation in the gospel. We should support such workers. Why? Third John 8 answers: "we ought to support people like these, that we may be fellow workers for the truth." The motive for the senders is coworker *koinōnia* (*fellowship*)! Put differently, we partner together for the gospel. "God invites us to be venture capitalists for the kingdom of God."[15]

Throughout Paul's letters, he calls those Christians laboring alongside him *coworkers* (*synergoi*), the same word that John uses in 3 John 8. Paul also uses the word *koinōnia* (translated "fellowship" throughout John's letters), most often related to the monetary gifts for gospel work. For example, in Philippians 1:3–5, Paul writes: "I thank my God in all my remembrance of you, always in every prayer of mine for you all making my prayer with joy, because of your *partnership* [*koinōnia*] in the gospel from the first day until now." The nature of their *koinōnia* is clarified in Philippians 4:10–18, where Paul speaks of his "needs" being met by means of their "full payment, and more . . . [by] the gifts you sent." He calls their love offering "a fragrant

12. Schnackenburg, *The Johannine Epistles*, 295.

13. "A common sight in the ancient Roman Empire was the vagrants who traveled about peddling their gods and begging for money from anyone and everyone." Bruce B. Barton et al., *1, 2 & 3 John*, Application Bible Commentary (Wheaton, IL: Tyndale, 1998), 149. Perhaps following the practice that Jesus had laid out in Mark 6:7–13 (cf. Matt. 10:1–40; Luke 10:1–20)—telling his disciples to take nothing and to expect to be welcomed into the homes of those on the side of the truth—and/or Paul's pattern as a tentmaker (e.g., 1 Thess. 2:9; cf. 1 Cor. 9:14–18; cf. 4:11), these evangelists took nothing.

14. Frederick William Danker, ed., *A Greek-English Lexicon of the New Testament and Other Early Christian Literature*, 3rd ed. (Chicago: University of Chicago Press, 2000), 276 (original emphasis).

15. Philip Graham Ryken, *Ecclesiastes: Why Everything Matters*, ed. R. Kent Hughes, Preaching the Word (Wheaton, IL: Crossway, 2010), 256.

offering, a sacrifice acceptable and pleasing to God." It is a beautiful image of money going *up in smoke* to missions. To provide prayer, housing, meals, notes of encouragement, and (notably here in 3 John!) money is to participate in the noblest endeavor in human history. Christ's *ekklesia* (vv. 6, 9, 10) is eternal, and Christ's church alone is eternally blessed. Why wouldn't we support its mission? "Would that our God would multiply both 'the sent' and 'the supporters.'"[16] Would that God would inspire us to gain all we can so that we might give all we can.[17] As important as the financial ethics of the sent are to the success of the spread of the gospel, the generosity of the supporters is no less significant. Giving is foundational, so let us give, give, and give!

Persistence in Resolving Conflict

The sixth lesson is that *the sad reality of Christian conflict can be resolved through persistent confrontation and imitation.* I say *persistent* because John has not given up on this church and its overbearing and overreaching leader, although I am sure he would have been tempted to. Every seasoned pastor feels John's pain, but few can withstand the heat of church conflict. John did not cower, retreat, or lose hope. Instead, as Gary Burge summarizes:

> He persisted, first by sending a letter (that was tossed out) and then by sending emissaries (who were rejected). But he did not allow this to discourage him. Third John is his second letter, sent with another emissary, Demetrius. I sense that John is determined not to let this church—or Diotrephes—go.[18]

Speaking of Diotrephes, John determines to deal with him through confrontation. In 3 John 9–11, we hear the sorry tale. But before I share that story, let me first share a true tale about two tails of my own. Before I was married, my roommate's girlfriend, Holly, asked whether I would watch her two fish. I agreed. About two days into my watch, I noticed that one fish was losing its scales. This concerned me. I assumed that the scales were important

16. Akin, *1, 2, 3 John*, 245.

17. As John Wesley preached, "Having, First, gained all you can, and, Secondly, saved all you can, Then give all you can." From Wesley's sermon "The Use of Money," in *The Works of John Wesley*, 14 vols. (1872; repr., Grand Rapids: Baker, 2007), 6:133.

18. Burge, *Letters of John*, 251.

to the fish's well-being. A few more days passed, and the matter was only growing worse. I changed the water and made sure that the fish was eating well. As I was watching it feed, I witnessed the crime and the culprit. One fish was attacking the other, biting off the scales. I was so upset. I couldn't believe my eyes. I grabbed the net, reached down in the water, pulled out the bad fish, walked over to the toilet, tossed the criminal in, and flushed it down to its deserved damnation.

John's action toward the one bad fish swimming around in the church's tank was just as swift but not as harsh or final. Once he knew what Diotrephes was doing, he took immediate action against him. The "son of thunder" thundered. But he did so, we can trust, with the whole church's best interest in mind, even the bad fish's. Christian confrontation is an act of love. John lovingly offers a public reproof.

John finds four problems with Diotrephes' behavior. First is his pride: he "likes to put himself first" (3 John 9), or, more literally, "loves to be first" (*philoprōteuon*). Has he forgotten that Christ alone "rightly deserves the preeminence (*proteuon* [Col. 1:18])"?[19] Has he moved beyond Jesus' teaching, a lesson that John himself learned well early on, that whoever wants to be first among others must be the servant of all (see Matt. 20:27)? God hates pride (Prov. 6:17), and John shares in that righteous anger. We laugh at Mark Twain's adage, "If I ever achieve humility, I'll sure be proud of it."[20] But we all know that it is no laughing matter to be led by a leader in love with himself.

John's second issue with Diotrephes is that this "all-too-independent leader"[21] refuses to "acknowledge our authority" (3 John 9). The "our" might reference the apostles, but more likely it refers to John and the emissaries he sent. Either way, Diotrephes does not acknowledge apostolic authority. In the contemporary church, some Christians couldn't care less about how they talk to or about their pastors. They treat them like hired help and not God-ordained authorities. But to the apostolic age, it was even more serious business to refuse apostolic leadership. John makes this nowhere plainer than in his introduction to 1 John: "that which we have seen and heard

19. Akin, *1, 2, 3 John*, 246.

20. Twain, quoted in David L. Allen, *1–3 John: Fellowship in God's Family*, Preaching the Word (Wheaton, IL: Crossway, 2013), 276.

21. Schnackenburg, *The Johannine Epistles*, 297.

we proclaim also to you, so that you too may have fellowship with us; and indeed our fellowship is with the Father and with his Son Jesus Christ" (1 John 1:3). John uses the first-person-singular *I* eight times in 3 John.[22] It is not because he is conceited, but rather because he holds "a position of theological, moral, and pastoral leadership over the churches of the Lord Jesus Christ."[23]

John's third issue with Diotrephes is that he is "talking wicked nonsense against us" (3 John 10). Against John, and perhaps Gaius and the brothers also (the *us*), Diotrephes makes unjustified accusations or "baseless charges."[24] There is no more common sin against church leaders (often by other church leaders) than slander, and yet slander is a very serious offense. It is hell-bent and hell-bound. Diotrephes's tongue needs to be tamed before it sets the whole church on fire (see James 3:6).

John's fourth and final issue with Diotrephes is his anti-gospel policy,[25] as depicted in 3 John 10: "And not content with that, he refuses to welcome the brothers, and also stops those who want to and puts them out of the church." He will not let the right people through the church door, and he seeks to toss the right people out the door. We do not know what his official ecclesial position was, if any. Maybe he was merely an influential lay-leader, a rich man whose big house hosted the house church. If he was a church leader, perhaps he was one elder among many who took the apostolic example of first among equals (Peter among the Twelve) to extremes. He changed a healthy balance into dictatorial heavy-handedness. Or maybe he saw himself, as many of this period started to do (see Ignatius's letters), as a monarchical bishop—one pastor ruling over a number of churches. Who knows? The issue, anyway, was not whether he was a Presbyterian or an Episcopalian. The issue also does not appear to be doctrinal. John never labels him as one of those apostate antichrists. Rather, the issue is how Diotrephes is wickedly throwing his weight around. Whether he has legitimately gained his power or usurped it, it is because of his attitude (he loves to be first) and his actions

22. In 3 John 1, 2, 3, 4, 9, 10, 13, and 14, and noted by Colin G. Kruse, *The Letters of John*, Pillar New Testament Commentary (Grand Rapids: Eerdmans, 2000), 220.

23. Akin, *1, 2, 3 John*, 239.

24. Schnackenburg, *The Johannine Epistles*, 297.

25. Akin sees a digression in Diotrephes's behavior: "What began as ambition (he loved to be first) moved to arrogance (he refused the elder), then to accusations (of no substance) and finally to action." *1, 2, 3 John*, 248–49.

(he is unloving toward his brothers) that John wants to come to town and knock some sense into him.

Christian leaders must follow John's example. With a "spirit of gentleness" and with our brothers' spiritual restoration as our goal (Gal. 6:1), we must not shy away from confronting others, even other Christian leaders. As Jesus taught us in his constitution on church confrontation (Matt. 18:15–20), we are to go in order to gain (v. 15). If the brother remains unrepentant, however, we next establish evidence (v. 16) and, if necessary, censure the sinner (v. 17). We are to gather in Christ's name to render an ecclesial judgment (vv. 18–20). This is the process that John has begun in his letter (3 John 9–10), and is on his way (v. 14) to help, if needed, the church to render a final verdict.

The sad reality of Christian conflict can be resolved through persistent confrontation. That is the first step. The second step follows. Having applied the act of confrontation, we turn next to the art of imitation. There is a connection between the two seemingly unrelated themes. As 3 John 11 teaches, we are not to "imitate evil" (namely, Diotrephes, whom John just confronted, and who "does evil") but rather to "imitate good" (namely, Demetrius, whom we are next introduced to, who "does good").

There are only two imperatives in 3 John—"greet" (3 John 15) and "imitate" (v. 11)—and "imitate" is the main one. With two antithetical parallelisms, verse 11 states:

> Beloved, do not imitate evil
>   but imitate good.
>
> Whoever does good is from God;
> Whoever does evil has not seen God.

The idea here is that those who know God imitate (i.e., do) good. One example of such a person is Demetrius. "Demetrius has received a good testimony from everyone, and from the truth itself. We also add our testimony, and you know that our testimony is true" (3 John 12). Unlike Diotrephes, who receives a fourfold scolding, Demetrius gets a positive threefold testimony: "everyone" (each person who knows him), "the truth" (the gospel truth with which his life accords), and the Christian community that John founded and leads (the "our") all witness to his worthiness.

If Demetrius was the letter courier, which is likely, 3 John 12 serves as John's personal letter of commendation. Robert Yarbrough notes Richards's work on first-century letter-writing, which "argues that letter carriers often played an active role in interpreting and explaining Paul's Letters." Yarbrough concludes that if "Demetrius serves John in this way, it is all the more important that Gaius be given reasons inducing him to listen to him."[26] Receive what Demetrius brings; heed what he says. But more than that, imitate his Christlike behavior. Imitate him as he imitates Christ (1 Cor. 11:1). Be willing to go into the heat of a church conflict with a message that is potentially explosive and somehow (by God's grace!) bring about "peace," the topic with which John concludes his letter.

Peace-Promoting Friendship

The seventh lesson is that *Christian friendship promotes the peace of God in Christ.* In 3 John 13–15, John concludes:

> I had much to write to you, but I would rather not write with pen and ink. I hope to see you soon, and we will talk face to face.
>
> Peace be to you. The friends greet you. Greet the friends, every one of them.

John has called those in the church *children*, *brothers*, and now *friends*. What can possibly bring together men such as Gaius and John—one a Gentile, the other a Jew, one likely a former pagan and the other certainly a first follower of Jesus?[27] What would motivate people from different towns and cultures to greet one another "by name" (3 John 15 NASB), to welcome strangers into their homes, and to provide resources for them? What would possess an old man to travel miles (before the inventions of trains, planes, and automobiles) to talk with people personally? The answer: the peace of God in Christ. When John ends this little letter with "Peace be to you. . . . Greet the friends" (v. 15), it is an unusual ending. This is the only place in the New Testament Epistles where believers are called *friends* (likely reflective

26. See Yarbrough, *1–3 John*, 383, and E. R. Richards, *Paul and First-Century Letter Writing* (Downers Grove, IL: InterVarsity Press, 2004), 207–9.

27. Stephen S. Smalley deduces that since *Gaius* is a Roman name in origin, it is likely that Gaius was a former pagan. *1, 2, 3 John*, Word Biblical Commentary (Nashville: Thomas Nelson, 1984), 344.

of John 15:13), and *peace* (not the more common *grace*) is the final blessing. Why end in this way?

John's conclusion is not some prophetic critique of the future hyperindividualism of Western civilization. It is a solution to the peace problem that so often plagues the church. It is difficult to stay angry at someone who wants to learn your name, greet you, pray for you, meet face-to-face, and support you if needed. Would that Christians today sought peace, the peace of God in Christ that is to be extended to all our brothers and sisters in Christ!

"The Minister's Fainting Fits"

While preparing the material for this chapter, I read the assigned chapter from Charles Spurgeon's *Lectures to My Students* that my interns planned to discuss the day after the sermon. It is called "The Minister's Fainting Fits." It is based on David's situation in the heat of battle, when he "waxed faint" (2 Sam. 21:15 KJV). Here, Spurgeon addresses pastors struggling with depression. He writes, "Fits of depression come over the most of us. . . . There may be here and there men of iron, to whom wear and tear work no perceptible detriment, but surely the rust frets even these; and as for ordinary men, the Lord knows, and makes them to know, that they are but dust." He speaks of Martin Luther, notorious for his depression, who on his very deathbed "sobbed himself into his last sleep like a great wearied child." Spurgeon's pearls of wisdom follow, such as this: "Good men are promised tribulation in this world, and ministers may expect a larger share than others, that they may learn sympathy with the Lord's suffering people, and so may be fitting shepherds of an ailing flock"; and:

> Who can bear the weight of souls without sometimes sinking into the dust? Passionate longings after men's conversion, if not fully satisfied (and when are they?), consume the soul with anxiety and disappointment. To see the hopeful turn aside, the godly grow cold, professors abusing their privileges, and sinners waxing more bold in sin—are not these enough to crush us to the earth? . . . How often, on the Lord's day evenings, do we feel as if life were completely washed out of us! After pouring out our souls

> over our congregations, we feel like empty earthen pitchers which a child might break.[28]

The apostle John had met Jesus of Nazareth in his late teens or early twenties. When he wrote 3 John, he had served his Lord as a pastor for at least fifty, if not seventy, years. Can you imagine all the sin, nonsense, heartache, and disappointment he had to deal with in his full life of ministry? We certainly get a taste of some of it in 3 John.

On the Tuesday night before I preached this little letter, I returned from an elders' meeting. I walked in the house, opened a bottle of wine, poured a glass for my wife and me, walked into the bedroom—where Emily was ready to sleep—handed her the glass, raised mine, and said, "To heaven!" She said, "Does this mean the meeting went well?" "Awful," I said. "My dear, that's why I said *to heaven*." To a time and place where I won't sin, Christian leaders won't sin, and Christian people won't sin. And where there will be no more ministers' fainting fits. To heaven, dear church! Raise your glasses. But until then, stay sober. Each day has enough troubles of its own.

28. From Charles Spurgeon, *Lectures to My Students* (Ross-shire, Scotland: Christian Focus, 2005), 177, 178, 180.

Select Bibliography of Commentaries Cited and Consulted

Akin, Daniel L. *1, 2, 3 John*. New American Commentary. Nashville: Broadman & Holman, 1993.

Allen, David L. *1–3 John: Fellowship in God's Family*. Preaching the Word. Wheaton, IL: Crossway, 2013.

Barclay, William. *The Letters of John and Jude*. Daily Bible Study Series. Philadelphia: Westminster, 1976.

Barton, Bruce B., et al. *1, 2 & 3 John*. Application Bible Commentary. Wheaton, IL: Tyndale, 1998.

Boice, James Montgomery. *The Epistles of John: An Expositional Commentary*. Grand Rapids: Baker, 1979.

Bray, Gerald, ed. *James, 1–2 Peter, 1–3 John, Jude*. Ancient Christian Commentary on Scripture, New Testament 11. Downers Grove, IL: InterVarsity Press, 2000.

Brown, Raymond E. *The Epistles of John*. Anchor Bible. Garden City, NY: Doubleday, 1982.

Bruce, F. F. "The Epistles of John." In *The Gospel and Epistles of John*. Grand Rapids: Eerdmans, 2004.

Bultmann, Rudolf. *The Johannine Epistles*. Translated by R. Philip O'Hara. Hermeneia. Philadelphia: Fortress, 1973.

Burge, Gary M. *Letters of John*. NIV Application Commentary. Grand Rapids: Zondervan, 1996.

Calvin, John. "1 John." In John Calvin and Matthew Henry, *1, 2, 3 John*. Crossway Classic Commentaries. Wheaton, IL: Crossway, 1998.

Comfort, Philip W., and Wendell C. Hawley. *1–3 John*. Cornerstone Biblical Commentary. Carol Stream, IL: Tyndale, 2007.

Dodd, C. H. *The Johannine Epistles*. Moffatt New Testament Commentary. New York: Harper & Brothers, 1946.

Jackman, David. *The Message of John's Letters*. The Bible Speaks Today. Downers Grove, IL: InterVarsity Press, 1988.

Kistemaker, Simon J. "Exposition of the Epistles of John." In *James, Epistles of John, Peter, and Jude*. Grand Rapids: Baker, 2002.

Kruse, Colin G. *The Letters of John*. Pillar New Testament Commentary. Grand Rapids: Eerdmans, 2000.

Law, Robert. *The Tests of Life: A Study of the First Epistle of St. John*. 3rd ed. Grand Rapids: Baker, 1968. Originally published 1909.

Lenski, R. C. H. *The Interpretation of the Epistles of St. Peter, St. John and St. Jude*. Minneapolis: Augsburg, 1966.

Lieu, Judith. *The Second and Third Epistles of John: History and Background*. Edinburgh: T&T Clark, 1986.

Lloyd-Jones, Martyn. *Life in Christ: Studies in 1 John*. Wheaton, IL: Crossway, 2002.

Luther, Martin. "Lectures on the First Epistle of St. John." In *The Catholic Epistles*. Vol. 30 of *Luther's Works*, translated and edited by Jaroslav Pelikan and W. A. Hansen. St. Louis: Concordia, 1972.

Marshall, I. Howard. *The Epistles of John*. New International Commentary on the New Testament. Grand Rapids: Eerdmans, 1978.

Painter, John. *1, 2, and 3 John*. Sacra Pagina. Collegeville, MN: Liturgical Press, 2002.

Plummer, Alfred. *The Epistles of St. John*. Cambridge Greek Testament for Schools and Colleges. Cambridge: Cambridge University Press, 1894.

Schnackenburg, Rudolf. *The Johannine Epistles: Introduction and Commentary*. Translated by R. Fuller and I. Fuller. New York: Crossroad, 1992.

Smalley, Stephen S. *1, 2, 3 John*. Rev. ed. Word Biblical Commentary. Nashville: Thomas Nelson, 2007.

Stott, John R. W. *The Epistles of John: An Introduction and Commentary*. Tyndale New Testament Commentaries. Downers Grove, IL: InterVarsity Press, 1976.

———. *The Letters of John: An Introduction and Commentary*. 2nd ed. Tyndale New Testament Commentaries. Downers Grove, IL: InterVarsity Press, 2009.

Thompson, Marianne Meye. *1–3 John*. IVP New Testament Commentary Series. Downers Grove, IL: InterVarsity Press, 1992.

Westcott, Brooke Foss. *The Epistles of St. John: The Greek Text with Notes and Essays*. Cambridge and London: Macmillan, 1892.

Wright, N. T. *Early Christian Letters for Everyone*. New Testament for Everyone. Louisville, KY: Westminster John Knox, 2011.

Yarbrough, Robert W. *1–3 John*. Baker Exegetical Commentary on the New Testament. Grand Rapids: Baker, 2008.

Index of Scripture

Index of Scripture

Index of Subjects and Names

Available in the Reformed Expository Commentary Series

New Testament

The Incarnation in the Gospels, by Daniel M. Doriani, Philip Graham Ryken, and Richard D. Phillips
Matthew, by Daniel M. Doriani
Luke, by Philip Graham Ryken
John, by Richard D. Phillips
Romans, by Daniel M. Doriani
Galatians, by Philip Graham Ryken
Ephesians, by Bryan Chapell
Philippians, by Dennis E. Johnson
1 & 2 Thessalonians, by Richard D. Phillips
1 Timothy, by Philip Graham Ryken
2 Timothy & Titus, by Daniel M. Doriani and Richard D. Phillips
Hebrews, by Richard D. Phillips
James, by Daniel M. Doriani
1 Peter, by Daniel M. Doriani
1–3 John, by Douglas Sean O'Donnell
Revelation, by Richard D. Phillips

Forthcoming

Mark, by Douglas Sean O'Donnell
2 Corinthians, by Trent Casto